Ciao Bella

In Search of My Italian Father

Helena Frith Powell

GIBSON SQUARE

For my father and my son

Also by Helena Frith Powell

Two Lipsticks and a Lover

More France Please

This third edition published for the first time in 2009 by Gibson Square

UK Tel: +44 (0)20 7096 1100
   Fax: +44 (0)20 7993 2214

US Tel: +1 646 216 9813
   Fax: +1 646 216 9488

Eire Tel: +353 (0)1 657 1057

   info@gibsonsquare.com
   www.gibsonsquare.com

   ISBN   9781903933947

Printed by Clays, Bungay.

Contents

Acknowledgements

A huge thank you to my publisher Martin Rynja for all his hard work and dedication. Also many thanks to my agent Lizzy Kremer for her inspirational feedback and enthusiasm, and to Rhonda Carrier and Diana Beaumont for their excellent editing. Thanks to my mother; if she had been less adventurous in her twenties there would be no story to tell. Thanks to Mary Jones for her ceaseless efforts on the publicity front and to Carla McKay for her ideas and sense of humour. Thank you also to Jacques Kuhnlé for his meticulous corrections as well as Valentina Motisi, Francesca Marchini and Chiara Monetti in Italy for all their help and kindness. As always thanks to Jonathan Miller for dropping whatever he's doing and helping me whenever I've asked him to.

Most of all thank you to Rupert, my husband and favourite editor, who first heard this story ten years ago on a boat on the Bosphorus and said I should write it one day.

Prologue

My first memory is of walking across Piazza di Spagna with my parents. I am almost three years old. They are arguing. I try to make things better by putting their hands together. My father seems keen on the idea. My mother less so. She rejects the gesture and instead crosses her arms. A month later my mother and I leave Rome to start a new life in England with a different man.

As soon as we leave Italy, my memory of Rome and my real father fades. I start to believe my father is an English artist. He brings me up in the British autocratic tradition. This involves being punished regularly and having to sit in my bedroom with the same meal (usually fish, which I hate) for days on end until I finish it. But he has many good sides. He is imaginative and spends hours entertaining me. In his studio, which smells of oil paint and smoke, he has three tiny magic wooden birds whose job it is to find me hidden presents on my birthday.

But neither my mother nor I are happy. My stepfather is demanding and spoilt. When he wants coffee in the morning, he bangs on the floor from his bedroom. My mother and I both dread taking it up to him. Any encounter with him can lead to an argument which you will have to concede before you're allowed to leave the room.

One day soon after my ninth birthday my stepfather travels to Morocco, apparently to find himself. "Hopefully he'll lose himself," jokes my mother.

I dread him coming back. The house is so peaceful without him. One night I go to sleep clutching my magic wishing troll.

"Please make mummy and daddy get divorced," I whisper in its ear.

Two days later a car lands in our garden. Inside the car is a drunken driver. But it wouldn't have mattered to my mother if there had been an alien inside it. Whatever landed on her doorstep was good enough to get her out of the relationship with my stepfather.

Inside the car is not an alien but something worse: a man with a red beard called Barry. He is short and wears flares with platform shoes. Not a great look. But, to begin with, he is funny and a light relief after the intensity of my stepfather.

My mother begins an affair with the red-haired man almost immediately. The first I know of anything is when we move in with him. My stepfather comes back from Morocco with a bag full of dirty washing and is furious to find no one at home.

Over the next few years we move house several times with Barry as he is careless about paying the rent. I nickname him Psycho because of his violent temper. The last place we live is a farmer's cottage. To escape the tension inside the house I have made myself a den in a barn. I hide in the middle of four walls made up of several bales of hay, reading or playing with an imaginary friend. One wet April morning I am hidden behind the bales. It has rained so much the smell of the hay is damp and strong. I find it a comforting smell. From above the bales I can see the farm buildings and our cottage, but no one can see me. My mother comes out to find me. She alone knows my hiding place; Psycho is not allowed anywhere near it.

"Your real father has asked if he can write to you," she says. "He's called Benedetto Benedetti."

My whole world changes. As an only child I have spent a lot of time wondering if I am in fact a princess who has been kidnapped into this miserable existence of constant fighting and poverty. This is surely proof? I feel special and wanted. I have a real father and there is a chance he may actually be relatively normal. Even if he has a silly-sounding name.

My Italian father writes to me. He sends me photographs of himself, his house and his horses. He is good-looking, the house impressive, but the thing that makes me happiest is the horses. I am in my early teens, that age before girls discover boys and when they find horses fascinating. I write back to him. He is a good pen pal. We decide it is now too late for him to be called Daddy, so he signs his letters Biologico. He always starts them with Ciao bella, which makes me feel exotic and special.

A year or so on from our first correspondence, life with Barry has become unbearable. My mother decides it is time to leave England before he kills us both. I am now fourteen years old. Our only problem is lack of money. So my mother writes to my father asking for help. He promises to send us enough to get us to Italy.

The weeks before the escape are tense. We can't risk telling anyone, or even packing anything. I am told to choose three things I want to take. I pick my Girl Guide diary, a little fur dog I have had since I was a baby and my copy of *The Lion, the Witch and the Wardrobe*. These three items sit on the table in my room ready to leave.

I am getting ready for school one Tuesday morning when my mother tells me today is the day. I cycle to school as normal and lock my bike. I tell my friends I am leaving. I give my bike key to my best friend Estelle. I also tell my English teacher about the plan. She thinks it's another one of my stories.

Half-way through my English lesson I see my mother rush past the window. I raise my hand and ask to be excused. The whole class looks on in amazement as I leave. Some of my friends rush out to wave me off. My mother and I get into her purple Ford Cortina and drive towards the coast.

We navigate with the help of the map of Europe in my Girl Guide diary. This has its disadvantages. At one stage, when we think we are about to hit the Italian border, we see a sign saying: Welcome to Switzerland.

After three days' driving we arrive in the Adriatic town of Rimini. This is the ancestral home of my new Italian family. We arrange to meet my father on the beach. We are early, or he is late, I no longer remember which. I go for a swim but when I come out I realise I am lost. Rimini beach is divided into numbered sections but they all look the same. I am now terrified I will never see my mother again, but more importantly that I will miss my appointment with my father. I start running on the beach, looking for something I will recognise. Suddenly I feel two strong arms around me. I look up into eyes that are shockingly similar to mine.

"Ciao bella," says my father. "I recognised you by your legs."

1

Two Hundred and Forty Steps

It is a Tuesday in the middle of November. I am in the Via Ricasoli, a road in Florence next to the famous Duomo. The sun is shining but the air is cold. This hasn't deterred the tourists, who have come from all over the world to gaze at the Baptistry doors and drink expensive cappuccinos in the Piazza della Signoria. But once you get away from the tourist trail, Florence is deserted. I am practically alone in this small road. I am surprised that I found it so quickly; I haven't been here for over twenty years. As I start to walk up the road, I have to move off the pavement to avoid some scaffolding. It's an odd thing about Italy: everything is in a permanent state of rebuilding.

I arrived this morning from my home in France on the overnight train. I have travelled to Italy to try to write a book about Italian women and to discover what makes them so glamorous. My previous book was about French women who appear superior to every other woman. But I discovered that the one thing they're scared of (apart from putting on weight and chipping their nails) is Italian women. So I am here to work out the reasons for this fear—and hopefully end up going back to France fully equipped to take on even the meanest Parisian. Fear of Italian women is nothing new. In the 18th century the Swiss philosopher Jean-Jacques Rousseau warned James Boswell before he set off on a Grand Tour of Italy to "Watch out for Italian girls—for several reasons."

My journey begins on a sunny morning at Montpellier railway station, where I am accosted by two American missionaries spreading the word. They do this in broken French until they realise I speak their language. They are sweet girls, from Carolina, probably about twenty, who explain that they have decided to base themselves in France to convince people to join the Church of Jesus Christ. They tell me it feels like the right thing to do. They have been lucky enough to find God and they want other people to enjoy the same benefits.

"You are not alone," the taller and more confident one says, looking at me earnestly. In fact it's lucky I'm not. I have far too many bags to carry and the good thing about these religious types is that they're very helpful. They see me into my seat on the train and push a leaflet into my hand before going to find more lost souls to convert. It is only when I look at the piece of paper I realise they are Mormons.

"If you ever feel like you need to talk, just call us," says my saviour, sounding like Vivien Leigh in *A Streetcar Named Desire*.

"I sure will," I smile, wondering how I am going to get my bags off the train without these angels of mercy. The carriage looks like it was designed by Coco Chanel. It is all cream. The seats are beige leather. Big enough for two of me and soft as a duvet. The carpet is thick as Devon milk and the walls are painted the same colour. An SNCF representative walks up and down offering drinks and snacks. Around me French people read or sleep; the atmosphere is as calm as the decor.

The train to Italy which I board at Nice couldn't be more different. There are people everywhere, standing, sitting, talking, pushing to get past. I have booked a sleeper but instead of a medley of calm cream and serenity I am shown into a drab carriage that is older than me. In fact it is probably older than my grandmother. There is a bed, neatly made up, with the Ferrovie dello Stato (Italian railways) logo on it. Above the bed is a faded black and white print of the Colosseum. Underneath someone has thoughtfully written Il Colosseo—Roma, just in case you were in any doubt. Underneath the window is one of the first phrases I ever learnt in Italian—E pericoloso sporgersi: it is dangerous to lean out of the window.

The neatly dressed guard is efficient but stressed. He has a lot of noisy people to look after. But oddly enough I feel at home. I love the Italian voices, Italian faces and Italian chaos. I can't wait to get there, although I am relieved I have booked a cabin to myself when I see the others all crammed with four people in them. The thought of sleeping with three strangers might be exciting in certain circumstances, but not this one.

As I am the only person with a cabin to myself, the Italian guard treats me like royalty. He knocks on my door with offers of wine and food, coffee and water at regular intervals. I eat some bread and Parma ham and try my best to drink the wine, which is from Lazio and totally undrinkable. At 9.30 I lie down in my bunk with E.M. Forster's *A Room with a View*. My bookmark is a photograph my mother took of my father and me on the beach at Rimini that first summer. He has his arm around me and is smiling at the camera. He is much taller than me and well built. His hair is thick and brown and slightly wavy.

He has a moustache. But rather than make him look ridiculous, which I have always thought moustaches do, it makes him look even more like an Italian film star. He looks intelligent—which is part of his attraction—if a little out of place, fully clothed and clutching a 1920s Fedora hat among all the half-naked sun-worshippers. I had never seen anyone on a beach wearing a 1920s Fedora hat. In fact I had never seen anyone wearing a Fedora hat before. I am skinny and gawky-looking with long brown hair. My purple bikini is slightly too big for me. I am totally flat-chested under my bikini top. I am also looking at the camera and smiling; our eyes are almost identical; brown and slightly almond-shaped with thick black eyelashes.

I think about our first embrace. He was wearing a white silk shirt, and my hair, wet from the sea, left a mark on it. I felt secure in his arms. His voice was loud and strong. With my head resting on his chest I heard it reverberate through his ribcage.

"Well," he said looking down at me. "At least in terms of looks I can't deny you're my daughter."

He stroked my cheek and I started crying, for no particular reason. He smiled as he put his arm around me and we walked towards my mother: "I must be some disappointment, but please, try to hide your grief. I am a sensitive man and easily hurt." This was the first time he made me laugh.

My parents embraced and we all sat down on the sun-loungers.

"Still smoking I see?" he said to my mother.

"Yes, aren't you?"

"No, never. Especially not in Rimini. The mayor has forbidden it."

The first picture I took of my parents together.

My mother laughed and raised her cigarette to her lips. Her hand was shaking slightly. I don't know if it was nerves at seeing my father again. She told me she bore him no animosity and that they had always behaved in a relatively civilised manner. But still it must have been odd seeing him after so many years. Actually, the shaking was something I had got used to seeing. Over the last few years she had acted like a frightened animal, always looking around the corner for the next disaster, her pretty face permanently worried. She would even frown in her sleep.

"But it is true," said my father. "There is a law. Anyone caught smoking will be tied up in the main square and flogged."

"I see you're still wearing that ridiculous hat," returned my mother.

My father tilted his hat and smiled. "Brava, you still have your legendary sense of humour."

It was an odd sensation seeing my parents together. It was difficult to digest that this man was my father. I had got so used to pretending other people were. But here he was; the truth, my real father. The idea was overwhelming. I couldn't stop looking at him, listening to his voice and examining his face. He really did look like me. Everyone had always told me I looked like my mother. But now I saw that they were wrong. I was the spitting image of this man I didn't know.

We left the beach and walked towards his car. I walked behind my parents, enjoying seeing them together. A group of boys standing on the other side of the street whistled at me. "Ciao bella," one of them shouted. I was amazed. It was only my father who called me that.

"Don't be alarmed," said my father, turning around to talk to me. "This is the normal mating call of the Italian male. All over Italy you will hear it. But of course when I say it to you, it is different."

We drove in his cream open-top Mercedes with red leather seats towards the city centre of Rimini. I had never been anywhere so hot and was glad of the breeze created by the movement of the car. We drove past large villas close to the sea. My father told me that when he was a child they had a house here as well as one in town. Rimini seemed very glamorous to me. First of all the sun was shining, a rarity in Berkshire where I had lived until now. There were poplars, palm trees and bright flowers planted alongside the road. Young people whizzed up and down on scooters, their hair blowing in the wind. On street corners people chatted and gesticulated wildly. As we drove past Rimini's famous Tempio Malatestiano, its bell rang out signalling midday. This was a sound I had only ever heard in films.

We were headed to my grandmother's house on the Via IV Novembre. It seemed odd to me that a street should be named after a date, but I was told it was to commemorate the end of the war in 1918.

We walked through the stone entrance hall to the building. I pressed the buzzer as instructed by my father. The door opened with a deep buzz. We got into an old wooden lift with steel doors. When we got out, we were greeted at the door by a woman who was dressed completely in black except for a green apron and looked about ninety. She was barely my height and was carrying a broom. She nodded curtly and led us into the house, telling us to wait in the hall. I looked around. The entrance was large, the floor was marble and there was a chandelier hanging from the ceiling. It was lit although it was mid-afternoon, the pieces of glass reflecting the light. It was one of the grandest things I had ever seen, although it didn't give out much light. I peeped through an open door to the drawing room. Along one wall there were French windows with all the shutters drawn. I was wondering why they had the lights on and the shutters down in the middle of the day when the woman in black returned and motioned for us to follow her. My father walked into the drawing room and my mother and I followed the woman down a long hall to my grandmother's bedroom. The door was open and on a chair in the middle of the room sat my grandmother smiling and clutching a string of Hail Mary beads.

My grandmother was so small that she made everything around her look outsized. For the first time in my life I felt gigantic. She was sitting on the chair, wrapped in a shawl that

would have looked normal on
anyone else but had the effect of
drowning her to the extent that it
was difficult to see where she ended
and the chair started.

"La mia bambina," she said,
reaching her arms out for me as she
got up from the chair. I approached
her and she hugged me with a
strength I would have thought
impossible for a woman her age and
size. She was at least eighty. She sat
down again, overcome with

La nonna.

emotion, and motioned for me to kneel in front of her. She
caressed my head and covered me with kisses, all the time
crying and repeating the words "La mia bambina è tornata. My
baby has come back."

It was difficult to know what to do or how to feel. I had no
idea that my being there would mean so much to her. I hugged
her back and tried desperately to remember her. It seemed so
sad that I meant so much to this woman I just didn't recognise.
Her smell was alien, a mixture of moth-balls and soap, her face
kind and her eyes the same brown as those of my father and
mine. I felt almost uncomfortable with the attention she was
lavishing on me. Partly because during my English upbringing
we were never allowed to show such emotions, but really more
because she was crushing me to her chest right into a large
silver cross she had hanging from a necklace. This was one of
my first, and more painful encounters with catholicism. She
smiled and cried and caressed my face again and again.
Eventually she looked at my mother.

"She's a lovely girl," she said.

My mother nodded and gave her a hug. They both cried a little in between talking and hugging. I was amazed at how upset my grandmother was; she didn't stop crying for about an hour and clutching me. When I called her "nonna", which I'd been told was the Italian for grandmother, she said she had waited twelve years to hear that word and not a day had gone by without her thinking about me.

I sleep well on trains and wake up ready to be reunited with Florence. Unfortunately, I discover I am in Rome. My travel agent has messed up my booking. The train whizzed past Florence about two and a half hours ago while I was still fast asleep. It seems incredible that I am unable to arrive in Italy without some major mess-up. I suppose though the wrong city is an improvement on the wrong country. Maybe next time I'll finally crack it.

It is eight o'clock in the morning but Roma Termini is already packed with people. The noise is deafening. One can hardly hear the train announcements over the chatter from the Romans. The place smells of cigarettes and coffee. Even though I generally don't like either, the combination is strangely familiar and reassuring. I lug my bags out into the main station to find the ticket office. There doesn't seem to be one. But there are machines everywhere purporting to do the same job. A friendly passer-by shows me how to work the buttons. Within seconds I have a ticket to Florence with a seat booked.

The journey is fine, except that I have never heard so many mobile phones ring. Every passenger in the packed carriage has at least one phone, which rings an average of four times during the trip. I take my phone out to see if it's switched on. What's wrong with me? Why is no one calling me? I haven't even had a text message for goodness sake. I notice there are even plugs by the seats where one can charge one's mobile phone, should the battery get dangerously low. Not much risk of that with mine. My fellow passengers are all Italian as far as I can make out. The man sitting next to me is reading the Italian newspaper *Il Sole 24 Ore*. I crane my neck to see what the news is but understand next to nothing. Opposite me is a young woman with a bare (and quite ample) mid-riff and long dark curly hair. You can tell she's Italian straight away, or rather you can tell she's not French. She is far too voluptuous, she is also wearing shocking red lipstick and it's not even breakfast time. I think she looks great. There is a flamboyance and a sensuality about Italian women I have always liked. A kind of daring that other nationalities lack.

We arrive at the Santa Maria Novella station. The contrast with Rome is immediately apparent. There are about half as many people milling about and the air is cleaner. I take a taxi towards the Pensione Annalena where I will spend the next two days. It feels great to be back in Italy after so long. The sun is shining and Florence is bright and welcoming. After France the people here seem very lively. I always thought it odd that joie de vivre is a French expression. Italians seem less uptight. I'm sure it's something to do with the language. Just struggling to pronounce French words makes me tense; whereas with Italian the words are rich and forceful. They can withstand bad pronunciation. You just need emotion to express yourself.

The sun feels hot through the window of the taxi. We drive over the river. There are lovers on the bridge gazing at each other and the Ponte Vecchio. The driver takes a narrow street heading south; he drives so fast I fear some of the pedestrians who have opted to walk in the road to avoid the scaffolding will be mowed down, but they all seem to jump out of the way just in time.

The pensione is housed in an old palazzo on the Via Romana. The taxi driver pulls up on the kerb just outside it. The building is huge. There is a shiny brass bell outside with Pensione Annalena written on it. I ring it and the large wooden door opens with a deep buzzing sound. A vast marble staircase leads up to the first floor. (Where are those missionaries when I need them?)

The pensione is a mixture of smart and shabby. Flamboyant statues guard the entrance, but inside the furniture is drab. The floors are terracotta and the ceilings high. I am greeted by a young blonde Italian receptionist who is, guess what, gossiping to a friend on the phone. She is slim and petite, wearing a cream shirt and black skirt. In fact she is dressed more like a fifty-year old than a twenty-five year old but maybe that's the Pensione uniform. She tells her friend to hold on while she checks me in and shows me to my room. Phone bills are obviously not an issue in Italy.

My room looks like it has been furnished entirely from an auction of bric-a-brac nobody else wanted. Nothing matches. The wardrobe is dark wood and rickety. Inside are a couple of misshapen wire hangers. The table is plastic and the rugs frayed. But the double bed is comfortable and it is clean. The bathroom is smaller than my loo at home. The shower was put in as an afterthought and soaks the whole room when used. After a quick shower I go back outside, armed with a map. I have arranged my first meetings with Italian women later on in the day, but as I have some spare time I decide to try to find my father's old apartment. I want to see how it makes me feel to be there again after so many years. It feels odd to be wandering around alone. I have had three children within five years and have got used to carting one or more of them around with me. It is a strangely liberating feeling to have only myself to worry about.

I remember it was at the beginning of the Via Ricasoli, maybe number three, or even seven. I walk backwards and forwards a couple of times. Two women come out of number seven; I dart in through the door before it shuts. The entrance hall is vaulted and to the right is a marble staircase. It looks very familiar. But then again one marble staircase is very much like another. I walk up; my father's flat was right at the top, and there were two hundred and forty steps. We used to count them in Italian. In fact he would take two at a time so he would count in twos. That was beyond my Italian. The first time, I got to about twenty before lapsing into English. By the end of my week in Florence I could count all the way to the top. As a method of learning foreign numbers it can't be beaten.

After a couple of days in Rimini together my mother decided to go home and start organising a new life for us. She wanted to find a job, somewhere to live and a school for me. My father offered to keep me in Italy and take me on a Grand Tour of the country.

"It's bad enough that she can't speak the language," he boomed. "But she's never seen her fatherland. I will show everything she needs to see."

I think my mother was relieved that he showed an interest in me, maybe it made her feel less guilty about the whole saga. She had made some pretty stupid decisions, most of them involving marriages, but now my father and I were finally reunited.

My father had started to teach me Italian on the drive from Rimini to Florence that first summer. He told me more about our Grand Tour of Italy, which would be starting with Florence.

"You English aren't so stupid," he said. "Already in the early eighteenth century you knew the best places in Italy to go to. And you even learnt to speak the language, insufferably of course."

He could never say something nice about the English without adding a criticism.

"All you need to speak Italian is Dante, or an Italian lover, or possibly both," he continued.

He recited the canto of Paolo and Francesca with considerably more skill than he drove his vintage Mercedes. I hung onto the red leather seat and wished there were a seat belt. The motorway was particularly scary, with huge lorries pulling out in front of us and my father more focused on poetry than the traffic. He told me to recite each line after him.

"Nessun maggior dolore che ricordarsi del tempo felice ne la miseria."

"What does it mean?"

"There is no greater sadness than remembering happy times in misery. Francesca is telling Dante about how they loved each other in life and for her it is a terrible thing to remember now they are in hell. Repeat."

I tried my best.

"No, we'll start with the kiss instead, it's easier to remember. Listen carefully:

Quando leggemmo il disiato riso

esser basciato da cotanto amante,
questi, che mai da me non fia diviso
la bocca mi baciò tutto tremante.

It means: when we read that the longed-for smile was kissed by so great a lover, he who never shall be parted from me, kissed my mouth all trembling."

"La bocca mi baciò tutto tremante," I repeated.

"No, no. You sound like an English matron who has never been kissed because she has a face like a goat. He is kissing her mouth, all trembling. Use the rrrr. Trrremante, not traemante. Madonna. Try again."

"La bocca mi baciò tutto trrremante."

"Brava. Better. Think passion, think love. Imagine you are kissing your lover for the first time. That way you won't forget. Da capo."

By the time we got to his flat in the Via Ricasoli, I was reciting it like an Italian, partly because we almost crashed every time I let out an English vowel sound.

My father's apartment had very large rooms, high ceilings and almost no furniture. It was full of books, tapes and records. There were books piled up to the ceiling in all the rooms except the bathroom and the kitchen.

That first time in Florence we arrived on a hot summer's day. My father showed me into a spare room, with nothing in it except a big bed, a wardrobe, which stretched along one whole wall, and piles of books. I walked over to the far wall and opened the shutters. The entire view was of Florence's famous Duomo. It felt as if I could reach out and touch it. The sun made the tiles tingle and I longed to go out and explore. My father said he had work to do, handed me a guidebook and 200,000 lire and told me to have fun.

I ran down the two hundred and forty steps and out onto the street. Florence was buzzing with Italian sounds and the air was warm. I walked all the way round the Duomo and wandered along to the Piazza della Signoria. I stood in the middle, turning around slowly to take in the Uffizi, the Palazzo Vecchio and the gallery of statues, among them a reproduction of Michelangelo's *David*. Beautiful, serene, a perfect man. My guidebook quoted D.H. Lawrence. "He may be ugly, too naturalistic, too big, and anything else you like. But the *David* in the Piazza della Signoria there under the dark great palace, in the position Michelangelo chose for him, there, standing forward stripped and exposed and eternally half-shrinking, half-wishing to expose himself, he is the genius of Florence." I felt intellectual for the first time in my life and decided to go and buy a Lawrence novel immediately.

I wandered towards the Ponte Vecchio through streets bathed in afternoon sun and crowded with tourists. My guidebook informed me it meant old bridge. Around every corner there was a church or palazzo. I felt like I was in a film about Italy. It didn't seem possible that a city could be so beautiful. Every building I saw would have been a national monument in Newbury which was mostly made up of supermarkets and car parks. Here they were just there, one after another, practically unnoticed. It was hard to take it all in; I felt like someone who hadn't eaten for days faced with a vast feast and unsure of where to begin. The Ponte Vecchio itself was alive with small shops, traders and tourists. From both sides of the bridge tourists were encouraged by those selling their wares to come and browse. There were portrait painters and people selling beads and watercolours of famous views of Florence. I walked onto its parapet and looked out towards the green hills surrounding the city dotted with villas and cypress trees.

It was almost impossible to get lost, however small and windy the cobbled streets got. To get back to my father's flat, all I had to do was look for the Duomo and walk in that direction. And if I lost sight of the famous cupola, my Italian was good enough by now to ask where it was, although there was no guarantee I would understand the reply. Unless of course it was from the fifth canto of Dante's *Inferno*.

I walked into the church of Orsanmichele. It was one of the few things I had read about in my guidebook. It was almost dark inside; the only lighting came from the Gothic stained glass windows, and compared with the temperature outside it was freezing. I moved as silently as I could past the worshippers and looked for the Gothic tabernacle my guidebook recommended. The congregation was made up mainly of women who looked and dressed like my grandmother. That is, tiny and dressed entirely in black. I wondered what or who they were praying for, and remembered my grandmother warning me before I left Rimini not to become like my father.

"He is a lost soul," she said. "Without God, we are nothing." I stood in front of the altar in Orsanmichele, made the sign of the cross as she had taught me and tried to find religion.

I got back to the flat to find my father listening to an opera. When he saw me, he stood up and walked towards me. I had discovered that when my father had something to tell me he would grab my cheek between his thumb and forefinger and gently shake my head. It drove me insane but there was no escape.

This is what he did now. "We are going," he announced in his loud voice, "to the best restaurant in Florence." He told me to go and get dressed "with a lot of attention" and meet him by the door in an hour. He told me I could choose any clothes I wanted from the wardrobe in my bedroom. I went into my room and lay on my bed. The sounds of the street came in through the window. I had opened it to let some air in but closed the shutter to keep the hot sun out. I heard voices, footsteps and, of course, scooters. They sounded like furious wasps whizzing up and down the street. From the next door room I could hear my father on the phone to someone. I wondered how he felt about having me here. He wasn't like my grandmother; it was hard to tell if my being here meant anything to him at all. He never expressed his feelings or showed me any affection, but I supposed that if he was willing to spend time with me he must be vaguely interested in me.

I got up and walked over to the wardrobe. I felt like a child in a sweet shop. Whoever had stayed here had expensive and good taste in clothes. There were dresses, skirts, shirts and trousers, all much smarter than anything my mother or I would ever wear. In fact my mother only ever wore jeans. I remember my father saying once that the first time she wore a dress my grandmother had asked her if she'd had them surgically removed. But my mother always looked elegant in her jeans. In fact it made me uncomfortable to see her dressed up. It normally meant she was about to get married.

The trousers in the wardrobe were all too long for me but there was a small black skirt that fitted well. I found a top that went with it, although it was practically see-through. I threw off my old purple cords and yellow t-shirt, which seemed terribly unsophisticated and put on my new outfit. My grandmother would not have approved. "La bambina è tutta nuda," she would have said. The child is totally naked.

"Brava, you look like a high-class hooker," was my father's verdict. And although I took this as an insult, he assured me it was a compliment. He looked dashing in some cream linen trousers and a pale green shirt. He had momentarily swapped his Fedora hat for a Panama which completed the look.

As we walked arm in arm through the cobbled streets to the restaurant, I told him how I had spent my first day.

"I loved the *David* in the Piazza," I said. "He's such a perfect specimen of a man, so beautiful."

"Yes, but how can you have such admiration for a copy?" said my father.

"A copy?"

"Yes, the real one is in the Galleria dell'Accademia, in the street I live in."

"What's the difference between them?"

My father stopped and looked at me. "The real one has an erection every Wednesday at six p.m. precisely. The tourists love it, especially the Americans. You should see the way they gaze at it. They queue for hours to get in."

I blushed.

"Surely you're not so English that you have to be embarrassed about an erection?"

"No, I just…"

"How many lovers have you got?"

"None."

"Well you're still a bit young. But you should think about the future."

I didn't answer; instead I pretended to look at a church we were passing.

"Cara, don't get offended. Sex is like any other bodily function. You are hungry, you eat. You are thirsty, you drink. What is the problem?" He laughed.

"Today I read the most wonderful thing," he continued. "I was doing some research into the British psyche, so as to better understand you bella, and I found this passage, written by a young British subject over one hundred years ago while visiting Florence. Listen!"

He stopped walking, took off his black hat and began reciting in a high-pitched voice in an attempt to imitate a young Victorian girl. "I often half envy the happy life of an Italian free from care and brought up so as to be almost devoid of conscience, indulging in every inclination natural to man, loving to be loved, and all without restraint. Yes I sigh after such happiness."

"All I want is for you not to sigh after it, but to have it," said my father. "So. Andiamo." He took my hand for the first time ever and marched me towards the restaurant. It was as if the strident action compensated for the tender one.

The restaurant was tiny, a total of five tables in a dimly lit interior. The tables were low and the chairs small, making it seem very intimate. The walls were painted red, which increased the cosy atmosphere. We were shown to a table by a large window, overlooking the river and the Ponte Vecchio in the distance. My father chatted to the waiters, who were delighted to meet la signorina Benedetti, if slightly amazed that there was one. I was proud to be introduced as his daughter; it made me feel like I belonged.

A waiter came and explained the menu to us in flowing Italian. I had absolutely no idea of what he said and asked my father to order something for me.

The wine arrived and I drank quickly. I still didn't feel completely comfortable with this man. It was so difficult to know how to treat him. We were close relations, but it was hard to feel familiar with a person I hardly knew. I couldn't help feeling shy, which was ridiculous. This was my father; biologically I was at least half of him.

"Why did you never marry again?" I asked after drinking a glass of Chianti.

"Why would I want to do a thing like that?"

"Well you did it once."

"Twice actually."

"What?"

"I was married before your mother. To a woman obsessed with fur and jewels called Franca."

"What happened to her?"

"She was a stupid woman. And I threw all her jewels and furs out of the window to the poor of Rome."

"Did you get a divorce?"

"Of course," he laughed. "It wasn't easy; we had to go to the Vatican court. My lawyer said the only way to get it over with quickly was to pretend I was a communist and sterile and this good catholic girl had to be given a chance to live again and raise the family she wanted. She had to be saved from this monster."

"So what did you do?"

"I didn't shave for five days and went to court wearing a full-length leather coat and a Russian hat with a huge Lenin badge on it. That was all it took. They said I was a monster and Franca was free."

"What happened to her?"

"I have no idea. I never spoke to her again. I expect she

My mother a few years before she met Benedetto.

found some rich fool to replace her furs and diamonds."

"And then my mother?"

"No bella. There were several hundred before your mother. You have no idea how easy it is to get women if you have youth and money. Especially money. The number of women that have said to me 'Oh that Onassis is such an attractive man.' I tell you, it's impressive. He looks like a goat. But they all want him."

"Several hundred?"

"Don't look so shocked, I didn't have anything else to do."

"Why did you and my mother split up?"

"She told me she was going to die if she stayed with me," he said. "Obviously I couldn't be held responsible for the death of such a beautiful young girl so I let her go."

"Was she very beautiful?"

"She was lovely with delicate features, big lips and those amazing eyes of hers. She was the most lovely girl I had ever seen, and totally natural, almost like an animal from the wild. She reminded me of a gazelle; slim and flighty. She had a perfect body and a face that would stop you in the street. And she had the most wonderful technique for keeping me interested. When she wasn't wearing her jeans she was naked, almost all the time. Formidable! You my cara have my looks and, as far as I can make out, her brain. This is the wrong way round."

I ignored the insult and continued questioning him.

"Did you fall in love at first sight?"

My father laughed. "No, of course I thought I'd like to take her to bed at first sight, but love, no."

"So when did you fall in love?"

"What happened was that she was the first woman ever to say no to me. And that drove me mad."

"Why did she say no?"

"A German secretary I had working for me warned her about me. 'He beds everyone,' she told her. 'I've only been here a few weeks and I've seen fifty come and go. If you want him to take you seriously then say no.' So that's what she did. I was amazed. I took her to see the moon in Capri, to the opera at La Scala and dinner at the Cipriani in Venice. And still she said no. It drove me to distraction. Then she even had the cheek to leave the country and go to Sweden for the summer. Your aunt Piera had to go and get her, I was in Rome tearing my hair out.

Formidable!"

"What's this?" I asked, staring down at something unrecognisable the waiter had brought me.

"Testicles," replied my father.

"Oh yes, and I suppose there are breasts for pudding?"

"If you wish my dear, I know a very good lesbian bar." My father roared with laughter. "But these are bull's testicles. I thought if you acquired a taste for animals' testicles, you might develop one for humans'."

"I'm not eating these."

"Go on bella, just try one mouthful. And if you don't like it, you can have anything else you like on the menu."

I circled the food with my knife and fork, prodding here and there, trying to work out which would be the least disgusting place to start. Finally I opted for a rather overcooked-looking part. It tasted like liver and I swallowed it quickly with the help of some wine.

"No, I hate it."

"Very well," said my father, beckoning the waiter. "I know what you will like."

What arrived was a tiramisu, a pudding made of coffee, cream, sponge, mascarpone and sugar put together in a miraculous way. It made my hitherto apex of puddings, a Knickerbocker Glory, seem like a stale cucumber sandwich.

After dinner we walked through the streets and squares I had explored earlier. In Piazza della Signoria he told me the history of Girolamo Savonarola, the fanatical monk who urged the people of Florence to burn any luxuries, such as books, paintings and other "blasphemous" belongings.

"Finally the corrupt pope and cardinals of Rome had enough of his influence and had him beaten, strangled and burned at the stake here in the piazza. Let that be a warning to your grandmother next time she decides to preach to us."

We walked past Dante's house and the small church in which he was married to Gemma Donati, a woman he had been promised to at the age of twelve, although some say he was already in love with his muse Beatrice by then. My father recited the whole of the fifth canto, leaving me to fill in the bits I had learnt.

"You know his love for Beatrice was really only a tool for his own creativity," my father told me. "It had nothing to do with her as a person. The fact that she died aged twenty-four was no bad thing for Dante; that way she was able to remain ideal for ever."

We stopped and looked at the Ponte Vecchio. The night air was warm and there was a full moon over the Arno.

"It's lovely," I said.

"I ordered it just for you," said my father. "It cost a lot of money, but it was worth it."

We walked on towards his flat. In front of the Duomo we stopped again.

"Bella, you have to choose your lovers carefully. The important thing when you choose a lover is not how big his penis is or how well he uses it, but that he speaks five languages."

"Where am I ever going to find a man who speaks five languages?"

"When you speak five languages," he said grabbing hold of my cheek, "this won't be a problem."

Finally I get to the top of the stairs. There are two hundred and forty. This must be it, although I don't recognise the door. It feels odd to be back here after such a long time, but strangely comforting. I wonder when he last lived here. I am happy to have found it but his presence is missing.

As soon as I get here and start remembering my first summer with my father twenty years ago I realise that a book about Italian women isn't the book I want to write.

Instead of spending my time interviewing Italian women in an effort to discover their secrets, I decide to recreate my first summer in Italy, to go to the places I went to when I met my father and see how I feel about the country and its people. I also want to understand my father and my relationship with him. He was maddening. And my Italian family—being so rich (then)—led such a different life from the one I was used to. Yet the odd thing is that here I feel instantly at ease; bizarrely more so than anywhere else. Until now I had never even given Italy much thought. My first contact with my father happened so late and things faded when my grandmother died when I was in my twenties.

I was raised in England but am also clearly half Italian. My English side I know. I may not eat Marmite, but I can understand cricket and enjoy a warm beer in the rain as much as the next man. It is my Italian side that is a mystery. Could I be more Italian than I ever thought? Is it purely a coincidence that I have given my three children silly Italian names?

Standing at the door of my father's old apartment, I decide to embark on my own version of the Grand Tour of Italy, following in the footsteps of the eighteenth-century aristocrats who visited Florence, Naples, Rome and Venice. But instead of antiques and Renaissance masterpieces I am in search of my Italian roots. Do they really mean anything to me? When I first came here all those years ago I felt a sense of belonging in Italy. Now I feel I belong in England. And to a certain extent in France which my husband and I have made our home. But it is still a home filled with English culture. I read Beatrix Potter to the children, we watch English television and eat toast and marmalade for breakfast. All those years ago when I was desperate for another life, any other life than the one I had, Italy seemed like a perfect option. How will I view it now?

The last time I was in his apartment, I was going through his belongings. I was so curious about this man whom I hardly knew and I wanted to know more. I'm not sure what I thought I would find but I started in his bedroom. Like the rest of the flat his bedroom was sparsely furnished. There was a huge bed, a bedside table and some shelves that were free-standing and formed a sort of curve at one end of the room. The floor was made of light wood and there was a director's chair with his name printed on the back of it. I walked over to the shelves and began to look through the books. They were divided into languages. Italian, French, Spanish, Latin, German and English. There were works by Goethe, Shakespeare and Voltaire. And of course Dante.

I looked down the shelves to the bottom one where the outsize books were kept. There were large dictionaries in every language. Next to them were five photograph albums. I pulled them out and settled down on the bed to take a look. I opened the first one a little nervously, not quite knowing what to expect and also worried that my father might come back.

To my amazement, the first picture I saw was of me when I was around two, in Rome with a dummy in my mouth. The

Spot the dummy.

photograph was black and white and filled the whole page. My mother was drying my hair. My hair was being blown around and I was laughing. I turned over the page and there were another six pictures, obviously from the same day. In one of them my mother was just visible. It surprised me that he had bothered to take so many; he seemed so detached from me. He was so against any human emotion, which he automatically condemned as sentimental and not worthy of a real Benedetti.

On the next page were photographs taken before they split up. There were photos of my cousins, my mother; and there was even one of the three of us together. This shocked me the most of all. I couldn't imagine that the three of us had ever been together like a proper family. We were sitting on a sofa next to my mother's sister, my father is holding me in his arms and I look like I'm trying to get back to my mother. I must have been about three months old.

I picked up another album. This one was filled with pictures from the hospital I was born in and the days following my birth. I looked strangely old compared to the other children with my black hair and thick eyelashes. My mother is in some of the pictures, looking very pretty, like some sixties film star with her hair blonde and piled high up on her head.

The other albums were more of the same thing: me in Rimini, me in Rome, me by the seaside somewhere, Florence. I wondered if he would ever have shown them to me.

I walk back down the two hundred and forty steps to the street. The tourists are still there; even the Via Ricasoli is busier. I decide to walk back towards the river and find a place to eat lunch. I have never known a city like Florence to inspire me to walk so much. I go to the Ponte Vecchio purely out of curiosity. To me it always seems prettier from a distance, but it's just one of those things you have to do. I am accosted five times before I reach the relative safety of the other side. People are either trying to sell things or just asking for money.

The goods on sale are not tempting. The fake bag vendors display all their wares on a sheet that they quickly pick up and drag to another spot should a policeman come along. I see one of them pick up his entire collection and follow an indecisive client until she gives in. There are Asian women selling shawls; men are selling a plastic toy that makes bubbles. Then there are all the artists and caricature painters. I remember them from before. They at least don't seem to have changed at all since I was here last. They occupy the same spot between the Uffizi and the Lungarno Acciaioli. They sit in a long line waiting for people who think the one thing they need is a caricature of themselves. I can't imagine why anyone would want such a thing. Business must be slow.

Mother and daughter.

I pick a restaurant for lunch in a small street called Borgo San Jacopo. It is called Camillo's and looks like just the sort of place my father would have taken me to. I am shocked, and a little ashamed, to discover that I am relieved to be on my own.

I have been to lunch before in Florence, but never alone. Never without my father telling me what to eat and more often than not how to eat it. The last time my father and I ate spaghetti with basil and tomato together, I mopped up the remains of the sauce with a piece of bread.

"What are you? Some kind of peasant?" he yelled. "You don't need to clean your plate." I have never been able to do it since without remembering his rage.

I arrive at Camillo's starving. I have had no breakfast. I had no dinner last night. The restaurant is just what I want: white tablecloths, lots of waiters running around looking busy, a dresser full of wine, a Madonna praying in the far corner and lots of happy Italians. I ask for a table for one and a waiter shows me where to sit.

I love eating alone. I sit and read and sip my wine slowly and enjoy the sense of freedom, of not having to talk. When I worked as a financial journalist, I would travel to Eastern Europe every month and one of the things I enjoyed most was eating out alone. I would dread anyone coming to talk to me, or asking me to join them. Being alone was such a luxury. Here in Florence at two o'clock on a Tuesday in mid-November I have that sensation many times over. There is no booming voice to tell me what to order. I am paying for this myself and can have anything I like. If I want to, I can even start with risotto and go on to pasta. But I'm not that much of a rebel.

Before I even walk into Camillo's, I know what I want: a rocket salad with parmesan followed by pasta with tomato and basil sauce. The latter is not on the menu. But one thing I learnt from my father is that if you're Italian you ignore menus. You simply go in and tell them what you want to eat. When the waiter arrives, I do just that.

"Of course," he says. "Straight away."

The salad arrives. The rocket is peppery and the parmesan much tastier than the parmesan you get outside Italy. I mix it with the olive oil; it is so fresh it almost melts. I can hear a conversation behind me. An Italian family is discussing what to eat with the waiter. They talk at great length about the benefits of one meat sauce versus another, and what sort of pasta to have.

The waiter suggests he bring the food for the two girls straight away, so they don't get too hungry. The grown-ups agree. They order the pasta and say they will think about the second course after it. This is also something I remember my father doing a lot. Ordering a starter and then seeing how he felt afterwards; deciding then whether he wanted to eat anything else and if so, what he wanted to eat.

My pasta arrives soon after I have eaten my salad. It is linguine: thin, flat pieces of pasta, handmade with eggs and flour. The tomato sauce is so fresh it tastes sweet. After almost twenty-four hours without food it is one of the best lunches I have ever eaten. And when the waiter comes to take the plate away, there is not a drop of sauce left on it nor bread left in the bread basket. My father would be horrified.

I leave Camillo's feeling light-hearted and walk over the Santa Trinità bridge towards the Lungarno Amerigo Vespucci. I am going to the house of a lady called Mariella Pallavicini. She is a close friend of the mother of a friend of mine who suggested I interview her.

"She's such a character," my mother's friend told me. "You have to meet her."

In fact my friend finds her rather scary as she has a glass eye. Her mother defends Mariella. "She can't help it," she says. "She lost an eye in a car accident when she was eighteen."

Meeting Mariella now becomes part of the book I want to write about my father. Maybe I will find I relate to Italian women in a way I don't relate to women from other countries. Perhaps I will change into an Italian woman with incredible ease, almost like responding to a calling I never knew I had, and then stay that way for ever. I will live out my days blissfully making homemade pasta in the style of Sophia Loren who, I am amazed to discover, has written several cookbooks. You'd think with all her money and fame she would just get someone else to cook for her. She once said "Everything you see I owe to pasta." Maybe that's why she insists on making it herself. Sophia Loren is for me the epitome of an Italian woman; fun, voluptuous and beautiful. She has a kind of style you don't get with French women. She is more natural than, say, Catherine Deneuve, but not quite as drastically natural (or a victim of nature) as Brigitte Bardot. The contemporary Italian icon is Monica Bellucci. A sexier woman is hard to imagine.

I stop in the middle of the bridge to look at the Ponte Vecchio. Its colours are bright in the afternoon sun and the crowds less troublesome. Either side of the three arches in the middle of the bridge there are collections of hut-like buildings, almost higgledy-piggledy in their arrangement. The colours are orange, yellow and brown. The buildings look so ramshackle it's a miracle they have survived since the fourteenth century and not fallen into the water below. Through the arches you can see the Arno continuing to the Ponte alle Grazie. I remember my father telling me the Ponte Vecchio was the only bridge in Florence not to be destroyed during the war. The others were all bombed by the Germans in 1944 in an attempt to halt the Allies' advance.

Mariella lives just around the corner from the Grand Hotel. The road is broad and elegant, the houses tall and imposing. I am already primed for something extraordinarily glamorous as the friend who made the introduction knows almost no normal people at all. All her acquaintances are minor royals, or at least counts or lords or something aristocratic. I have also spoken to Mariella and she sounds suitably eccentric.

"There are two buttons with Pallavicini written on them,"

she tells me. "Ring them both, there's no point in waiting outside longer than you have to. The servant will let you in."

I don't think I have ever heard anyone outside Africa refer to a servant. I am intrigued to see what he or she will look like. A kind of Roman slave perhaps? Or some Sicilian peasant brought in to work for a pittance? I ring both bells as instructed. Once I am inside, I have to wait for the front door to close behind me before the wrought-iron gate leading to the interior of the palazzo will open. I cross a courtyard decorated with large plant pots and walk up a wide stone staircase to the first floor. As I reach the top of the stairs, the door opens.

I almost fall over with the shock. Forget the Sicilian peasant and the Roman slave: I am standing in front of Max from *Sunset Boulevard*. He is short and sturdy, wearing an old-fashioned uniform and white gloves. His hair is dark and cut very short, his face expressionless. He nods as he lets me in and takes my coat.

"Madame is on the telephone," he says slowly. "I will show you into the drawing room." The man even sounds like Max. This is uncanny. I am desperate to ask his name. Or if he had a previous life as a movie star. Or maybe it actually is Erich von Stroheim, the actor/director who played Max, and he's just incredibly well preserved.

Max shows me into the drawing room, which is also like something out of *Sunset Boulevard*. There is a chandelier and a grand piano, obligatory props for the aristocracy. The carpet is thick and cream-coloured. There are two over-sized sofas in the middle of the room covered with material with elaborate floral patterns. On the glass coffee table there are several outsized art books that look too heavy to pick up. In the middle is a silver vase holding a bouquet of mixed flowers. There are faded black and white photographs of beautiful and elegant women in backless evening dresses on the grand piano. Another vast bouquet of flowers, mainly lilies, stands on an inlaid table along one of the walls. I walk over to look at them. Their perfume is strong and good. Elsewhere the room smells slightly of old smoke and expensive scent. The walls are covered with large gilt-framed paintings. The ceiling is almost as high as my entire house.

I walk over to the window and look at the view of the Arno and its bridges. This has to be one of the best addresses in the world. I touch the curtains; they are a deep blue colour, silky and as thick as a sheepskin. Scarlett O'Hara could make a great dress from them.

Max offers me a coffee. I decline and he walks away slowly. Suddenly there is the sound of music. It's an opera I think; I vaguely recognise it. Whatever it is, it's dramatic. And very loud.

A woman comes out of a room adjoining the drawing room. When I say she comes out, she sort of dances out. She moves like a predatory tiger, arms high, hands like claws, legs lifted high with each step she takes towards me. I watch in amazement as she approaches. What will she do next? Jump on me? She is wearing the uniform of the classic Italian grande dame; black Chanel suit and diamond earrings. Her hair is thick and blonde, stylishly cut. Her lipstick red. She is a little shorter than me, so around five foot six. She is slim. Her face is attractive, her eyes large and blue, her smile slightly mischievous. The music stops and she takes my hand.

"I could make love to Rossini, even at my age," she announces. I don't know how old Mariella is, but she has a daughter who has just turned fifty so she must be at least seventy.

I'm kind of stuck for an answer but opt for a meek "Me too" and a smile.

She leads me to one of the sofas, which we sink into. "Tell me what you're doing here," she says.

I explain about my father and that I have lived in England almost all my life and have always thought of myself as English. Until I moved to France there was no reason to think of myself as anything else. But in France they tell me I speak French with an Italian, not an English accent. My mother is from Sweden, although she too has lived in England most of her life. Where do I really belong? Would I rather make love to Rossini than the Rolling Stones?

"Being Italian is all about duty to the family," she tells me. "Duty to your parents, to your children, to God. They all come before the self. I remember the first time I kissed a boy aged seventeen at a dance. I only kissed him because of the disappointment I felt that the boy I really liked had gone home. And it was an innocent little kiss. But the next morning I woke up and the first thing I thought was 'What have I done to my parents and to Jesus?'"

She shows me pictures of her two daughters. They are blonde and beautiful.

"My children and my grandchildren are the most important things to me," she says. "They come before everything, they have to; it's the only way to live. And I try to teach them about their roots, their identity. I tell them about their grandparents and what they did and what that means that they themselves can achieve in life. I think that is one thing that is very much missing from family life now, there is no sense of identity."

I remember my Italian aunt Piera saying that first summer that my mother had taken me away from my roots. At the time

I thought it was propaganda against my mother, but now I begin to think maybe my mother was wrong to wrench me from my family. In the years that followed our move from Italy it often felt like my mother was the only family I had. Her relations were all in Sweden and we only saw them once every few years. But through my stepfather I was to meet two people whom I am still in touch with, even though we severed links years ago.

The first was his mother, a lady called Eve. She was like a grandmother to me. She influenced my view of England and made me feel at home there. She reminded me of Mrs Tittlemouse. Everything in her home was perfect and so very English. Her sofas were covered in Liberty print material, her garden immaculate, even her cats seemed English. At one stage she lived in a thatched cottage covered with roses and wild flowers. I remember going there to stay with her when I was about five. She made me a marmalade sandwich and buttered the bread before she cut it which I thought was incredibly impressive. Then she cut the crusts off, which made me feel very special.

I think Eve is one of the reasons I feel such an attachment to England. Her husband was also a memorable figure. He was an RAF pilot during the war and extremely dashing. He was universally grumpy with everyone but seemed to like my mother and me.

I remember once driving down a small Devon country lane with him and my mother in his Jaguar. He was driving in the middle of the road.

"Aren't you worried about other cars?" my mother asked.

"Why should I be?" he thundered. "It's my road."

When he heard much later on that I was planning to go to

university in Durham, he wrote me a very stern letter. "The towns in the north of England are dreadful," he wrote. "And if anybody tells you any different, they're lying." I went to Durham anyway and loved it. He died several years ago but I am still in touch with Eve who is as gentle and lovely and as much fun as always although she's almost ninety. My children adore her and call her great-granny. I love listening to her recount to my children the same stories that she told me as a child. England may have changed a lot since then, but Eve has not.

The other person I grew very close to is the women into whose arms my stepfather ran when my mother moved in with the drunken driver. She is called Claudia and I first met her when I was nine years old. I was playing football at the time and had just accidentally kicked the ball through a window. This didn't put her off and we are still in touch on an almost weekly basis. She was possibly the most stable and constant influence I had throughout my childhood. She has bought a house close to ours in France so we spend lots of time together. Her two children are godparents to my middle daughter Bea and my son Leonardo. She also severed links with my stepfather years ago.

"Children love to hear about where they come from," says Mariella interrupting my thoughts. "How can they have a future if they have no past? Where were you brought up?"

"My mother remarried an Englishman when I was three," I explain. "So we moved to England."

"But you knew your father?"

"Not until I was fourteen. Then I came out here one summer."

Mariella looks horrified. "But you're married to an Italian now?"

"No, an Englishman. But we live in France."

"The English are such cold lovers, don't you find?"

"I don't know, I don't have any experience of any other kind of lover."

Now she's truly horrified. "What? You're practically a virgin. What a disaster."

She tells me the story of an English aristocratic lady who came to stay one summer in Mariella's villa in the hills above Tuscany. She was seduced over dinner by a local Italian count. Before pudding they vanished for half an hour. When they came back to the table, the lady's dress was covered in dust.

"They had obviously been up to the attic or somewhere," says Mariella. "I told her to wipe her dress but she was so happy she just didn't care. She was like a child who had just eaten a really good cake. She had needed to meet an Italian man. I do know one very attractive Englishman though, the Duke of Beaufort. Now, he is charming."

She asks me if I would like to see the house where the seduction took place. I would, very much. Will the count be there, I wonder?

We walk down to her car in the street below.

"The house was built in 1560 and they say it might have been designed by Michelangelo," she says, taking a deep drag of a cigarette. "But in my view, if he'd designed it, they would know about it. You'll have to drive. I can't face it any more and the servant is going out."

There is a motorbike parked in front of the car, making it impossible to move it. Mariella blows smoke at it in disgust. I offer to move the offending vehicle. Mariella shakes her head. "No, I'll call the servant. By the way, the road is very windy, will you be OK?"

"Yes, am I insured?"

"I'm not worried about insurance," she says. "I'm worried about survival."

Once the motorbike has been removed to somewhere it is guaranteed to be ticketed, we set off. Mariella's car is a Volkswagen and easy to drive. We head south out of the city towards the commune of Scandicci.

Mariella tells me she is the only person that uses the house now. She goes there for a couple of months in the summer. It is not open to the public, although sometimes they have weddings and other events there.

Once in Scandicci, we drive up a windy hill. Cars are coming down towards us fast on what I thought was our side of the road. After about three miles we turn off to the left down a track lined with olive trees and cypresses. We carry on for another mile or so before turning right into the tree-lined drive of the house. We park just outside, next to a vast chestnut tree whose branches have collapsed onto the ground and taken root again in several places. Mariella points the tree out and tells me this is very unusual. "Horticulturists have come from all over to investigate my multi-rooting tree," she says proudly.

A man and a woman wearing black and white uniforms greet us. They are obviously delighted to see Mariella and help her out of the car.

The villa, I Collazi, is perfectly proportioned. Like many Tuscan villas it is painted a muted yellow colour. Beyond the misty hills you can see Florence's Duomo. We walk up the stone stairs to the front door; Mariella leans on my arm for support. In some ways she is surprisingly fragile, despite being such a strong character.

At the top of the staircase we are greeted by two stone lions bearing the family crest with the word "liberty" written above it. We walk across a courtyard of large stone slabs. The villa is not vast but it is certainly big enough to be described as a stately home. It is one of the most elegant houses I have ever seen. It is made up of a main section and wings either side. As far as I can see from the outside, there are three floors. The entrance is colonnaded and reminds me of several buildings in Florence itself.

We walk into the great hall of the Colazzi. It is bigger than the whole of my five-bedroom house in France.

"This is where I had my coming-out ball," says Mariella, lighting yet another thin cigarette. "I looked fabulous all dressed in silk. Whenever we have events here, the chandelier is lowered and all the candles are lit. The fires burn for several days in advance to warm it up."

The flagstones are at least two foot square, stone and ancient. I wonder how many elegantly clad feet have danced over them in the past.

The tour continues. As we walk through the house, we are accompanied by the female maid carrying an ashtray.

"This was the nursery," says Mariella as we walk into a room with ink portraits of the entire Medici clan all over the four walls. There is still a cot in the corner. "I hated it; I was frightened of all these faces staring down at me." She gesticulates around the room with the hand that is holding the cigarette. The maid tries in vain to follow it with her ashtray.

The next room is one of several drawing rooms. Here I am shown a seating plan with the Queen Mother on it. There are signed photographs of the Queen, as well as Charles and Diana, casually propped up on a side-table.

"Princess Margaret loved it here," Mariella tells me. "She

came to stay for several weeks. My mother and she were very close."

Mariella doesn't offer to show me upstairs, but tells me that there are "around thirteen" bedrooms. The gardener takes me on a tour of the grounds. We start on the steps at the back of the house. Below us is the rose garden and the lemon orchard. They look a little sad now in mid-winter, but I imagine during the summer the colours and smells must be wonderful. There is a constant sound of cars from the nearby road. This is one of the sad things about Italy: you are never alone. We look out over the hills around. The view is splendid. I always thought that image one has of Florence surrounded by misty hills, cypress trees and pines was exaggerated. From the back steps of the Collazzi I see it isn't. If you put your hands over your ears and ignore the traffic, you really do feel like you've walked onto a Merchant Ivory set. Unlike the countryside around Rome, which has been ravaged, the Florence countryside is protected. The gardener points out another villa on top of a hill to our right.

"That belongs to the signora as well," he says. It is smaller than Collazzi but looks lovely.

"We have a hundred and twelve lemon trees," the gardener explains. "They will soon be put away for the winter." I ask him what they do with all the lemons.

"Make limoncello of course," he smiles. "And the signora gives a lot away to neighbours and friends."

To the east of the house is the swimming pool, which is kept clean although there is nobody to swim in it. It is twenty metres by ten metres and if you stand at the far end of it away from the house, the façade of the villa is perfectly reflected in it. It is framed as if it were a painting. Only the movements of water boatmen swimming back and forth break the perfectly flat surface.

When we get back from our tour of the garden, Mariella is already in the car, still smoking. She is keen to get back home to her "work", which consists of managing portfolios of shares. We say goodbye to the guardians of Collazzi.

On the way back to Florence she tells me about her childhood.

"We come from a different world, my generation. When I was a child, it took two hours to make a phone call to Milan. Now you can get there in two hours. I was sent to university accompanied by a governess. My grandfather wouldn't leave the house without wearing a hat. It's all so different now. You belong to this world, I don't."

I wonder if she means Italy or just the modern world. Do I belong in Italy? It seems so strange that I feel so happy in her company after such a short time. Is it because she's Italian or just because I like her? Maybe a bit of both. In spirit she seems closer to my age than hers. I find her fascinating, much more open than a French or English woman of her age and class would be, and much more fun. Despite her posh surroundings and servants she seems extremely natural and unstuffy. Maybe it's a sign of real class as opposed to anything very Italian. But one thing that I do think is Italian, and I have experienced again and again with other Italian women, is generosity.

Once back in her apartment, Mariella shows me her office, where she follows the stock markets with obsessive regularity from three desks. She has prospectuses from New York, London and Milan. She asks me what I think of General Motors. I have no idea, I tell her. They make cars, don't they?

"I took a couple of hours off to show you Collazzi, but I

must get back to work," she says. Before she does though, she wants to send a postcard to the friend who introduced us. She looks through one of her desks for a suitable one. I have never seen a room with so many bits of paper in it. There is no computer, so I guess Mariella does all her work with pen and paper. There isn't even a typewriter. There is a bed in the room, although I am unsure if this doubles as her bedroom as the bed is also covered in papers.

"Let's send her this, a picture of Collazzi," says Mariella, taking out a card with a line drawing of the villa on it. Then she sees another card. It is a delicate painting of a servant girl carrying a jug of milk. She tells me early on in their marriage she and her husband moved to Brazil for a few years. They wanted to have some of their favourite works of art shipped out there. She tells me you have to declare any work of art that is taken out of Italy to the authorities.

"We did all this, of course," she says. "But what we didn't know was that the state has the right to buy the work of art and at face value. We lost six of the most precious paintings that ever belonged to the family, including her," she says pointing at the girl in the postcard. "It broke my heart to lose them. I never got over it."

Mariella is crying as she tells me this. And it is only now as tears fall from her real eye that I notice which one is false.

2

Nothing Gay about Gabriel

I know where I want to go next but I don't know how to get there. I am on the Ponte alle Grazie, the bridge after the Ponte Vecchio as you walk eastwards along the river. It is 9.30 in the morning and it is my last day in Florence before I continue my Grand Tour. My plan is to go to Piazza San Marco, where I remember a museum my father and I visited on that first trip. It was the only museum I went to with him that left a lasting impression and I want to go back there. I don't remember its name, but how many can there be in one square, even in Florence?

The problem is that I have left my map at the hotel. I head over the bridge, following a sign that says Santa Croce. That sounds familiar. There are rowers on the Arno gliding effortlessly through the water. At least it looks effortless. A jogging club runs towards me across the bridge. One enterprising man has a sporty double-buggy with twins inside. He's obviously giving his wife the morning off. Unlike most of Florence, the streets here are wide and open. You can see to the hills beyond the city.

San Marco is on the northern side of the river, I'm sure; I have a vague feeling it is the other side of the Duomo. Once I get over the river, I will go into the nearest hotel, explain my predicament and get them to give me one of those maps they hand out. But meanwhile the sun is getting warmer and as usual Florence inspires me to walk.

The Piazza Santa Croce is surprising in that it is just off a small side street but is one of the largest piazzas in the city. One minute you are walking down a tiny little alley and the next there is a vast square in front of you. It is rectangular and lined with marble benches. Its size gives it a stately elegance. I sit down to look at the Basilica of Santa Croce, which stands at the far end of the square. There are people occupying the other benches, either locals reading a newspaper or tourists looking at maps. The locals are well dressed and stylish. I am always surprised whenever I come to Italy at how good people look. I remember my father telling me that for an Italian looks are all-important. The bella figura is not just a saying but a way of life. Waiters in Italy look smarter than most office workers in England. There is an attention to detail that is very different from the Anglo-Saxon way, and it's almost more apparent in Italian men. When I arrived at Roma Termini a few days earlier I spotted a good-looking young man (like you do), probably aged around twenty, walking towards me. He was wearing jeans and trainers with a white shirt. Normally quite a scruffy look. But his shirt was so perfectly ironed you could see the creases and the care that had been taken over it. The effect was that instead of scruffy he looked well dressed. I wondered whether his mother did his ironing for him or whether part of the Italian male's education is to learn to do what it takes to look good.

"Being called ugly is the worst possible insult for an Italian," my father told me during that first summer. "Worse than being told you're a cuckold, which comes a close second."

A man sitting on a bench opposite me wears tailored cream trousers, a salmon pink shirt and a leather jacket. The jacket is cut like a blazer and the same colour as his shoes which are polished and look expensive. His hair is neat and clean. The woman sitting next to him is more striking. She is wearing gold trainers and carrying a matching gold bag. She must be around fifty and has long bleached blond hair. Oddly enough she doesn't look vulgar, but rather elegant. Italians are a lot more daring in what they wear than others. It's not a look a French woman would go for. Her jacket is made of white fur. It looks incredibly cosy. It's not that cold today but Italian women wear fur whenever they get a chance. I remember my mother telling me how astounded she was by the amount of fur shops in Rome.

"It's not as if it ever gets cold there," she told me. "But that doesn't stop them, bloody women." My mother is very left-wing, so automatically opposed to things like fur. When I was growing up I believed that Margaret Thatcher was truly evil, on a level with Franco and Hitler. Her hero was (and still is) Che Guevara. Her most prized possession is a stamp from Cuba with his image on it, which she keeps in her jewellery box. In fact there is no jewellery in her jewellery box, my mother is not one for feminine trinkets. She keeps important things in there like her Che Guevara stamp and her father's old reading glasses.

There was a poster in our kitchen of Ronald Reagan and Thatcher; a take-off of the original *Gone with the Wind* poster with Reagan as Rhett Butler sweeping Maggie off her feet. "She promised to follow him to the end of the world; He promised to arrange it," it read.

"They ought to do one with Blair and Bush," she said to me recently when I asked if she remembered the poster.

It was only once I left home that I understood that my mother's hatred of all things American might be a little irrational, especially as she's never even been there.

The tourists in the piazza are easy to differentiate from the locals. They wear the classic tourist uniform of trainers (the non-gold variety), rucksacks and baseball caps. They may be lost but at least they had the foresight not to forget the map in their hotel room. On the edge of the square, stall holders and newspaper stands are opening up for business.

I call home. Olivia, my eldest daughter answers the phone. There's no school in France on a Wednesday so she's at home. I have been looking forward to talking to them all. Despite my feeling of liberation the day before, I miss them terribly. I think Olivia, who is now seven, would fit in very well in Italy. She looks very Italian, out of the three children she is the most like me. My husband Rupert says she's like a mini-me; the same brown eyes and brown hair, the same little nose (although hers has a charming ski-jump shape), the same body, the same temperament and ambition. She never sits still. I asked her a few months ago if she could stop moving for a second. She was driving me mad, fiddling about constantly.

"That's not my job," she told me.

"Hey Mummy," says Olivia. "Do you want to talk to Bea?" She's obviously too busy taking over the world to talk to me.

I am passed from one to the other, the only person who seems vaguely interested in talking to me is my husband, but it's good to hear their voices.

Although Santa Croce dates from the end of the thirteenth century, the façade is neo-Gothic. I think Gothic was bad enough the first time; the thought of reviving it seems absurd, but I don't dislike the overall effect. It is at least striking: all dark green and white, if a little ornate. There is a main block in the middle with a wooden door. On either side are two smaller copies of this middle section. It is very fiddly though, and reminds me of one of those matchstick statues, for some reason.

The most important thing about Santa Croce is the dead who are buried or commemorated here. Its tombs and cenotaphs read like a Who's Who of the other world: Michelangelo, Alberti, Dante, Galileo, Machiavelli and Rossini are among the notables buried or commemorated here. Inside I walk around from tomb to tomb, wondering if the dead in here sometimes rise and compare notes about their lives. There would be some great conversations, maybe ferocious arguments. I can imagine Alberti and Michelangelo going head to head on the nature of perspective.

I stop in front of Michelangelo's tomb. I have to say that for one of the greatest artists who ever lived, his tomb is pretty naff. It was designed by Giorgio Vasari. The three figures surrounding it are meant to represent painting, sculpture and architecture. I guess he was only following the trends of the day, but it's all very fussy. And the actual tomb, a sort of brown marble box stuck in the middle, seems strangely out of synch with the rest of the monument. Fat little cherubs hold up a painted curtain around an elaborately framed painting of the pietà. It is impressive, the biggest tomb I have ever seen, but it lacks elegance.

I walk along a road called the Via Verdi, which I guess is named after the composer. Not one of my father's favourites: "too sentimental," was his opinion of *La Traviata*. It is still early and the streets are relatively empty. I continue for another half an hour away from the river, not really knowing why I am choosing certain roads over others but revelling in the adventure of not having a clue where I will end up. Suddenly I am in a square that looks familiar. To the left is a building I have definitely seen, before with small blue terracotta roundels on the loggia. It is the Spedale degli Innocenti. I look around the square. A sign tells me I am in the Piazza della Santissima Annunziata. Good news, but where exactly is it? I walk over to a newspaper stand at the other end of the square. I hate to give in but I need to find my Holy Grail.

"Excuse me," I say to the vendor. "Am I by any chance anywhere near Piazza San Marco?"

The man smiles. "Yes, you can see San Marco, it's just up there," he says, pointing to a square at the end of the road.

I have butterflies in my stomach when I get there. But I don't recognise it at all. There are several buses driving around and I am unsure of where to start looking. I am about to ask someone when I spot a building that looks like a museum. I walk around the square until I reach the front door. A brass plaque tells me this is the Museum of San Marco and that it is closed practically every day apart from today. I go in and pay my four euros. It is an elegant building and has the added advantage of being practically empty. All the tourists must be milling around the Baptistry doors or the other more obvious sights.

I walk around the cloister; the pillars are thin and create shadows on the walls. Between the arches is a small garden with a perfect lawn and a small sign telling you not to go anywhere near it. There is a serene feeling about the place, which I suppose comes from it having been a Dominican monastery. I am beginning to think I must be in the right building but wonder how I can find my way back to the place I remember from over twenty years ago.

I walk around the cloister once again. There is a room with some paintings in it, another with some statues. But no sign of what I am looking for. Then I see a notice leading me upstairs. I walk up. There at the top of the thin carpeted stairs is the fresco I have been searching for. It is the *Annunciation*, painted by Fra Angelico, who my father had told me was a Dominican friar who was born in the fourteenth century. The cloisters the Virgin sits in look like the ones downstairs. She is on a simple wooden stool, looking serene in a flowing blue cape. Her skin is translucent, her cheeks rosy. She is the epitome of youth and innocence. In front of her the angel Gabriel bows. He is wearing pink, nothing gay about Gabriel, and the obligatory halo. But it is his wings that are so remarkable. They are multi-coloured, starting with light blues and pinks at the top and moving through the spectrum to purples and russets at the bottom.

All the colours in the fresco are pure and clean. The composition is simple. The perspective is slightly off, giving it a naïve feeling that adds to its charm. The last time I was here, my father told me the story of my birth. It was the first time I had ever heard it. My mother never spoke about my past and because I loved her so much I didn't like to ask her. She had once told me the reason she left my father was that she just couldn't stand it any more. He never left her alone for a minute to be herself.

"I had to get away," she told me. "It was killing me. I just wanted to be free to think and say what I wanted. I was so sick of him talking at me all the time I just couldn't stand it any longer. And when he wasn't lecturing me he was sleeping. I was young and wanted to have fun."

"Bella, this picture always reminds me of your birth," he

said. "There was a copy of it hanging in the hospital in Stockholm where you were born. Your mother insisted on you being born in Sweden for patriotic and medical reasons. I wanted you to be born in England. But I travelled with her to Stockholm; I had never been to Sweden before and I wanted to see the land of Bergman."

I remember a group of Japanese tourists stood behind us while their guide told them the history of the fresco. My father ignored them and carried on with his story, practically drowning out the tour guide.

"One evening your mother decided it was time for you to be born. Despite the fact that it was mid-December and colder than you can imagine, she went jogging over the star-lit bridge that linked the flat we had rented in Lidingö with mainland Stockholm. The next day her contractions started. We went to the St Eriks hospital in the centre of town. 'Don't stand there looking daft,' she told me when we got there. 'There's nothing you can do anyway. Go and see a film.' By the time I came back from the film, you had been born."

The Japanese gave up and moved on. My father completed the story.

"A nurse led me to the rows of babies in their sterile cots and white blankets. There were over fifty babies in the room but there was no need for her to point you out. Among all the blond Swedes, you were the only baby with thick dark hair and long, black eyelashes that reached half-way down your cheeks. Formidable."

This was the one painting in Florence I really loved all those years ago. Now, standing in front of it all so many years later, I am again struck by how perfect it is. It radiates a kind of peace and harmony. Did I believe my father when he told me it reminded him of my birth? At the time I had, but he was so wrapped up in his intellectual pursuits that I wondered if he ever really thought about it. He would probably call such reflection sentimental, which is akin to obscene stupidity in his view. I always felt that being his biological daughter had little bearing on his feelings or treatment of me. His love was not, like a mother's, unconditional.

I walk around the cells on the first floor. There are around thirty-five of them. In each of them Fra Angelico or one of his followers has painted a fresco. They are all in the same simple, naïve style of the *Annunciation*. I walk into one of the few cells you can actually enter. There is a tiny window about eight inches long and four inches wide. It is covered by a miniature wooden shutter. I carefully open the shutter. It is much thicker than you would expect. It has a black metal handle. The view is of the Duomo in the distance. Inside the cell there is nothing but white walls and the fresco. The floor is made of shiny terracotta tiles. In the days when the cell was the home of a friar, I guess there must have been a bed or at least a mattress there. Thinking about my home and all the clutter that goes along with lots of children and family life, I reflect that it must give one a sense of inner peace to own nothing in the world but a bed, a fresco and a view of Florence's Duomo. Some of this inner peace rubs off on me. I leave the San Marco museum feeling serene and positive.

I think back to my mother's decision to leave Italy. I can't imagine an Italian woman doing the same thing. One thing I have learnt from Mariella is that the family is by far the most essential thing to them. We have definitely lost some of that in England. When you make sacrifices in your career for the sake of your family, you're judged as irresponsible or idle. In Italy it's the other way round.

My mother didn't have an Italian attitude to family values. She severed all links with my father when she left Rome with me aged three. It was as if my Italian family didn't exist. When I asked my father why he had given up trying to get in touch with me he told me the last straw was a postcard from England from my mother saying: "Since I remarried, the child has stopped looking like you."

I can't imagine what it must be like to lose a child now that I have my own. I have only been away from mine for a couple of days and although I am enjoying rare time to myself, I think about them endlessly and wonder what they're up to. They are still so young and I worry that Leonardo will think I've gone away for ever. I don't think this is particularly Italian, all mothers miss their children when they're parted from them, although the family is definitely a more central part of life here than it is in England. Here you eat together, which may sound trivial but is very important. I read somewhere that forty per cent of families in England don't eat together. A statistic I find terribly sad. After two days in Florence I am beginning to feel more Italian. I am speaking the language more fluently, craving pasta and coffee on a regular basis, and thinking about my family a lot.

The other thing I am thinking about is my hair. It is distinctly un-Italian. This getting in touch with my inner Italian woman doesn't only have a spiritual element. I need to look like an Italian too. I am at an advantage in that I already have brown eyes and brown hair. I also have thick eyebrows and long eyelashes. So far, so good. But I have not yet eaten enough pasta to be able to sport that voluptuous Italian look and my dress sense is far too conservative. Out should go the Audrey

Hepburn cream trousers and black polo-neck look and in should come the studded jeans, cowboy boots and sexy crop-top. Italy, my husband says, is the country of Bling. And I don't fit in. Yet. I decide to start at the top; with my hair.

Just at this moment I pass a hairdresser's. From outside it looks like a nice enough place: lots of shampoo bottles in the window and white walls. There are yucca plants in the reception area and a grey leather sofa. The BH salon in Borgo Ognissanti, just off the Lungarno, looks like as good a place as any to begin my physical transformation.

As soon as I walk into the salon, I almost do an about-turn and run out screaming. They are playing rock music. Loud rock music. Oh God, how unrelaxing. How incongruous after the serene calm of Fra Angelico's frescoes. But by now the receptionist has caught my eye. She is very pretty, extremely slim and wearing very low hipster jeans and a tiny black T-shirt with a rhinestone heart on it. The diamonds are emerald green. Maybe I should ask her where she bought it. As she puts the phone down I see her nail varnish matches the rhinestones, as do three or four streaks in her otherwise black hair. What an unusual idea. She asks how she can help.

"I'd like to get my hair cut," I shout over what I can only assume is a punk-rock revival that I seem to have avoided up until this moment. "And maybe some colour?"

"No problem," she smiles. She is joined by a good-looking man in a white Rasta hat. He is wearing jeans and a red and white T-shirt with some logo plastered all over it, which I'm sure is incredibly trendy but is totally lost on me. This is going horribly wrong. Whatever happened to slick-looking types dressed in black and Sade being mellow in the background? This is as far from the salon at Harvey Nicks as you can get; I am WAY out of my comfort zone.

"I'll do your colour," says the Rasta. Great, now I'm going to have my hair dyed by a man with a knitted tea-cosy on his head. I smile weakly.

"Come and sit down."

I am led to a chair next to a boy in his early twenties who is cutting a girl's hair. He looks up at me and smiles as I approach. He is dressed all in black, so an improvement on the Rasta, but the soothing effect is somewhat ruined by the vast serpent tattoo edging up his neck from underneath his T-shirt. Other than the Beckham-esque touch though, he's quite attractive. I catch myself wondering briefly where the serpent starts. Then Ricky, my new Rasta friend, puts a gown on me. There are mirrors and lights everywhere; the whole place looks super-clean and white. The only splashes of colour are the stylists, the clients and the posters of people with mad haircuts.

"Here is our colour selection," says Ricky, sitting down next to me. What, no bright green? I'm tempted to ask, but I stop myself in case he doesn't think I'm joking. Ricky goes into a long explanation in Italian as to why I should have this or that and the benefits of mixing two colours and so on. I nod rather inanely; conversation would be futile anyway, the noise is so deafening. He really is a sweet-looking boy, with lovely coffee-coloured skin and delicate hands. He is also extremely friendly; in fact I would say he is positively flirtatious. But then I tell myself to stop imagining things; I had green hair before he was born.

Ricky goes off to mix my colour. Then my stylist appears. She is about nineteen, quite short, with gorgeous shoulder-length blond-brown hair cut in layers, green eyes and the most porcelain skin I have ever seen. Her smile is totally addictive.

"I'm Marina," she says holding out her hand. I introduce myself. She addresses me in the informal tu. Suddenly I feel about twenty years younger. I might even think about having a serpent tattoo and green highlights. And the music, which is now something fairly mellow by Simply Red, may be loud, but hey, so what? I even find myself singing along.

"How would you like your hair?" Marina asks.

I struggle to find the right words in Italian; I mumble something about a bit of life, not so flat, more interesting, it just hangs there and then finally admit it. "I'd like it like yours." And in fact while we're at it, could I have your face and body too?

Marina smiles and nods as she plays with my hair. Then she leans closer to me, rests her hand on my shoulder and asks if I'd like anything to drink. It's an amazing thing about Italian women; they are so tactile. As she wanders off to get my glass of water, she doesn't just take her hand off my shoulder; she sweeps it along my back. Incredible. You don't get that at Harvey Nicks. In fact the only time I ever saw it in London was with my Italian friend Allegra. We were in Oriel's wine bar in Sloane Square. She had showed up looking totally Italian and glamorous as usual, wearing all black bar a bright orange coat. As we left, she bumped into the waiter. Instead of just saying sorry and moving swiftly on, Allegra stopped dead in her tracks, took hold of his arm, looked deep into his eyes and cooed: "I am soooo sorrrrrreeee." The man was a goner.

Ricky comes back with my colour followed by another gorgeous-looking girl who starts talking to him, in English. When she goes, I ask him where he learnt his English. He tells me he is from the Seychelles but has lived in London, where he trained with Toni & Guy in St Christopher's Place, and moved to Florence a few years ago to run the BH salon. I ask him what he thinks of Italian women.

"They're terrible," he says smiling. "So naughty, and NEVER faithful. Believe me, I do their hair all day long, and they LOVE talking about sex, it's their favourite subject."

He tells me he met a girl on the train two days ago. He was in the restaurant carriage, chatting in English with his friend. This girl, a very pretty Italian, was eyeing them up, and eventually she talked to them.

"We invited her out yesterday," Ricky tells me. "She said she couldn't come because her boyfriend was there. But that she could come out tonight."

"And are you going to go out with her?" I ask.

"No, I'll be too knackered after work," he grins. "But my friend's going."

I ask Ricky why Italian women behave like this.

"They think the same way as a man," he tells me. "And they have to have good sex, otherwise it's finished."

"But aren't they all catholic?" I ask him.

"Yes," he says. "And it's so convenient. They just go to confession, get forgiven and start all over again the next day. What could be better?"

Ricky puts a rotating contraption over my head that emits heat and will apparently do wonders for the colour of my hair. Then he goes away. Almost as soon as he leaves, about thirty young women come trailing into the salon and queue up behind my chair. A photographer runs around with an official-looking woman carrying a pen with pink feathers streaming out of it. It is obviously some modelling competition. I sit there feeling very old and unattractive with brown gunk all over my head and a wok-like contraption acting as a kind of rotating halo. I decide it's best to rise above the situation (halo and all) and immerse myself in *A Room with a View*.

Ricky comes back after fifteen minutes. He leads me to a sink where I am to be rinsed. I am ashamed to say I am quite looking forward to those delicate fingers gently massaging my scalp. But sadly Ricky delegates this job to the shampooing queen from hell with a Mohican and bigger hands than my feet. I feel like I have been mauled by a ravenous tiger when I am finally released from the shampooing chair and put back in front of a mirror.

At last it's time to get my hair cut. The lovely Marina appears again, looking serene. She is one of those classic Italian women who I fear will explode after the age of thirty, but for now she is perfectly ripe and gloriously lush. Her chest, it has to be said, is probably her most striking feature after her smile. Her breasts are firm and plump, like two tennis balls bouncing under her jumper. Her tight cream wool top not only accentuates their shape but also rides up just above the waistline of her trousers to show a little bit of belly. This is not a skinny French girl. This is a full-blooded southern Italian lass who will make love and cook home-made ravioli with equal gusto. I am not surprised when she tells me she comes from Salerno, not far from Naples.

Marina starts to cut my hair. She takes a chunk in one hand, combs it straight up above my head, then she leans into me (tennis balls and all) and cuts it in mid-air.

She is like a dancer, creating a pattern around my head as she lifts, snips, leans and combs. The whole spectacle is quite amazing. We exchange few words. Partly because I am so engrossed in this whole scene, but also because the punk revival has returned on the loudspeakers. She tells me she was in London two weeks ago.

"It was nice," she shouts. "But so hectic. We worked on a hair show all day and then at night, dancing, dancing, dancing."

I ask her if she likes Florence. She nods unenthusiastically. I get the feeling this is a girl who will end up back in the south as soon as she has found some macho Italian bloke to marry her. Perhaps I have an outdated impression of the south of Italy, but as far as I can understand southern women in the main want to breed and cook. I remember my father told me that women in the south had never really escaped from the culture of slavery that they were born into. He quoted a poem by the Nobel Laureate Salvatore Quasimodo who talks of a land far away in the south where women wearing shawls whisper about death in the doorways. They could probably do more with their lives.

Despite the fact that it is almost closing time and all her colleagues are off to a party, she takes great care with my haircut. She dries my hair and then goes through an incredibly thorough process, checking its length all over.

"We need to lighten up the fringe some more, and the sides," she tells me. So the whole dance begins again and I wonder if I'll have any hair left at all by the time Marina finally goes partying.

Suddenly she stops and I am presented with the finished product: a shorter-haired but definitely more Italian-looking woman. Ricky comes over to say goodbye. For one awful moment I think he is going to ask me if I want to go out for a drink. He might not have enough energy for an Italian nymphomaniac he met on the train but how tiring can an old English bird be? Of course it would be interesting to say yes, if only to see what is under the tea-cosy, but really I think the whole haircutting experience has been enough to satiate my longing for youth. Luckily Ricky doesn't ask. Instead he smiles warmly and shakes my hand.

"Enjoy your haircut," he says as I leave.

I went to a hairdresser's in Florence that first summer in Italy, but not to have my hair cut: to have it permed. It looked totally ridiculous, but to me anything at all was better than the thin straight hair I had. I remember walking into the salon with some money my father had given me and pointing to a picture of a girl with ringlets. As my father said at the time: "We all want what we haven't got. That's why I always prefer young women to those who are old like me."

I arrived back in his flat with strange curly hair but was unaccountably pleased with it. My father laughed and announced we were going to the Galleria dell' Accademia to see Michelangelo's *David*, so I could "experience a real man". We walked down the stairs and left out the front door. The Galleria dell' Accademia was just a five-minute walk away.

"Of course, Michelangelo was a queer, as most of your English men are, but *David* is a work of genius and only homosexual in his creator's dreams," he explained as we jumped the queue of tourists waiting to get in, thanks to some card he flashed intermittently.

"Isn't this a bit rude?" I asked, nervous at being branded a queue-barger, a terrible thing to be in England.

"Bella, queuing is for the proletariat. They have the time. They have nothing important to do but their shitting jobs. You don't have the time to waste; you have a lifetime of art, music, history and literature to catch up on. You cannot afford to waste even one minute in a queue again as long as you live. So,

Andiamo. Rude," he mimicked my accent. "Bah you English are so bourgeois. Show a little flair, be a little frivolous. Dare to be different, bella. You behave like a pecora."

"A pecora?"

"Yes, a sheeps."

"Sheep?"

"Exactly. If you want to be a sheeps all your life, you can queue. If you want to be an interesting and magnificent woman, come with me. I will introduce you to your first sexual encounter. Here you will lose your artistic virginity. I hope the physical one will not be disappointing in comparison. Let's go."

We walked into a large marble hall where Michelangelo's *Four Prisoners* stood alone, one in each corner. My father removed his black hat as a mark of respect, something he also did in churches, which I found odd, as he was always so rude about religion. The muscular figures trying to free themselves from the stone were dramatic and powerful. I thought they were wonderful and told my father so.

"Yes, but they're only half a man. Come with me and meet a whole one."

We wandered through another room and came to a standstill in front of *David*. He really was beautiful. A tower of masculinity.

"His hands are too big," said my father. "But otherwise he is in good form."

I nodded.

"So, when the time comes to lose your virginity, we find you one of these. Agreed?"

"One that speaks five languages?" I wanted to show him I'd remembered what he told me the previous day.

My father laughed and grabbed my cheek. "Bella, for losing

your virginity, you only need the language of love."

I now find myself back in the Via Ricasoli, walking towards the Galleria dell' Accademia, showing off my new haircut. I have a desperate urge to see the real thing again before I leave Florence. There's nothing like a new haircut to waken a girl's urges. Thank God I've grown out of perms. The museum is much further up the street than I remember. I look at the shops as I walk past: leather goods, art, trinkets and mementoes of Florence, all the usual things. Every twenty metres or so there's a bar. What would happen if Italians decided to give up coffee one day? Millions of small bars all over the country would go out of business. Or maybe they could survive on the food and ice cream they sell? Anyway it's an unlikely scenario. I think Italians are more likely to give up pasta before caffeine.

I can see where the museum housing *David* is before I see the actual building. There is a long queue stretching all the way down the street. I walk to the door to see if there is any possibility of pushing in. Without my father I don't have the guts to queue-barge. I start to walk the length of the line. Most of the voices I hear are American. I look at my watch. It's half past five. And it's Wednesday. They're obviously all queuing to see the famous erection. I keep walking past the end of the queue, back down the Via Ricasoli towards the Duomo and then on to my hotel. David's erection may be magnificent, but I am in search of something else.

I turn right along the Via dei Pucci into Via Cavour towards the Palazzo Medici. There is something here Mariella has told me to visit, the Chapel of the Magi. It was decorated by a pupil of Fra Angelico called Benozzo Gozzoli. As soon as I walk in, I am overwhelmed by sensations. Colours, light, details, images, stories and faces all descend on me from the walls of the chapel. It is one of the most magical places I have ever seen. The frescoes tell the story of the procession of the Magi. But the details are incredible, from the beautiful, almost angelic face of Magi Casper, said to be an idealised version of Lorenzo de Medici, to the natural landscape that frames the procession and the horses, reminiscent of Paolo Uccello but somehow more successful.

It is almost too much to take in. I find my breathing gets heavier. I feel dizzy trying to focus on it. This is something that has happened to visitors on the Grand Tour before me. It is known as the Stendhal effect. It was named after the French writer who said he collapsed from "a pitch of excitement wherein the celestial sensations of the fine arts meet the passions" during a visit to Florence in 1817.

I don't collapse, mainly because I don't want to mess up my new haircut. Instead I walk outside for some fresh air. There is a small garden in the Palazzo Medici. It is late afternoon but there is still some sun on the far wall above the fountain. I go and sit on the edge of it and close my eyes. I am alone in the garden. Thanks to the thick stone walls the Florence traffic is silenced. The sun is strong and warming. The images from the chapel turn round in my mind. I think about my father and my first visit to Florence with him. I had come from a miserable existence in a damp and dark England to meet a father I didn't know in a country filled with light, flavours and art. The contrast couldn't have been stronger and the memory has never faded. Now I am back more than twenty years later. But the mystery of my father is as intense now as it was then. In fact it's even deeper. I don't even know where he is, let alone what he thinks of me.

3

Fish and Fidelity

I get on a train bound for Reggio Calabria. Just the name makes me nervous. It conjures up images of the deep south, of poverty, of violence, families with at least ten shabbily dressed children and the mafia. For many Italians Africa starts at Naples. There is a book by Primo Levi called *Christ Stopped at Eboli.* The theory being that beyond Eboli, just south of Naples, civilisation ends. Reggio Calabria is not even worth talking about. There you're way beyond salvation.

Luckily I am not going that far south, although part of me is curious to go to the toe of Italy. I imagine it is peopled with short women, all of an indeterminate age wearing black from head to toe and aged men sitting around outside bars playing chess or backgammon, drinking Fernet Branca. It is hot and stifling; there is a menacing stillness in the air.

But it is to Naples I am heading that November morning, to revisit an area I knew well as a teenager.

When I first came back to Italy as a fourteen-year-old, my aunt had a house outside Amalfi, south of Naples. My father and I went to visit her that first summer at her holiday home where she spent a few weeks every year.

"This is a woman," he assured me as we got off the train at Naples, "who is even more stupid than your mother."

I was intrigued to meet her; his opinion of my mother was not high. In fact as far as I could make out, the only people he liked were Mozart, Bach and Dante.

We hired a car from the station and headed for the coast. I had never been anywhere so glamorous. The contrast with the dull towns of Berkshire could not have been more marked. Everything was bright, a sharp contrast to the cloudy light I was used to. Bright flowers and palm trees lined the road. The sea glistened in the distance as we drove along the windy mountain road towards my aunt's house in Conca dei Marini. I was feeling car sick, but got no sympathy from my father.

"Who controls your stomach?" he demanded. "Your brain. And who controls your brain? You!"

I focused on controlling my stomach via my brain instead of throwing up over the leather seats.

When we arrived at my aunt Piera's house, she and my uncle Bertrand were having breakfast, although she looked like she was about to go to a cocktail party. She greeted me warmly but embraced me carefully so that I hardly touched her. Her scent was subtle and smelled expensive. Her hair was perfectly rounded into a slick, black bob. She was made up, but in a very natural manner. She was wearing a beige silk sarong and billowy silk shirt over her thin figure. According to my calculations based on my father's age, she must have been in her mid-forties.

She didn't even look thirty.

"You look wonderful," said my father.

"Ah caro, I only just got out of bed," she said, clearly lying. This was something I would learn about my aunt over the days that followed. Even if it were perfectly possible to be honest, she preferred to lie or at best embellish the truth.

We sat down in a large, light room. A giant wooden fan in the middle of the ceiling rotated slowly above the breakfast table, making a dull thudding noise as it turned. There were perfectly polished terracotta tiles on the floor; the walls were all painted a brilliant white. The house had an Arabic feel to it; all the doorways were arched.

At least in terms of interior design, my aunt was way ahead of my father: the house looked like something out of a magazine. She and Bertrand were fitting inhabitants. He was very tall, dark and good-looking; in fact he resembled Gregory Peck. At the time he must have been all of thirty, but to me he seemed terribly old.

The house was built on several levels, all of which had terraces, making it seem huge and sprawling. It was made of stone but the outside walls were barely visible because of the creepers and plants that wound their way up them. There was honeysuckle, bougainvillea, magnolia and wisteria; the smell all around was sweet and exciting. My bedroom was on the top floor, next to a small oval-shaped indoor swimming pool and large terrace. I felt like a film star. I had never experienced such luxurious surroundings. I unpacked my clothes but they looked strangely out of place and shabby in my new home.

I walked downstairs and through the garden to the orchard of lemon and fig trees. I had never seen either growing before and it reinforced the feeling I had of being somewhere truly exotic. The lemons were as big as grapefruits. I hadn't even recognised the figs as figs until I saw one squashed on the ground in the same way they arrive in boxes in supermarkets at Christmas.

Behind the house, the steep, uninhabitable mountains of Conca reached towards the sky. In front of it was the sea. It was several hundred feet below but I could just about hear the sound of the waves lapping against the shore. From the terrace outside the dining room, I could see the small pink church of Conca. It stood alone on a piece of flat land half-way between the house and the sea, its bell towers looking out towards the horizon on the water. I could imagine the locals making their way down the narrow, winding path to Mass.

Conca dei Marini was a place about thirty years behind the rest of Italy. It was famous in Italy for the convent where families would send girls that had fallen into disrepute. The Convento di Santa Rosa was still there when I first went to Conca, but by then it had been turned into a hotel. People went to the edge of its walls to enjoy the stunning view, instead of throwing themselves off, as so many young girls did, rather than face a life of incarceration.

The inhabitants of Conca wore mainly black, which made them look as if they were perpetually on the way to a funeral. They were all very short, and never looked me in the eye. There was never any communication between them and "i francesi" as they called my aunt and uncle. My aunt had a habit of always speaking French in public so they couldn't understand what she was saying, so the locals assumed she was French as well as my uncle. Both sides had a kind of contempt for the other. The locals hated the people who came to enjoy the summer. The heat in the south of Italy is lovely unless you're farming in it.

My aunt and her northern allies found the south an incom-
prehensibly backward place where they did nothing but accept
taxes from the north, go to church and have babies. Of course
contraception was out of the question for this deeply religious
community. "If it were up to me," my aunt would say, "I'd put
the pill in their bread."

I had been very curious about her, this Italian aunt of mine.
I had imagined a feminine version of my father. To some
extent I was right, although she was smaller than him and more
delicate. Her cheekbones were high and her skin olive coloured.
She had a tiny nose that was peppered with minute scars that
looked like over-sized pores, the result of a car crash while in
Spain making an anti-Franco film with her first husband, a
Spaniard. Her eyes were the same as mine. I liked the fact that
she and I looked similar. It made me feel I belonged. In
character she was forceful and domineering, something I
certainly was not. But maybe that was more as a result of my
upbringing. Maybe if I'd had her background, I would have
been more confident. It would be interesting to see who out of
my father and aunt managed to take over proceedings when
they were together for any length of time. Under any other circumstances I would have given my father the better odds, but
as this was her turf they were about even.

The main difference between her and my father was that
she seemed a bit more rational. And less obsessed with sex. But
maybe I didn't know her well enough yet.

My aunt had been married before she met Bertrand to
Eduardo Arroyo, a bohemian Spanish artist. My father told me
that she was just too stupid to hold on to a man like Eduardo;
Piera insisted it was she who left the artist.

"It was an impossible life," she told us on that first morning

Bertrand or Gregory Peck?

as we sat sipping caffe lattes and eating ciambella, a light Italian sponge cake. "Party, party all the time. C'est pas possible, une chose pareille." My aunt liked to throw in the odd French phrase; she had lived most of her adult life between Paris and Rome and felt very Parisian. "I know we were young, living in Paris, but I was studying and, tu sais, it was impossible. We lived like beasts; apart from painting stupid portraits of Napoleon, all he did was eat, drink and make love. Like an animal, c'est vrai, n'est ce pas?" She turned to my father for support.

"Carissima, if he made love like a beast, I am sorry. I am your brother and cannot help you in these matters. But maybe, if I knew, I could have given him some hints at least."

"Ah, you're impossible," said my aunt. I soon learnt she lacked a sense of humour when it came to herself and found anyone or anything that didn't coincide exactly with her views "impossible".

She asked Bertrand to get some more coffee in order to change the subject.

Bertrand was not the butler as I had first thought when he dutifully carried my suitcases into the house, but my aunt's lover of ten years. My mistake, however, had not been a serious one. He did double as a servant, always fetching things for her, constantly having to respond to the call of "Oh Bertrand" and some order.

They had met in a bakery in Paris. She had chosen a brioche for her breakfast and found she had no money to pay for it. A tall dark stranger stepped out from the long queue behind her and offered to pay on her behalf. They ended up having breakfast together, followed by rampant sex and ever-lasting love. At least that's my aunt's version. Personally I can't imagine Bertrand, even in his youth, having the courage to come up with such a gallant gesture. I rather imagine he was behind her in the queue and she asked him to subsidise her breakfast. She was probably very charming and he was clearly taken with her. She must have been even more attractive then, added to which she had some of my father's eloquence and charm.

Bertrand was a good catch for her. He was aristocratic, related to the French photographer Henri Cartier-Bresson, well educated, artistic and extremely kind. He was also young, and as my aunt always said: "There is nothing as boring as a young man when you're young and an old man when you're old."

Bertrand moved in with her the week after they met, but even when her divorce was finalised they didn't marry. I've never really understood why; my aunt claims to be above such petty bourgeois conventions, but she did it once. My father said it was Bertrand's escape clause, that he dreamt of the day he would run away and live happily ever after with a girl he could boss around. I wasn't so sure; after ten years of being told what to do, escape would be a frightening concept.

My father said he had some work to do. I had not really understood what he did as a job. He told me he was a writer but I hadn't seen any books. My mother said that when they were together he worked as a film producer, then director, and opera critic. He never seemed to be short of money. He paid for everything with cash. I suppose it was in the days before credit cards. When a restaurant bill came, he would hand over a large note and let me keep the change. It was one of the most profitable jobs I ever had.

My aunt, Bertrand and I left him to do whatever he had to do and set off towards the quay in their Alfa Romeo Spider. It was a windy drive and I had to concentrate hard on not throwing up again. It was a convertible so the fresh air helped me fight the sickness. My aunt and uncle chatted in Italian about the menu for that evening; luckily neither of them tried to bring me into the conversation.

Once we had arrived in Amalfi, we walked down the quay. Around thirty boats were moored there. There was little sign of life on any of them. I followed my aunt, whose white chiffon wrap billowed delicately in the breeze. We eventually stopped in front of a yacht called *La Mela*. She was beautiful, old and wooden, with cream-coloured sails spread out across the deck.

The customary confusion that always seemed to accompany any excursion with my Italian family followed. Ropes were muddled up, winches were put in the wrong place, the anchor was heaved up and dropped four times, boats blocking our exit had to be moved. Antonio, the harbour master, got more and more exasperated and I think by the time we finally left he hoped we wouldn't make it back.

We headed for the open sea and then veered right towards L'isola dei Galli, which was visible from the terrace of the house. By this time it was already three o'clock and the sea was totally flat, perfect for my first sailing experience. Every way I looked, there was a new view to take in. In front of us was the blue infinity of the sea reaching up to the horizon. Behind us, the town of Amalfi nestled into the mountain. It looked as if it had been designed from the sea, with a symmetry that you could really only enjoy from there. There wasn't a single building out of place. Further down the coast, mountains took over and there were only very few houses, perched in splendid isolation. I felt the warm sun on my skin and lay back on the deck. It was impossible to look at the sky; the sun was fiercely bright. I lay with my eyes closed and let myself be rocked by the gentle rhythm of the boat moving forward in the water. Bertrand had turned out to be a more competent sailor than I had imagined.

"Stop! Helena wants to swim," my aunt commanded after about forty minutes. We had reached the huge gaping black opening in the cliff that gives Conca dei Marini its name. Bertrand slowed the snail's pace down to a stop and threw in the anchor. I dived into the water and felt it cool me down. I had never been anywhere quite so hot. How she had known I wanted to swim I had no idea. It didn't take me more than another day to understand that it was actually my aunt who wanted to swim but for some reason she found expressing her desires either too vulgar or too mundane. She climbed down the stairs to join me in the water and suggested we swim around the boat five times as an "aperitif".

While she swam, she told me about the importance of breathing properly and made strange puffing sounds when she breathed out. She suggested I do the same. It was difficult,

Off the Amalfi coast.

partly because I felt like laughing and partly because I have never found it easy to keep my head above water.

"Oho, lunch," I heard my uncle calling.

Then came the challenge of getting back into the boat. I was forced to tread water and observe the farcical sight of my otherwise supremely elegant and in control aunt trying to get back on board the boat. I knew I shouldn't laugh but watching Bertrand struggle to pull her up was too funny. At one stage I caught his eye. I thought I saw a glimmer of humour. Just to be on the safe side I let myself sink into the water so any sniggering would be hidden. The sea was almost as warm as a bath on the surface. The lower down I went, the cooler it got. The water was soft. I lay back in it and let my hair spread out around my head. I closed my eyes and let the sun dry my face before getting back on board.

Bertrand had transformed the boat. A wide plank of wood had been erected between the sides and this now served as a table. There was a tablecloth on it. Laid out there were tomatoes, melons, mozzarella, Parma ham, basil and white soft bread. My uncle clearly hadn't had time for a dip. The melon had been sliced into crescent-moon shaped slices, and he had also cut prefect tranches within the slice so it was easy to eat. The tomatoes were cut and he now mixed them with slices of mozzarella and bits of basil. The thin slices of ham were laid out on a white plate.

"You sit here," my aunt motioned to a place for me on one side of the table. She sat next to me and my uncle sat opposite us. The meal was simple, but it was one of my most memorable. Perhaps it was the sea air but the flavours were more intense, as if I were eating for the first time. The melon was like biting into sunshine, the ham salty and tender. The bread was soft and doughy. I realised as I took my first bite of a tomato that I had never tasted a real fresh tomato until that moment. It was sweet and plump. I experienced mozzarella cheese for the first time. I had always loved creamy things. But here was something creamy that was savoury at the same time and so smooth you almost didn't need to chew it. The mixture of mozzarella, basil and tomato with a little olive oil drizzled on them was divine. I had never experienced anything like it. This was way before the foodie revolution hit Britain. In those days, my idea of a great meal was egg, beans and chips in a Little Chef.

We sat in the sunshine, the salty water drying on our skin, looking at the sea and the view of the coast, eating hungrily. I wondered if there was anywhere as perfect in the world. My aunt asked me about how I liked Italy. I said I loved it. Of course, who wouldn't? But actually I hadn't really thought about it. I had arrived and been put into this family and their world. I was so busy trying to assimilate everything that I hadn't had a chance to formulate my own opinion. In an effort to be honest, I tried to explain this to my aunt, in English, but she quickly got bored. I don't know whether it was the strain of having to talk in English or just listening to someone else. Our little chat soon turned out to be a lecture, all in Italian, which I just about followed.

"You have had your roots taken away from you," she said. "This is the most violent thing that can happen to a person. Your mother had no right to do this. It's lucky you are back now before it got too late. But you must take in your culture, your heritage, your family. This is where you belong." I liked hearing her say it, but wasn't convinced. I belonged with my mother, in England, that was where I lived. Italy was great, but could it ever become home? My mother had gone back to sort out a place to live and a school. In a few weeks' time the summer would be over and I would say goodbye to this life again. Now that I had found them there seemed to be no doubt that I would return but I couldn't imagine ever living in Italy, becoming Italian.

My aunt liked to sail. However there always came a point in the day when she got terribly bored of it. But she could never admit to being restless. Only a fool would ever have had enough of the deep blue sea and beautiful coast we sailed along. So she blamed me for having to go back home, saying I looked tired and had had enough. She had the most extraordinary capacity to mould events into whatever suited her and make them facts, while completely ignoring reality. We saw more evidence of this as we walked along the quay towards the car.

"This," she announced to a couple of women with tanned, leathery skin and gold everywhere she had stopped to talk to, "is my little sister Helena."

I must have looked stunned because one of them asked me if I found it too hot, coming as I did from Rimini.

"No," I stammered trying to sound as Italian as possible. "I like it very much."

"Helena lives in England where she works for the BBC," continued my aunt. "That is why she has that appalling accent."

The two leather-heads nodded understandingly before walking on.

We walked back to the car via an ice-cream shop. There were so many flavours and colours I didn't know where to start. My aunt asked me if I had ever tried zabaglione ice cream. Tried it? I couldn't even pronounce it. She bought me a zabaglione and chocolate ice cream. It took me a while to recognise the taste but then it hit me. It was eggnog. One of my favourite things in the world. But something I was only ever allowed when I was ill. My mother used to make it for me as a special treat.

A couple of hours after we got home, guests arrived for dinner. They were a couple who owned a house in a nearby village and were friends of my aunt's from Rome. The man was a large flamboyant artist called Giovanni. His wife, Cristina, was a rather mousy woman half his size. During the evening I was introduced to two themes that would dominate my visit to my Italian family: fish and fidelity.

"Giovanni is a painter and his mother was one too. She painted the girl with the basket of flowers in your room," my aunt explained as I was introduced.

"Oh, it's lovely," I said.

"Thank you," said Giovanni, bowing and kissing my hand dramatically. "Where's that Bertrand? I need another drink," he said wandering off and leaving me with his wife. I tried to talk

Giovanni in hat and Bertrand on Giovanni's boat.

to her, but she was monosyllabic and hard work. I kept asking her questions and only ever got a yes or no answer. She really was the mousiest person I had ever met.

My aunt had cooked a dinner that began with a mushroom risotto. We ate outside, at a table overlooking the sea. It was black and peaceful except for the boats moving slowly below us.

"Marriage," said Giovanni to me under his breath, filling up our wine glasses, "is to be avoided at all costs."

"Why?"

"Because my dear, it is the dullest state to be in and goes on for ever."

"So why did you do it?"

"Money."

"Just money?"

"There's nothing just about it. I was forced into it, by

hunger. You see, I'm a penniless aristocrat."

"But I'm sure your wife is very nice."

"Not at all. It is only rare self-control that stops me from strangling her daily. I have plotted her murder countless times. Sometimes when we're out on the boat, I think, yes, I could just do it now. Sneak up behind her, walking oh so slowly, hands stretched out, ready to grab her by the neck. Then I would squeeze the life out of her, throw her overboard and say she fell. But something in her miserable face stops me," he said, snapping a grissini in two.

"Well, maybe deep down you like her." I was rather shocked he was telling me all this. What would I do if the mouse suddenly died horribly? Go to the police and relate our conversation?

"Deep down I hate her more than I do on the surface," he said and turned to Cristina who was tugging at his sleeve. "More wine dear?"

"Giovanni, you know I only ever drink one glass. You're drinking far too much again, and boring poor Helena with your drivel."

"Well, at least I'm selective about who I bore, whereas you just bore everyone," he said turning back to me. "Do you think some of your English friends might like to meet me? I find young women very attractive."

"But you're married," I protested.

"My dear Helena, if everyone had your attitude, I wouldn't have had sex for over thirty years. Imagine what that would have done to my creativity. The whole world would be a bleaker place than it is today."

"Fidelity is something for the petite bourgeoisie." My father now joined in the discussion. "It gives them something to talk about when it is breached. Besides, who are we mortals to suppress such a powerful instinct?"

"Well, you should try to be strong, I suppose, isn't that the idea?" I looked at the two men next to me with their stubborn expressions and realised that it wasn't their idea of how to live.

"No wonder England is such a dull place," said Giovanni. "I don't see what the big deal is anyway. Who wants to own someone that doesn't want to be owned? Much better just to relax about these things."

"Hear, hear," said my father. "You, my cara figlia, sound like Jane Austen."

I wished I'd known enough about Jane Austen to come up with an intelligent response.

"Voilà," said my aunt, placing a huge grilled fish in the middle of the table. "Fish, the food of sex. You know, Helena, in ancient Greece fish was the symbol for sexuality."

"No, I didn't." I felt my stomach turn at the smell of it. "Oh God, I don't know how to say this, but I don't like fish."

"That figures," said Giovanni, as my aunt looked at me in horror.

My aunt couldn't have looked more horrified if I'd announced I was a lesbian with a penchant for sadomasochistic sex with nuns. Her face dropped. In fact she almost dropped the fish.

"It's not possible," she said. "To dislike fish is to dislike life itself. It is a negation of sex."

"No," I tried to defend myself. "I just don't like fish, there's nothing more to it than that." I was fed up with them always intellectualising everything. Why couldn't something just be as it was for no deep or meaningful reason?

"Bah," said my aunt. "That is a typically superficial Anglo-

Saxon way of looking at it. You know, dear Helena, that there is a reason for everything. And the reason you don't like fish must be something to do with your sexuality. This is a problem you have to address. Try some." She put a piece of fish on my plate.

I poked at it and then decided the only thing to do was try it. All eyes were on me as I put it in my mouth. It was disgusting: salty and unbelievably fishy. I tried to hide my abhorrence and smile at the five faces staring expectantly at me. I felt like a pilgrim at Lourdes who is rolled into the waters in a wheelchair and expected to walk out. I had to disappoint them.

"No, sorry, I just don't like it," I said.

My father laughed. "I knew it. I'm destined to have a frigid daughter."

"It would be an apt punishment for you," said Giovanni.

For the first time since I arrived in Italy, I felt like running away. I suddenly missed my mother terribly and wished she had stayed with me to face all these mad Italians. For the first time since I arrived in Italy I wished I were somewhere else.

"But you should know, dear daughter, that I didn't eat fish until I was twenty-one," said my father. "So there is hope for you yet."

My aunt didn't look convinced. "That's not true," she said. "You were much younger. And anyway, it's different for a woman."

"Cara Piera, what would you know about truth?" asked my father, thus ending the conversation.

From that moment my aunt made it her personal aim to make me appreciate fish. Everywhere we went, she made me try it. I tasted every variety, seafood included, and hated it all.

She seemed to take this aversion to all things from the sea as a personal insult.

The next morning I woke around eight. Out on the balcony the sun was already hot. I sat and looked at the sea. I could make out the island of Capri in the distance and L'isola dei Galli, shaped like the head of a cockerel, where Rudolf Nureyev had lived.

I tried to let the sun and the view in through every pore, the smells of the lemon orchard and the early morning, the sea gently moving below me. I thought about my relations; they were so domineering it was hard to ignore them. They had an uncanny way of undermining the way I felt about myself, almost making me feel I needed to completely crumble and start again, to be rebuilt in their mould. I took ten deep breaths and tried to relocate a part of me that had been hidden by operas, Italian, new clothes and poetry. There was no sound from downstairs where the others were sleeping so I took my Walkman onto a sun-lounger on the terrace. I lay in the morning heat listening to Blondie, thankful that for once nobody was telling me what to do.

At about eleven o'clock the rest of the house was ready to go. We all piled into my aunt's red Alfa Romeo Spider and headed towards the port and the unfortunate Antonio, who had surely been dreading our arrival for hours. It was already unbearably hot and I longed to get into the sea breeze. There was something liberating about not having to wear clothes to keep warm, but it was also stifling to feel hot almost constantly. The most magical moments were the mornings and the evenings, when the sun had not yet become ferocious or was setting and it was still pleasant to be in.

We walked towards the boat carrying our supplies. My aunt

seemed very happy. She told me I looked good. I was of course wearing one of the many outfits she had given me, a pair of white flowing trousers with a broad waistband and tiny black and blue flowers printed on them. To go with them I had picked a little white T-shirt with short sleeves and a round neck. I think it was made by some smart designer because the label was cut out. My father told me Piera did this so Bertrand didn't realise how much money she'd been spending. Now that I had been furnished with a whole new wardrobe I couldn't imagine ever wearing my old clothes from England again, they seemed to belong to a different life.

"Of course she looks good in your opinion," said my father. "You told her what to wear."

It was true that from the moment I met my aunt I was no longer in control of my own appearance. In fact since meeting my Italian family I was no longer in control of much. That morning I had enjoyed a rare moment of freedom. But I was aware that their aim was at least to improve me; obviously this meant making me more like them, but at least it was progress. I had not been aware of my shortcomings until I arrived in Italy. As a Berkshire schoolgirl there was really no need to know anything about Dante, Leopardi or even Mozart. Eating well and living well were not issues I had to grapple with daily.

Once on the boat, we sailed out of the port towards the open sea and steered a course towards the south and Paestum. Bertrand busied himself tidying ropes and organising things below deck. My father didn't know what to do with himself. I had never seen anyone more unsuited to the sea. He fiddled about and read and walked uneasily from the stern to the bow several times. I felt it was the fact that he had no control over things on the water that he didn't like. It was a medium he knew nothing about and for once my aunt was in a position of relative power.

I was lying in the middle of the boat. As it was a small racing boat there wasn't a huge amount of room. If you wanted to sunbathe there was basically one spot. Right in the middle. My aunt had a couple of mattresses laid out and as a way of whiling away a few hours it was great. I would lie there and day-dream, enjoying the sound of the water as we sailed through it. Finally my father settled down next to me and pointed out a large white house that perched in splendid isolation to the right of the town of Amalfi. It was almost like an over-sized bird's nest, perched on the cliff. It looked like it would be impossible to get to it any other way but abseiling.

"It belongs to a famous American thinker and writer called Gore Vidal," he explained. "You probably wouldn't have heard of him."

Something in me snapped. I was fed up with being constantly criticised. "If I'm such a disappointment to you, then why are you wasting all this time with me?" I demanded.

My father looked slightly surprised, then he smiled. "You must understand it is very important for me to have a daughter I can insult. But I also love you as you are my daughter, and you must not be afraid of disappointing me. I will always understand you. A person who is disappointed is only someone stupid who was filled with illusions before." He put his arm around me and drew me towards him. I rested my head on his shoulder and breathed in the smell of him, a blend of expensive aftershave and something comforting.

"But you have a lot to learn to become a really important woman; draw your strength from me, I am here to teach you," he said, tightening his arm around me.

I felt like crying with happiness, like a girl being told she is loved for the first time by the man of her dreams.

"What do you want to be when you grow up?" he asked me.

"An actress," I replied.

"Really?"

"Yes, I think it would be fun. And I could travel and go to Hollywood."

My father laughed. "Hollywood, ah yes, the American dream. Do you think it is so great?"

I nodded.

"Bella, I have been there and it is a place full of people made of plastic. But you have to make up your own mind. I assume, unless someone is keeping any other offspring from me, that you are my only child; in fact you are the last of the Benedettis as Piera has no children at all. As such I am relatively pleased with your choice of career. But I think you could be a special kind of actress, the kind that will write her own films. Greta Garbo mixed with Ernest Hemingway."

The idea appealed to me, an actress who writes her own roles. I smiled.

"You must start immediately," he continued. "Writing is like exercise, you have to do it all the time."

We arrived at the marina of Paestum mid-afternoon. By then I was starving. Meals with my aunt were always a few hours later than the rest of the world as she usually had breakfast when most people have lunch. Bertrand carried an enormous picnic basket to a shady spot beneath some trees. My father took a couple of minutes to find his feet, but once he had, he was back to his old self.

"I will tell you all the history of this wonderful place," he boomed as we settled down and my aunt began to unpack the food and wine. "Of course some of you may know more than others. Example, I am sure my dear sister is aware of the fact that it was founded in the sixth century BC by a group of Dorians who had been expelled from the city of Sybaris, a wonderful place across the mainland in the Ionian Sea."

My aunt nodded sagely and buried her head deeper in the picnic hamper. My father grinned and continued.

"The Dorians named this, their new colony, Poseidonia, after the most important of their gods. Darling ignorant daughter, what is Poseidon the god of?"

I thanked all gods everywhere. It was just about the only one I knew. "The sea."

"Incredible." He squeezed my cheek. "Now, we will lay our hearts before this marvellous feast before continuing with our little lesson."

To start with we ate fresh figs and Parma ham. I had never tasted fresh figs before. I was shown how to peel their skin carefully to reach the purple, juicy interior.

"Just like the *fica* of a woman," my father commented. "It is no accident they are more or less the same word. You must always look to the root of a word to understand the meaning of the word. *Ficus* in Latin is fig, *fico* is fig and *fica* is a woman's sex. What is amazing about women is that they all think they are the only woman on earth in possession of one, whereas they all have one and they're all more or less the same."

I suddenly went off my *fico* and moved onto the mozzarella and rocket salad.

My father stopped eating to continue his lecture. "So, Poseidonia flourished and quickly became the most important city in the Gulf of Salerno. Not much is known of the decades that followed. Eventually it was overgrown by the jungle and not rediscovered until the eighteenth century. The Temple of Hera, for example, was searched for throughout the Middle Ages and the Renaissance, but not discovered until 1740. I'm sure Piera will explain who Hera was."

My aunt looked up from the peach she was demolishing. "Of course, she is the goddess of marriage and of life, and especially the sexual life of women."

"Brava. So my dear daughter, a sexual neophyte, will meet her goddess in this most magical of places." He leant towards me and squeezed my cheek.

We packed up the picnic and Bertrand took the hamper back to the boat.

"Very nice bottom," commented my father, watching him go. "Did you hire him just for that?"

My aunt looked disgusted. "You are an impossible old man," she said crossly.

"Careful cara, if I'm old, what does that make you? There are not so many years between us as you like to pretend. What do you think of his bottom, Helena?"

"I really hadn't noticed it," I said, trying to look furious. I was shocked my father would talk about my uncle in those terms.

My father laughed. "Let us all pray to Hera that she awakens the dormant sexuality of this young girl; I cannot bear to admit to society that I have a frigid daughter. Or maybe you're just a little bit lesbian, *leggermente lesbica*? Whatever, Hera will sort you out."

I ignored him and started walking up the path that led to the ancient city of Paestum.

It was the first time I had ever seen a Greek ruin. It was easy to enjoy the atmosphere of the place as we were the only

At Paestum, alone for once.

people there. I imagined what it must have looked like in its full splendour, with white-robed inhabitants wandering up and down the straight, broad roads. There were remains of three Doric temples, the Temple of Hera, the Temple of Neptune and the Temple of Ceres. The fact that they were ruins made them almost more magical, as it was left up to the imagination to complete the picture.

We walked around the city for about an hour, my father, as always, full of information and theories. My aunt tried to drag me off and give me a mini-lecture about the ancient Greeks herself. I wondered not for the first time since my arrival in Italy if I would ever be left alone. My mind kept drifting away from the ruins to all the shops with gorgeous clothes that would soon be closing. My aunt had promised to take me shopping and I was keen to get back to land. I scolded myself for being superficial; here I was in one of the most magical places in the world, breathing in the history of ancient Greece. How could I possibly even think about clothes? I looked at my father, who was strutting in almost regal fashion down the main road of the city, and wondered if he ever had any superficial thoughts at all. I suppose, even if his mind was filled with Dante and Bach, he still had to decide what to wear in the mornings.

The weather changed slightly on our return trip and the sea turned choppy, making me feel sick; a feeling I now dreaded more than I used to because of the reaction it provoked in my new relations. It was almost as bad as not eating fish. The conversation was heated. My aunt and father battled for supremacy. The discussion centred on the Odyssey and different translations of it. My aunt had worked on one by a poet friend of hers and was adamant that it was far superior to others. My father called her an ignoramus and backed up his arguments by quoting from the various versions, something my aunt couldn't do. She moved on to the French translations in the hope of cornering him there, but he was too quick for her. He went on to the German ones, which left her floored. My aunt, sensing defeat, wisely changed the subject.

"This must all be so boring for our little bambina who we are so lucky to have back after so long."

"Of course it's boring; she doesn't understand a thing about it."

"That's not true," my aunt defended me. "She's very intelligent."

My father laughed. "As usual, cara Piera, you are far removed from the reality of the situation, which is this. As I have told her, she has my looks and her mother's brain. A most unfortunate way for things to have turned out."

I focused on the horizon and wondered whether he was right.

A s I did with my father all those years ago, I travel to Naples by train. As soon as it pulls into Naples central station in the Piazza Garibaldi, I realise I have arrived in a very different place to Florence. For a start it is almost impossible to move due to the amount of people. They don't even seem to know where they're going. They just push in every direction. They are also very short. I am beginning to feel like the jolly green giant by the time I find the taxi stand. It is much warmer than Florence, almost balmy.

"I want to eat a good pizza," I explain to the driver. "And see some of the city and maybe walk on the beach." It's very important to get one's priorities right on these trips.

My driver explains in a thick Neapolitan accent that the best pizzas are to be had at Brandi in the centre of town, close to the Royal Palace. This is where they invented the Margherita, he tells me. He starts his ancient Fiat and heads off. But instead of driving on the road, which is totally packed with traffic, he chooses to drive along the tramlines, at a speed I would normally reserve for the motorway. I wonder briefly what will happen if a tram comes towards us, but don't have time to worry for long as a car is doing just that. We now have a game of chicken, which the other driver loses. My taxi driver's argument is that the other driver has no right to be on the tramline.

"Oh, are taxis allowed to drive along them?"

"No," he replies. "But this is Naples and everyone does what they want."

On either side of the tramline the traffic is totally blocked.

This seems to me the most disorganised place I have ever been in. I have never been to Bombay, but I imagine it is like this in rush hour. Cars everywhere, lots of smoke, noise, people shouting and the sound of large ships blowing their horns in the distance. We enjoy another four or five games of chicken on the tramline before arriving at the Piazza Reale. It probably wasn't the least stressful way to get there but it was certainly quicker than the road. I already feel polluted from the fumes and walk towards the sea in the hope that the air might be a bit fresher. I also want to work up an appetite for the famous Brandi pizza.

In the eighteenth century Naples was one of Europe's great cities, along with Paris and London. Stendhal called it the most beautiful city he had ever seen. It must have changed a lot since then. To me it looks seedy and slightly sad. Like an ageing beauty. It is an odd mixture of a glorious past and seedy present. You can see how lovely she was but she's never going to recover. A sort of Norma Desmond of European cities.

I walk past the Royal Palace towards the sea. The air is humid, almost clammy, despite the fact that it's November. There are palm trees swaying in the wind. The buildings are big, dirty and imposing. It is a world removed from Florence and its Renaissance elegance. The Neapolitans are a world removed as well. They are very short and not particularly attractive, rather swarthy and dark. Many of the women are dressed in the classic uniform of the south; black dress, shawl and a shopping basket as an accessory. Some of the younger women though, especially the ones working in the boutiques that line the cobbled street next to the piazza, are very attractive. They are typically Italian, with long tumbling dark curly hair, red lips and voluptuous figures.

The sea is rough and grey, not at all the sparkling blue I remember from my first visit here. I decide it is best viewed from a distance and head back towards the Royal Palace. As I walk past, I notice one of the carved figures in the alcoves. It is of Gioacchino Murat, one of the past kings of Naples. He is a proud figure, probably around three metres tall, with his hand on his chest and an impressive moustache. Even more impressive though is the bulge in his trousers. It is bigger than Nureyev's. I wonder if as king you were allowed to specify that any commemorative statues included this detail, or if he had to bribe one of the sculptors. I look at the other kings as I walk past, all worthy men I'm sure, but none with a groin that compares to Murat's.

The pizzeria is a two-minute walk from the king's crotch. It is in a small cobbled alleyway and hard to miss as there are signs all over announcing its existence and the date of its establishment: 1780. Since then the restaurant has expanded and now sits on both sides of the street, so there really is no missing it as you walk up the Salita Santa Anna di Palazzo. I walk in and ask for a table. I have been told by my aunt that people in Naples are friendly. Maybe this waiter is not from Naples. He tells me to sit down in a tone I would normally reserve for my dog. In fact, I wouldn't even talk to my dog like that. The children possibly, but never the dog.

The interior is brightly lit and stark. The tablecloths are linen though, which surprises me in a pizzeria. There are three other people eating in my half of the restaurant; I can't see much of what's going on across the road but I can see the pizza oven at the back of the room. It starts to rain heavily and people run up and down the small street, bumping into the waiters who move between the two parts.

I sit for about five minutes soaking up the atmosphere. Actually there is no atmosphere. To be honest I already hate Brandi's Pizzeria. So far it has nothing to recommend it. But one of the main things I wanted to do on this trip to Italy was to eat a pizza in Naples. I remember eating one that first summer with my aunt and uncle; it was one of the best things I had ever tasted, with a super-thin crust, melting mozzarella and ripe tomatoes. I remember my aunt telling me that the only pizza to order is a Margherita. "It's a classic," she said. "Like an Armani dress. There is no reason to go elsewhere."

After ten minutes of soaking up no atmosphere I ask one of the waiters if it's possible to see a menu. He looks at me as if to say, "Oh God not another difficult customer" and shoves one in my general direction. There is some information on it about the history of the Margherita, which was not, apparently, named after the flower but one of Italy's most illustrious queens, who took a liking to the pizza with tomatoes and mozzarella. Mr Brandi himself is quoted in 1929 as saying his Margherita has "a well-cooked base, deliciously flavoured topping and a nice thin crust all around". Sounds perfect. I'll have one of those. If it's good enough for Queen Margherita then it's good enough for me.

Eventually one of the grumpy waiters comes to take my order. I sit back and wait for the taste sensation to arrive. If they have been making Margheritas here since 1780, they must be pretty damn good at it by now. Another ten minutes passes. Then another. It probably took less time to invent the Margherita than to get it to my table.

Finally it arrives. The smell is sublime. I take my first bite. It is very moist, in fact I'd say almost too moist. And the base is well-cooked in parts, but shockingly soggy in others. The crust is far from nice and thin as Mr Brandi described. It's doughy. Which is fine, but something I would expect from Pizzaland in Guildford, not the Mecca of pizza restaurants in the heart of Naples. The topping is tasty, but I don't get that flavour rush I had all those years ago. Maybe Mr Brandi has got bored of knocking out Margheritas. Or maybe he saves his best efforts for royalty. Whatever the answer, I leave feeling disappointed and disillusioned. I thought the one thing one could be sure of in Naples was a good pizza. Seems I was wrong.

I walk out into the half-rain half-sunshine. I have to get back to the railway station to take a train to Rome. I want to find a tram to take me there. If I'm going to play chicken again, I want to be in a tank-like contraption, not a little Fiat that offers as much protection as a baked-bean can. There are two women in front of me so I catch them up and ask them where I can catch the tram to the station.

"It's number one," says one of them. "Follow us."

I walk behind them on the thin pavement, concentrating on not falling into the road, where I would surely be flattened by a car or scooter within minutes. I have never seen so much traffic as I have in Naples. The air smells bad. I hope they don't still hang out their pasta to dry as they used to do. They would end up with pasta tasting of car fumes instead of the hot winds from Vesuvius and the cool breezes from the sea.

The women walk slowly, possibly because we are on an almost vertical hill. It must be hellish to climb up in the summer. They are both short; the older one is wearing a black dress and the younger one is in blue jeans and a jumper. They talk as they walk. As they're walking so slowly, I am close enough to hear their conversation.

"Yes," says the younger one. "I am from Portici, but I don't know if I'll stay here."

"Only the good Lord knows that," says the older one.

I want to beg to differ. I mean, that's not strictly true. The woman herself, for example, might have an idea way before God does. He has a lot on his mind; does he really care whether or not some random woman is moving from Portici?

All of a sudden the younger one stops to talk to someone else. The older one continues. Now what do I do? I opt for movement and follow her. She smiles at me and so I join her. She doesn't know the younger woman, she tells me; she just met her on the bus.

"She is very sad and lonely," she continues. "No one wants her, not even her mother. I think she's a bit simple. But she has her health, thank the good Lord."

We get to the tram stop, where there are already about twenty people waiting. I'm tempted to ask my new friend when the next one is due, but feel sure the answer will involve the good Lord. After a few minutes it arrives. I have never really imagined hell but I think a Naples tram is as close as I will get until I actually go there. It is packed, smelly and stuffy. God knows what it must be like in the summer. According to my new friend, He probably does.

I get back to the station in good time for the train to Rome. In fact in extra good time, as it is delayed by an hour. I stand around, terrified someone will steal my handbag. A friend of mine from Milan has warned me about the city. "You walk into Naples fully dressed and you leave naked," she says. "And you don't even know how they do it, they're so clever."

Finally my train arrives. I will be in Rome by this afternoon. Of all the places I am going to visit it is the one I am most excited about. It is where I first felt that I belonged in Italy.

4

A Date with Caravaggio

You know you are in Rome from the sound of the streets. Most of the city centre is cobbled, which makes the cars' tyres sound "thud, thud, thud" as they race along. I think if I were kidnapped and blindfolded and brought to Rome, I would know where I was just from the sound of the tyres. The cobbles, despite being loud as well as aesthetically pleasing, have a worrying side-effect. As part of my transformation into an Italian woman, I bought a pair of shoes in Naples with four-inch heels. They have pointed toes and can best be described as provocative. A Frenchwoman would consider them hopelessly vulgar. I rather like them, particularly as they make me four inches taller. The only drawback is that the thin heels catch in the space between the cobbles and make walking treacherous. It's even worse because I am running. I have a rendezvous with my aunt and uncle at four o'clock in the Piazza del Popolo. I am already ten minutes late due to the fact that I have been stuck between cobbles for most of the way there. But I have heard three "ciao bellas" so far, so the effort is worth it.

I arrived today from Naples and caught a taxi to an

apartment my aunt has rented for me. It belongs to an actress friend of hers called Carla. It is half a minute's walk from the Trevi Fountain. Unless you're wearing four-inch heels that is.

It is small, but well furnished with antiques and unusual paintings on the wall, including one of a white woman giving a black man a blow-job. From the expressions on their faces, both seem rather pleased with the arrangement. I feel quite happy here, cut off from the noise of the street. It is rather like the cell in the San Marco monastery, although the view is not as impressive and I think the monks would be rather shocked by the paintings. I play a CD of Rossini's overtures and blast my neighbours with the music, before falling asleep on the sofa.

This is why I am now running through the Piazza di Spagna in high heels.

What is it about high heels anyway? They make you feel more confident, more sexy, but also more vulnerable. You become both predator and prey. I had a boyfriend who insisted I wear them at all times; they put your feet in the arched position of orgasm, he would say. An Italian woman I lunched with in Florence told me that she would rather go to hell in high heels than paradise in flat shoes. This is all very well, but as a way of getting around Rome fast, I think I would rather be in trainers. And of course there's not a taxi driver in sight: they are all in the cafés talking about Lazio's poor form and drinking short black coffees.

Just as I get into the large square of Piazza del Popolo, and make my way towards the column in the centre (covered, of course, for essential repairs), my phone rings.

"Cara, we are a little late. It's all Bertrand's fault. We shall be with you in no less than half an hour. We can't wait to see you."

Great. This would annoy me less if I hadn't raced to get here, risking life and limb, and broken ankles, and if I hadn't also phoned her minutes before leaving the apartment to see if she was on time for once. She was then, or so she said. Now I have half an hour to waste. Luckily there's a bright blue clear sky, with even a little heat in the sun. Or perhaps I am just warm from the effort of trying to stay alive in my shoes. I wander around the column a couple of times. Close by there is one of those human statues painted with gold leaf. He or she is designed to look like a mummy. If you drop some money in the hat, the figure will move. The mummy is surrounded by three young Roman girls. They are very amused by this. First, they drop some money in the hat. The figure bows, grandly. This isn't enough for the girls, who walk round the back of the mummy. They want to see if it's a boy or a girl. Laughing and pushing each other forward, they see a gap in the costume. One of them puts their hand in. Then they all jump back as the mummy lunges towards them. They run off laughing.

This is something I like about the Italians. They are impulsive, ready to laugh, full of fun and mischief. In a similar situation in Paris, the girls would hardly notice the mummy. For a start they would be too busy smoking; second, laughing is considered vulgar.

As I walk round the column for a second time, a dark-skinned Indian-looking man offers me a red rose. I can't think of anything I need less, so I shake my head and say no. He is insistent, very charming, with white teeth. Have it, he says, as a present. No, I couldn't possibly, I don't want it, I say, but he looks so kind that I don't want to hurt his feelings, so I take it, and give him five euros. He is as reluctant to take the money as I was to take the rose.

There are two cafés at either side of Piazza del Popolo. The

Bar Canova where my father always used to go, and the Rosati where I go now. There's a good crowd, jostling and laughing, pushing their way to the counter and drinking coffee. The barmen in Italy normally call me signorina instead of signora, which makes me feel good. I remember my father would always call bus conductors and barmen dottore or maestro. It's a good way to get their attention and a method I employ to order my caffe latte.

There are three young men standing next to me arguing about something. Actually they're probably not arguing, it's just the way Italians talk. I remember when I first came back to Italy, one of the first things I asked my mother was why everybody kept arguing. She told me that was just their way and that when her parents had visited her in Rome to meet Benedetto they had asked exactly the same thing. They were amazed by the noise and didn't really relax again until they got back to the calm north. "The only things that were quiet in Rome were the statues," my grandfather used to say.

The barman is quick in his work. Unlike most men he is able to multi-task, warming up the milk for my caffe latte at the same time as he makes the coffee. The noise of him putting the saucer on the zinc counter and the teaspoon clinking is a sound I have only ever heard in Italy. He presents me with my caffe latte. The foam is almost solid and deliciously creamy. Through it I can smell the promise of the coffee below.

It's now half past four and I am back out in the square. The sun is getting lower, sending a brilliant light over the church of Santa Maria del Popolo, the place we are going to visit if my aunt and uncle ever show up. I am being taken on a tour of the Caravaggios of Rome. This is probably not my first choice of things to do on a gloriously sunny day in Rome, but with my

Italian family there is never a choice. I would rather sit on the Spanish Steps in the sunshine, or maybe even wander along the river or around Piazza Navona. Despite living in France I still haven't got out of that very English habit of feeling that if the sun is shining I need to be in it.

I hear calls of "Cara, cara" and I turn to see my uncle and aunt crossing the square. She and I have kept in touch over the years since that first summer in Italy. Every so often she phones me to ask for my address. A week later a large box appears in the post, containing the previous year's Armani and Versace collections. Inside the boxes are detailed labels written out carefully in her spindly handwriting for each garment with instructions such as "for the evening" or "for the mountains" or "to be sexy" or "to wear at home". Even from a distance she continues to dress me like a Barbie doll. They walk towards me and we embrace.

After all these years, they both look virtually unchanged. She is dressed all in black, wearing the cut-off trousers that are fashionable now with boots. A look I haven't dared to try. Her hair is neatly cut and styled. She wears an elegant black velvet hat. She seems genuinely pleased to see me. Bertrand is still tall and thin and actually more handsome than he was. His thick black hair is peppered with a couple of grey hairs, but age seems to agree with him. He just looks like an older version of Gregory Peck than when I first met him.

"You look well," I say. "Really well, and young. What's your secret?"

"We don't eat meat, we cook in water, not olive oil," he says. He might also have added that while I have been rushing round the world writing stories, producing three babies and staying up all night trying to get them to sleep, he has produced a slim volume on the importance of the monkey in art. My aunt's life is even better. Her typical day is as follows: she wakes up at around ten. Bertrand has by then produced an exquisite breakfast for her of freshly squeezed grapefruit juice, sliced fresh fruit, tea and fresh bread. Then she spends about two hours in the bathroom putting on make-up, doing her hair and getting dressed. By this time Bertrand has gone shopping for lunch. They cook lunch and eat it. Then they have a sleep, or maybe read, or perhaps this is when they're at their most productive, secretly playing the stock market or writing bestselling crime novels under a pseudonym. They resurface at around four or five. Bertrand then goes shopping again for dinner while my aunt goes shopping for clothes or gets her hair done or something equally exhausting. Then they cook an exquisite dinner, Bertrand does all the chopping and boring stuff while my aunt, an excellent cook, oversees the operation and gets to do all the good stuff like adding the finishing touches to the risotto before it is brought to the table. After dinner Bertrand washes up and then they go to bed. It's no wonder the woman hasn't aged in twenty years. If I'd lived like her, I'd still look fourteen.

"We must begin the tour," says Bertrand. "The last time I went on this tour was with my uncle Henri Cartier-Bresson. He didn't like Caravaggio to start with, you know, but he told me that he learnt a lot about framing a photograph from him. There is one particular painting that converted him. I'll show it to you."

The three of us walk arm-in-arm across the square. It is just like old times. We are still talking about culture instead of anything else, but at least now they seem keen to include me, rather than just use me as a pawn in some intellectual battle.

It was too good to last.

"Take your glasses off," says my aunt. "You look terrible in them."

"But I can't see without them," I protest.

"Bah! What do you want to see anyway?" she asks.

"Caravaggios," I'm tempted to respond, but instead dutifully take off my glasses. It's amazing how certain people in life make you feel like a hopeless little girl again. My aunt invariably has this effect on me. She also makes me feel scruffy. It doesn't matter how good I felt when I left home, as soon as I see her I feel second rate. It's rather like going out feeling like a million dollars and walking into a smart clothes shop with impeccably dressed sales assistants who look at you in disgust. You leave feeling deflated, ready to go home and drown yourself in the bath or at least get changed.

We walk up the steps to the Santa Maria del Popolo church. I am now holding on to my aunt not so much from affection but from necessity. The combination of high heels and no glasses is practically suicidal. We enter the church. It is dimly lit. Candles burn in the small chapels that line each side of the nave. There are only a few people in the church and they are moving slowly and silently. I concentrate on making sure my heels don't clatter like a showgirl's as we walk towards the paintings. Furtively I put my glasses back on.

"Ecco," says Bertrand, who switches easily from his native French to Italian. "*The Conversion of Saint Paul.*" We are at the Cerasi Chapel, in front of the first Caravaggio of the tour. My aunt grabs my arm and starts whispering as she always does in front of anything awe-inspiring, be it a great painting or an Armani coat.

"Look at the horse," she whispers. "It's almost impossible to tell which legs belong to the horse and which to the peasant holding him."

The other painting is the *Crucifixion of Saint Peter*. Here I am told to take special note of the peasant's dirty feet. I look up at the paintings. It is the light and the colours that most impress me. And the horse. Have you ever tried to draw a horse? It's the most impossible thing to do. I tried once for my daughter and was told it looked like a dog. I felt like the man in *The Little Prince* who is asked to draw a sheep and fails miserably. But Caravaggio has got this horse thing totally sussed. This is a horse that looks like a horse; it has a glossy coat, muscular thighs and a black and white mane. Nothing dog-like about this beast.

"You will notice the composition," says my uncle.

Will I?

"The painting is cut diagonally in half by the shape of the cross," he continues. "And you can see how Caravaggio uses light to tell the story. The other interesting thing is his naturalistic approach. Look at Saint Peter, he is not a hero or god-like character, but simply an old man suffering and scared. This may look natural now, but when Caravaggio painted like this it was revolutionary."

The electric light goes out in the chapel. The three or four people gathered wait to see if someone more generous than them will put a euro in the box to illuminate it. The church feels empty without the paintings. My uncle strides over, as always the perfect gentleman. I have never seen my aunt pay for anything. She is rather like the queen in that she never carries cash. My uncle is in charge of all that, but I wonder if it is her money he is spending. There is a loud clunk as the lights come on again. Then silence. The Caravaggio worshippers are in quiet contemplation. Even my uncle stops lecturing me, which I am thankful for. Partly because I am enjoying the moment of reflection. I lean on the cold marble rail, look at the vast paintings and listen to the worshippers shuffling towards the altar in the semi-darkness, the smell of candle-wax all around. But mainly because I hate being lectured.

Then he starts again. He is giving me a potted history of Caravaggio.

"He was as famous for his volatile temper and character as his art," begins my uncle. "But he was also famous for his controversial painting methods. He shunned any preparation in favour of working directly with oils."

I say yes at the right time now and then but the words start to float over me. Now and again a word penetrates my mind: virtuoso, chiaroscuro, technique. But most of the time I feel myself falling into a daydream.

I think my inability to concentrate on anyone telling me anything about art must be a throwback to being dragged around museums as a child by my stepfather. In retrospect it was a good thing that he did make me spend hours at the Ashmolean museum in Oxford dissecting drawings by Michelangelo, although I preferred the shrunken heads in the Pitt-Rivers museum. At least he gave me a taste for art and a desire to know more. But as a ten-year-old girl I would rather have been anywhere else. I remember my feet aching and stifling yawns as I wondered if we would ever get out of there so I could eat the Knickerbocker Glory I'd been promised. My stepfather was a strict teacher and would not have put up with me yawning, much like my aunt. She was always asking me if I was tired. "Tired, no," I would often feel like responding. "Bored to tears, yes. Tired of being talked at and lectured to, yes, yes, yes."

Odd that they should have anything in common really; they

only ever held each other in contempt, although they never met. But both my aunt and stepfather were intent on shoving fish and art down my throat. My stepfather's methods were more brutal; he would leave my uneaten fish in my room until I had eaten it. My worst ever dish was a Swedish one my mother used to cook; funnily enough it's the only thing I remember her cooking. It was made of anchovies and potatoes and known as Janson's Temptation, but it never tempted me. He would literally force-feed me it while I gagged and tried to swallow as much in one go as I could. I still can't eat anchovies. My aunt's method was to tell me that not eating fish was the sign of some deep psychological flaw, like being hung up about sex.

My father and stepfather only met once. I was probably about four by then, and my father had travelled to Stockholm where my mother was living at the time to try to see me. My stepfather told me the story when I was older. He said that Benedetto had told him that when my mother was a little girl she used to bring stray dogs home. Her parents would immediately have them put down; they didn't want any dogs around the house.

"What she did to dogs then, she does to men now," Benedetto told the young art student. But this didn't put him off; in fact my stepfather was a man who was positively encouraged by adversity.

He had met my mother on a train she had taken north to get away from my father for a few weeks. She was headed home to spend some time thinking about things. She had argued with my father before leaving and was upset. She says she can't remember what the row was about now, but she told me they usually argued about him sleeping or talking too much. He told me she was so passive it drove him insane. "You could put some

My mother at the time she met my stepfather.

dynamite under her bottom and she still wouldn't react," he said. I've never seen my mother angry and I guess to a raving, ranting Italian this kind of calm must seem passive. She was sitting in a compartment alone, her knees drawn up to her chest, her head bowed on top of them. The train stopped at Orte station north of Rome. It had started to rain heavily and the track was flooded. They sat there for several hours. As it began to get dark, my future stepfather finally plucked up the courage to speak.

"I would love to see what you look like," he said. As soon as she lifted her head he fell in love with her. She was incredibly pretty with different coloured eyes: one green and the other a mixture of colours, mainly brown. He convinced her to travel with him to Aylesbury, where they spent a week together. When it was time for her to return home, they agreed he would follow her to Rome shortly afterwards. She was going to send some money to a friend of hers in London that he would use to get there. From there they would travel, with me, to England and a new life. By the time he arrived, my mother would have split up with my father.

When he called my mother's friend, he had never heard of him. My mother had of course got back to Rome after what she viewed as a holiday romance and forgotten all about it. My stepfather, though, was a nineteen-year-old in love and desperate to get to her. So he walked into a department store, asked for some change and as soon as the cashier opened the till, grabbed as much cash as he could before running out. He used the money to travel to Rome and made straight for the Piazza di Spagna, which he knew she lived close to. Imagine my mother's surprise when she was out walking with me one morning and she heard a voice shriek her name across the square.

Apparently I didn't much impress him. My first act was to grab his cigarettes, take each one out and break it. An early act of defiance that would not be repeated until I finally severed links with him. The following week the three of us left for England by train. I once asked my mother why she ended up marrying him.

"Because I couldn't get rid of him," was her response. This might seem like a strange reason, but I think I finally understand her. He was the most tenacious man I ever met. He was also one of the most insecure. I think she probably thought the only way to make things better was to make him more secure, so marrying him was a natural step.

"Santa Maria del Popolo is only one of three Caravaggio sites we are visiting," says my uncle. "Next up is the church of San Luigi dei Francesi, the French national church."

We walk back across the Piazza del Popolo. The mummy is still there, motionless, and the rose seller, who smiles at me. My aunt and uncle may be unchanged in appearance, but they move more slowly than I remember. Perhaps I have got used to leading my life at a rush, racing to stop a child from falling over, panicking about being late for the school run, meeting a deadline. They, unencumbered by such things, stroll at a pace that is so leisurely it is positively funereal. Fortunately Bertrand has a lot to say about the city and the architecture.

"You must remember, cara, that the baroque is the most important architectural feature of Rome. Everyone thinks of Ancient Rome, but that is a small, almost insignificant part. You must remember that for nearly one thousand years, barring that unfortunate period when the Pope went to live in Avignon, Rome was the richest city in the world. Bernini was baroque's finest exponent. Incidentally, you know why it's called baroque?"

I don't. But I have a feeling I am about to find out.

"It's after the word baroca, which is the name given to a misshapen pearl. Anyway, Bernini is as important a figure in Rome as Gaudi is in Barcelona. For example, he built the Fountain of Triton in the Piazza Barberini and the Four Rivers Fountain in the Piazza Navona."

We arrive at the church. The Caravaggios here depict three scenes from the life of Saint Matthew: *The Call of Saint Matthew*, *The Martyrdom of Saint Matthew* and *Saint Matthew and the Angel*. The martyrdom seems a little melodramatic to me, lots of furious characters scowling and wearing nothing but sheets.

"You see the man with the beard," whispers my aunt. "That's

Caravaggio, he painted himself in." I suppose this was rather like Hitchcock, who always appeared in his own films. But had I been the artist, I would have painted myself into *The Call of Saint Matthew*. This is an altogether more impressive work. None of the melodrama of the other one, but a fight between good and evil being carried out with elegance and subtlety.

"Look at the sheet wrapped around the angel," whispers my aunt. "The detail is incredible." She is referring to *Matthew and the Angel*, the third painting. Sheets were obviously all the rage that year. But she's right, the detail is incredible. I can safely say as far as paintings of sheets go it's the best one I've ever seen.

It is a short walk to the next church but at the pace we go at it takes a long time. We stroll along arm in arm again, me in the middle.

When we get to the Church of Sant'Agostino, there is a woman begging in the doorway. She looks like a gypsy. She has a baby in her arms who is drinking a bottle of milk. I have never seen my aunt or uncle give anything to beggars and today is no exception. Instead my aunt tells her favourite story about me which I must have heard a hundred times, but like listening to anyway.

"When you were little and your mother left to think about things and whether she could carry on living with Benedetto," she says, "you came to stay with me in Rome. You would wake up very early in the morning and tried everything to wake me up. Nothing worked. In the end you got your milk bottle and came and hit me on the head with it until I got up. You were so wonderful."

To me I sound spoiled; if one of my children hit me on the head with a milk bottle, I wouldn't be too impressed. But I suppose that's the luxury of other people's children; you don't

Bound for England with my mother and future stepfather.

have to teach them how to behave.

We walk into the church. The painting we are here to see is the *Madonna of the Pilgrims*.

"Look at the feet," whispers my aunt. Once again Caravaggio has painted a pilgrim with extremely dirty feet, which are turned towards us as he kneels in front of a Madonna with black hair wearing a pinky-purple dress. She is carrying a child who looks like he's at least five years old and should really be standing alone, but that's not what children do with Madonnas.

"This is the painting that converted Cartier-Bresson to Caravaggio," whispers my aunt. "Suddenly in front of this he said, 'Now I get Caravaggio'."

He had a point, it's a lovely painting. But now I'd like to get away from it. There's only so much Caravaggio a girl wearing four-inch high heels can take in one day. Luckily my aunt has also had enough. She suggests my uncle go for a coffee as we have something to do. The way she says "something to do" immediately perks me up. The longing for a chilled glass of wine and some grissini sticks vanishes. That tone of voice can only mean one thing: Armani. I daren't ask where we're headed but am delighted to note that we are walking in the direction of Via del Babuino, where many of the designer shops are.

Alexander the Great couldn't have had a warmer welcome when he came back from conquering the world than we get at Emporio Armani. Smiling sales assistants rush to greet us. The manager slams down the phone on whoever he is talking to and sashays out from behind the till to embrace my aunt.

"Signora Benedetti," he says, "how delightful, we haven't seen you for a few weeks."

"No, I've been travelling in Asia," lies my aunt. "This is my daughter."

I am prepared for this. It's nothing unusual. At least she's not trying to pass me off as her sister. And there is a seriously good reason for the lie. My aunt gets a huge discount in Armani, a privilege only accorded to direct descendants, rather like a hereditary title. In fact, much more useful than a title.

The manager is in raptures. "Isn't she beautiful, wonderful, so tall, so elegant." Much as I appreciate this Italian form of social exchange and exaggeration (you must be told how beautiful your daughter is even if it's not true as it reflects well on you and you have been our best customer for the last forty years), I am beginning to feel slightly embarrassed as the whole staff has now come to inspect this long-lost daughter and make the right noises. Eventually we are released, but not before my aunt has secured the hereditary discount.

We walk around the shop picking out things to try on. My

aunt is great fun to shop with. Her attitude is to try everything. She keeps feeding me garments in the changing room.

"Take your bra off," I'm told after I try on a little grey silk and cashmere top.

"Much better, that's really sexy," she says as I walk out braless. She's right of course, the top is really special but only works without the bra. "I'll buy it for you. But don't wear it when there's no one special to see, it's not worth it."

My aunt has found a coat she likes but they don't have her size. This sends her into a death spiral. The manager, thankfully, is on hand to help. We crowd around the till as he keys in the details of the coat on the computer. There is silence while my aunt stands fanning herself with an Armani brochure.

"We've located one," says the manager. Sighs of relief all round. "It's in Via Manzoni, Milan."

"When can you get it by?" asks my aunt. The colour has just about returned to her face.

"The day after tomorrow," says the manager.

"Call me the minute it comes in," says my aunt. "On the mobile."

We leave with a little chic packet inside which my grey top is beautifully wrapped in tissue paper. We say goodbye on the corner of Via Margutta and I hobble back to my apartment by Fontana di Trevi. I have some rare time to myself. My aunt and uncle have plans for dinner so I am free to do and eat whatever I want. My aunt once told me that when she was married to her first husband they lived in Paris. His parents were dead. One of their friends said to him, "You don't know how lucky you are, to be young, living in Paris and an orphan." Tonight, as I feel free for the first time in hours, I know what he meant.

5

Birds Obsessed with Sex

That next morning I go and look at the Trevi Fountain. I watch the water gushing from the mouths of the horses, the white marble, the tourists admiring the scene and among them a woman holding up a giraffe. Why, I wonder, would anyone hold up a giraffe by the Trevi Fountain? Then I realise that she is Italian-looking but surrounded by Japanese people. She is clearly a tour guide. The giraffe is a prop to show the tourists where she is. She is obviously banking on nobody else holding up a giraffe and making off with her tips. I think about picking up a giraffe from somewhere, but she's right: there's not a hope of finding one anywhere. I go back to looking at the Trevi Fountain. What do I really think of it? I think it's ghastly. Although it would be quite fun to bathe in it, as Anita Ekberg did in *La Dolce Vita*. Sadly if you tried it now you'd be less likely to get snogged by Marcello Mastroianni and more likely to get arrested.

I sidestep the woman with the giraffe and go into the nearest café for a caffe latte. I am fast becoming a coffee addict. This is partly because the government has brought in a rule banning smoking in public places. Once you have negotiated your way past the smokers in the doorway, you can breathe freely in the interior. It makes the whole experience so much more enjoyable. I recall my father's anger so many years ago at a smoker who lit up at the table next to us in a restaurant in Rome:

"Put that cigarette out," he said. "I have no objection to you killing yourself with that filthy habit, but you have no right to kill me." At the time I was a teenager and of course like most teenagers was desperate for a cigarette. I had started smoking on the journey down with my mother. She would ask me to light her cigarettes for her as she was driving and I was soon hooked as well. I'm sure now he must have known I smoked; every opportunity I had I would rush off and have a cigarette in secret. He must have smelt it on my breath and clothes. But he never said anything to me about it.

When I finish my coffee, I decide to walk towards Piazza di Spagna. I'm not sure which direction it is in but I follow an instinct and miraculously arrive there in about five minutes. There are building works at the east end of the square making it difficult to walk into. I have to negotiate my way around two large cages where men are digging up the road. There are cars and scooters trying to get past too, as well as other people. A typical Roman scene of chaos.

Finally I reach the square. However many people there are in the piazza, it always seems serene. Maybe it's the graceful sweep of the Spanish Steps, or the elegant buildings that flank it. But whatever chaos is going on, Piazza di Spagna seems peaceful. I sit down on the steps. It is November so the stone is cold. There aren't many people on them today, despite the sunshine. In the summer they are packed with travellers, students and hippies. I remember when I was here with my father one summer's evening towards the end of my stay. It

My father aged around forty.

must have been the middle of August as I went home to start school at the end of the month, having arrived at the end of June. That evening the steps were packed full of people, mainly young. They were chatting, laughing, playing guitars and singing. There was a man selling a selection of posters to cater for all tastes; Che Guevara to Marilyn Monroe to Padre Pio.

"They are like spectators and actors at the same time," said my father. "Watching a play in which they are the stars. They are living in a theatre, with no responsibility. Formidable." Today there are some young Romans feverishly sending text messages, to each other judging by the laughter and reactions.

On either side of the steps there are memorials to two great British traditions: poetry and tea. The Casina Rossa, literally little red house, built in the early eighteenth century, was the final home of the poet John Keats, who died here of tuberculosis on February 23rd 1821, aged only twenty-five.

If you ever want to see the difference between the British and the Italian character distilled, this is the place to come.

Stand on the Spanish steps and look up at the marble plaque on the side of Keats's former home. Because of its height it is not something your eye automatically picks put unless you stop somewhere underneath it. There is a memorial written in both Italian and English. In Italian it reads:

The English poet John Keats (except they call him Giovanni Keats which sounds a lot more glamorous), a mind as marvellous as it was precocious, died in this house on the 24th of February 1821 in the twenty-fifth year of his life.

Then the English: The young English poet John Keats died in this house on the 24th of February 1821 aged 25. That's that then. A slightly more eloquent version of "John Woz Ere", but only slightly.

On the other side of the Spanish steps is the Babington's Tea Rooms, opened in the late nineteenth century by Anna Maria Babington and Isabel Cargill, who came to Rome with the dream of opening an English tea shop here. An odd ambition for two Victorian ladies, but I suppose it was better than living in Victorian England. You can still enjoy the most expensive cup of tea in the world there.

I walk down the Via Frattina. This is the road where my parents lived with me when I was a baby. When I went there that first summer my father told me how I used to walk down the street with him and insist on sitting on every step. We had continued our Grand Tour after a few days with my aunt and Bertrand on the coast.

"You wanted to try them all out with your bottom," he said. "Formidable. I would tell you to mind your head when you stood up as some of the shops had glass cases on the walls. Attenzione, I would say, tapping my head. You would say attenzione too and do the same." I wonder what my children would make of the bustling streets of Rome.

After my parents' divorce my father moved to a spacious flat that occupied two floors of a palazzo on the Via Margutta, a cobbled street famous for its eccentric artists and sculptors. It is also famous for being Gregory Peck's home in the film *Roman Holiday*. As in Florence, there were hundreds of steps up to his flat and no lift.

But the flat in Rome was much more like a home than the one in Florence. The rooms were well furnished and the kitchen looked almost used, although there was nothing in the fridge apart from Royal Jelly. The most impressive part was the drawing room, which had a huge window overlooking the Villa Borghese park and the Palazzo Medici. There was a spiral staircase that led up to a library where he had a few hundred books.

On our first day together in Rome my father and I walked out of the flat into a gloriously sunny afternoon onto the elegant Via del Babuino with its designer shops towards Piazza di Spagna. I felt exhilarated; there was something in the Rome air that made me feel good. Maybe it was a childhood memory. I told my father, who smiled and squeezed my cheek.

"It's normal, bella, you are with the last male descendant of a highly specialised and inspiring family."

He told me about my grandparents. Settimia came from a small hamlet between Emilia Romagna and Tuscany. There were only four houses, built close together near a volcano which used to spout lava but from which a small river later ran giving the place its name, Ruscello. When she was 17, she left for a small town nearby called Perticara along with her three sisters. Don Luigi, the local priest, had read in the paper that teachers could earn 100 lire a month and that since the

Gigino and Settimia.

unification of Italy there was a lack of them. So he paid for my grandmother and her sisters to train as teachers as a kind of investment in their future.

It was here that she met my grandfather. She was teaching a class when she heard a horse whinnying and a loud crash. She looked out and saw its rider had been thrown to the ground among the pine trees. She went out and my grandfather stood up, covered in pine needles and bleeding from a head wound, caused by a branch that had lodged itself on his head like a crown of thorns. To the diminutive teacher he resembled Christ bleeding on the cross and she fell in love immediately. Despite this, she kept him at bay and didn't agree to marry him for another two years.

He was the local hero because of his good looks, family and money. He came from a rich industrial family. They owned a company called Tessuti Benedetti (Benedetti Cloth). I had seen the logo on the tea-towels at my grandmother's house. By the time he met my grandmother he was twenty-six, the right age for a man of his class to marry. She was twenty and although she had a very plain face, her body, though diminutive, was perfect. She was also the right kind of girl to marry, which his girlfriends hitherto had not been. He knew, of course, that as a *padrone* in Italy in the 1930s he could carry on seeing as many of them as he wanted.

"Gigino your grandfather always lived with servants and in great luxury," said my father. "He lost his virginity at the age of 13 to one of the chamber-maids who worked in his parent's mansion. I did the same when I was 14, although not with the same woman ha ha. When he was a lot older and suffering from the effects of a riding accident, he used his valet to prop up one of the daughters of the same chamber-maid while he again exercised his *droit de seigneur*. Formidable!"

I was horrified by this idea but didn't want to seem prudish so let him go on.

"Your grandparents stayed mainly in Rimini and Carpegna, the country house, Piazza di Spagna was your first home. This will always be your spiritual home in Rome."

We stood in the middle of the square and I looked up towards the top of the steps of the Trinità dei Monti church. My father pointed up to a spot just above the end of the first flight of steps. There were two swallows making love in the air. So furious was their passion that they forgot to maintain their flight and plummeted to the ground. A small crowd had gathered below to watch and several people gasped and moved closer to see what had happened. There was silence as the birds lay stunned side by side. Shakily one of them got to its feet, straightened out its wings and flew off. The other one followed soon after and we watched them fly over the steps up towards the gardens of the Villa Borghese.

"Thank God," said one of the men watching. "It all went well." I couldn't believe even the birds in Italy were obsessed with sex.

My father took my hand and announced he was going to take me somewhere that would make me feel at home: the Keats museum.

"I think, mia cara, your life has lacked symmetry so far," he said. "I am thinking about the consequences of my biological responsibility and I think it is my job to inject a little order. So far, I have to admit, I like you. My opinion of your comportment is not so enthusiastic, but you will learn. And you are horribly ignorant, so let's start to educate you with some poets from your beloved homeland."

Whenever he was rude about England I felt angry and protective. Later on I realised that perhaps for him England was the enemy, the country that had taken me away from him. But at the time I just swallowed my fury and kept listening.

We walked up the steps to Keats's House in Piazza di Spagna. I knew nothing of the Romantic poets but was fascinated by the small apartment filled with books and memorabilia. I was most intrigued by Byron, whose name I had at least heard. There was a poster of him looking suitably Byronic (occupational hazard I guess) and a poem.

> Here's a sigh to those who love me,
> And a smile to those who hate;
> And whatever sky's above me,
> Here's a heart for every fate.

After our initial visit to the museum I often came back on my own. I spent hours walking around the rooms thinking

Gigino and transport.

about the poets travelling around Italy, feeling very intellectual and pleased with myself. I even read some poetry. It was a relief to be learning something that wasn't Dante.

The room Keats died in was tiny with terrible wallpaper. Maybe he had had an Oscar Wilde moment. I looked out of the window and wondered if he knew this would be his final view. Not a bad one to have.

"Look here," my father pointed to a fading letter in one of the glass cabinets addressed to a lady called Fanny. "She was Keats's muse; writers all need an ideal called a muse. This is someone to write to that is not present in person but present in spirit. Now I have found you again, I confess to you that my muse is Helena."

I was amazed; he always treated me as if I was something to be teased and not taken at all seriously.

"What does it mean to be someone's muse?" I asked.

"It means you are in their thoughts when they are alone

writing and you help them to work better, you inspire them."

"How do I inspire you?"

"Partly because, like my book, you need me. I feel the same strong demand from my book as from my biological daughter. But if I do not understand and treat both with respect, I will be a bad writer and a terrible biological. So I am a father of two now."

We walked out of the museum into the glaring sun across the piazza, past the boat-shaped fountain. Students and drop-outs from all over the world sat chatting and smoking on its edge, some dangling one hand in the cooling water. We wandered down the Via Frattina. Almost all of the houses were designer shops. I stopped outside the window of Gucci. An elongated model stood dressed in a cropped top and silver hipsters. I caught sight of myself in the reflection of the sparkling glass and felt horribly unfashionable, despite the fact that I was wearing a favourite from my aunt's cast-offs, some pale peach linen trousers with a matching shirt. I was taller than the average Italian, but far too thin. I had really no shape to speak of at all and felt I looked gangly and clumsy. I longed to dive into Gucci and re-style myself. My father read my thoughts.

"Bella, I know you think I am incredibly rich and should buy you the whole shop just because we are related by blood, but I am not as rich as you think. I am only rich enough not to have to waste time looking for money. And if there is any money left when I die, then you can have it to waste on whatever you like."

I laughed. It didn't occur to me then that he would fritter it all way before I had a chance to spend any of it. He had so much. And he took me shopping anyway. We went to a small boutique just opposite the Spanish steps where he bought me some fuscia pink satin skin-tight trousers and a diamond-encrusted T-shirt that went with them. I loved my father taking me shopping. Clothes until now had just arrived via friends who had older children or been bought in uninspiring shops in Newbury. Now I was introduced to a world of shopping I had no idea existed. My father marched me around boutiques in Rome and within minutes had all the staff running around me and suggesting various outfits, rather as Julia Roberts does in *Pretty Woman*. I felt like a princess. I remember when we went to buy the pink trousers it was ten thirty in the morning and the shop was just opening.

"This is a shop where all the whores of Rome come," my father said. "That's why they open so late. They know all the whores have been up all night and they won't surface until midday at the earliest."

Despite my father being a mortifying shopping partner (he did nothing but come out with stupid comments like the above and flirt with the female staff) it didn't take long before shopping took over from horses as my favourite hobby. I still have those pink trousers and can just about fit one of my legs into them. But I just can't bear to throw them away. Maybe Olivia and Bea will wear them one day, although the girls are already so French they would probably find them slightly lurid.

Later that afternoon over tea in the Babington's Tea Rooms my father revealed his life-plan for me. I was to forget about my dream of becoming an actress and instead become a writer, like him.

"You see bella, with me as a father you have no other choice. It is in our blood. I have been trying to write since I was a young boy. And the fact that you can write in English is wonderful. How many Italian books do you think get

My mother and me in Rome shortly after my birth.

translated? Almost none. Maybe the odd bit of rubbish by Umberto Eco. When you write in English, you have America, Australia, Canada, New Zealand, England all there ready. What a market! You must start straight away, think of a story, any story and write it. Now!"

"But what if I can't think of anything to write?" I protested.

"Just write the most extravagant thing that comes into your head. And remember, something I am learning as a biologico and a writer, you are like me, extremely possessive and jealous, but the persons of a tale are like daughters or lovers and if the writer is too possessive, too jealous, they will scarcely live. If you give birth to a person in a novel you have to manage their life with a prudent touch, forbidding strictly your own possession to oblige him to do something. The writer alone with his typewriter can write in complete freedom, but you will have to respect the freedom of your creations. If you don't, the delicate balance of the novel will be broken. It is the same with you: I propose to you all myself, good and not good. But I will never impose something on you."

I was surprised. "You've done nothing but tell me how to behave since we met."

"That is different. I am trying to understand your juvenile errors, but I have to admit they stink of mediocrity. We Benedettis are never mediocre, bad often, but never mediocre.

My parents and Piera in Rome.

So I am trying to suggest to you that you lift yourself up a level and become an elegant creature, as opposed to a shitting one. But I will never oblige you to follow me, as I never oblige my characters to do what I want. They are thinking and living persons, as you are, and I have a lot to learn from you, like you maybe will learn from me. One thing I will tell you now is that when you write you must never just tell a story, you must show it. If good writing were just a question of telling any stronzo could do it."

I couldn't imagine what he could possibly learn from me as he never really asked me anything, but I sipped my lemon tea, tried to take on board what he'd told me and planned my first novel.

I sat down in front of a notebook he had given me as soon as we got back to the flat. I decided on a romantic theme. A tale of a girl stuck in an unhappy marriage who falls in love with an impossible hero. It was much more difficult than I had imagined. Not only couldn't I think of a sensible plot, but the characters didn't seem to come alive in my hands. Finally I decided that half a chapter was a beginning and I would show it to him. He was in the library reading the libretto of Wagner's *Parsifal*.

He took my notebook and read it silently.

"Porca miseria! Sei proprio stupida. Ah Dio, and you, the last of the Benedettis. This is a disaster. It is good for only one thing. To show someone how not to write."

"I didn't think it was that bad."

"It's worse. Listen to this, for example. 'I walked down the aisle, my mind full of thoughts of Rupert and his caresses. By the time I got to the altar, I was in tears. I cried, oh how I cried.' Dio. First of all it is sentimental rubbish. Secondly you tell us everything. Try to leave a little to the imagination of the reader. And then repetition. Listen how stupid it is. I shit, oh how I shit. Cara, you have to start again, and try to choose something a little less like the shitting sentimental life you hope to lead. I thought you were like me, now I see you also have a lot of your grandmother in you. This is the kind of drivel she likes."

"Well, show me how to do it properly."

"Bella, I can't. You have to learn yourself. I can only direct you."

"So direct."

"You have a different life to the average fourteen-year-old. Write about it. I will give you the first line." He paused for a moment and then reached for a piece of paper. "Pen." He snapped his fingers in the air. Rather sulkily I handed him mine. He scribbled for a minute and then gave me the piece of paper. "Ecco, your first line. Now you just have to add the novel."

I read it out loud. "'I spent my childhood cradled in the arms of my mother's revenge,' that's not bad."

"Of course; it's brilliant, you are dealing with a genius. Now get to work. Tonight we go to the opera. Maybe it will inspire that miserable little brain of yours to produce something worthwhile."

The overture of *La Traviata*, with its mixture of solemnity and happiness, bounced around the walls of the opera house and back to the stage, where the curtain rose on the opening scene. I remembered it well from listening to it several times in Florence. But hearing it live was completely different and I was swept into it within the first few bars. At the end of the first act I was praying the ending would somehow miraculously change and they would end up together.

"I love it," I told my father in the interval as we stood

drinking champagne in the sumptuously decorated bar.

"Bella, of course you do. You are about as stupid as that stronzo of Alfredo. And it is sentimental, which is your favourite emotion."

"I'm not sentimental," I defended myself.

"Yes you are, you long to be in love as you call it. But you should try to use the term less often. Love is a big and difficult thing and not so common. At present your emotions are egotism, that is all. And if you met some poor stronzo tonight, provided he was stupid enough, you would fall in love immediately."

"Rubbish."

"I tell you, it's easy. Your little heart is fluttering with the feelings of Verdi's music." He pinched my cheek and shook my head ferociously, a habit I was beginning to hate. "The most important thing to remember about *La Traviata* is that Violetta is fulfilling every woman's fantasy of being a whore as well as pure. The father tells her his angelic daughter's reputation and life is in her hands and if she sacrifices Alfredo she will become pure. Of course she falls for this. The other thing to remember is that since Eve up until the present day, there has never been a pure woman."

The remaining acts passed in a mixture of my tears and reprimands from my father, who didn't think crying was the done thing at the opera. Still, he said when we left, as it was my first *Traviata* ever he would forgive me.

"Next time we see a real opera, no more of this shitting sentimentality."

"Shit."

"What?"

"The word is shit."

"Hmm. Bene," said my father. "But shitting sounds better."

We went to a restaurant near the opera house, which was famous for its late nights and the clientele that poured in after performances. It was already buzzing with people and waiters running around. The floor was covered in sawdust and the tables with bright red linen cloths. We sat down at a round table and studied the menu.

"I suppose the only thing to have after a night at *La Traviata* is Fettuccine Alfredo," said my father.

"Yes. I'm hungry," I said. "Shall we order?"

"Cara. I am sure *La Traviata* has given you an appetite, but try to be a little more elegant about these things. Instead of saying you're hungry, how about 'Everything I see has transformed itself into plates of spaghetti and I don't understand why.'"

I looked at him and thought about sulking but decided he probably had a point.

"Even you are beginning to look like a plate of pasta," I smiled.

"Brava," he roared with laughter.

We walked into Alfredo's restaurant where my father was greeted like a conquering hero.

"Ah maestro," said the waiter. "Such a pleasure to see you. How wonderful that you're here." We were told we could sit anywhere we wanted in the restaurant and chose a table outside.

"Why is he making such a fuss of you?" I asked my father.

"That's his job," he replied.

After about ten minutes the waiter called for us to watch the mixing of the Fettuccine Alfredo which took place on a round table with a vast glass statue in the middle. The ritual of

Fettuccine Alfredo is as follows: a waiter in a white uniform comes out carrying a plate with however many portions you have ordered and places it on the round table in the middle of the restaurant. He then throws industrial amounts of parmesan cheese and butter. This is mixed in with incredible dexterity. If the customer is important enough, the chef will bring out the special gold spoon and fork used only for the mixing of Fettuccine Alfredo given to the original Alfredo by Douglas Fairbanks and Mary Pickford. The pasta almost flies a couple of feet above the plate, as the cream, parmesan and fettuccine mingle to become the dish. This finished, he looks at the table to see how many men there are, gives them the lion's share and leaves the women with the remainder. One lucky recipient gets the plate he did the mixing on, which is the best bit.

I was given the gold cutlery to eat with, so now I have something in common with JFK, among other famous guests of Alfredo's.

Ever since that dinner with my father I have been searching for Alfredo's. Every time I went back to Rome, I would try to remember where it was, but I never managed to find it. It isn't until this trip when I arrange to meet a girlfriend for lunch and she suggests we meet at a restaurant in the Piazza Augusto Imperatore that I begin to think I may be on the right track. The name sounds familiar, although the restaurant she has asked to meet me at is called Gusto, so it's not the one I am looking for, but I have a feeling it is in the same square.

The minute I walk into the square, I know I'm in the right place. It is an ugly square, a monument to Fascism. Mussolini strongly identified himself with the emperor Augustus so set

about destroying a whole neighbourhood and a couple of
Roman monuments to build a square in his honour. The result
is terrible, but what can you expect? Mussolini was good for
two things, my father always told me: making the trains and the
operas run on time.

I recognise the restaurant straight away. Above the door is
written Alfredo—Imperatore delle Fettuccine. As you walk into
the vast room, there are signs everywhere proclaiming that this
is the true home of Fettuccine Alfredo. There is an expression
in Italian: la verità vera. The true truth. Which of course
implies there is a false truth. It is the same for fettuccine: there
is true Fettuccine Alfredo and false Fettuccine Alfredo.
According to the propaganda around me, I am in the right
place for the true experience. And there are faces of superstars
smiling at me from all the walls to testify to this fact. They
include the Duke and Duchess of Windsor, Joan Crawford,
Frank Sinatra and J.F. Kennedy. But are they the real ones?

The restaurant is almost Art Deco in style. It hasn't changed
at all since I was here with my father. I am inexplicably excited
at finding it again and call my friend to change the location for
lunch.

"I don't understand you," she says as she walks in. "Why do
you want to come to this old place?"

I explain and she nods understandingly. This is another big
difference with Italians. If you explain that something is family
related, they forgive anything. I remember once being on a
business trip in Rome and having to cancel a meeting because
my aunt showed up unexpectedly. In England I would have lied
and blamed something to do with work. In Italy it was perfectly
acceptable to blame my aunt's arrival; they totally understood.

The friend I am having lunch with is called Valentina and is in fact a friend of my mother's. She used to work with her. Valentina is for me the epitome of an Italian woman. She is very pretty, with long dark hair and brown eyes. She is voluptuous and sensuous in a way a French woman would never be. Partly because French women don't do curves; for them there is one look and that's pencil-thin. At least for the Parisian. The other thing Valentina has is an incredible warmth and kindness. This is a girl who despite the fact that she had only met me once moved out of her bedroom in Milan when I needed to come and stay. Because she comes from Milan she is dressed in black. Black trousers and a black cashmere jumper. Milanese women are famous for wearing hardly any colours at all.

I am keen to meet her for two reasons. One I owe her lunch, and two I wonder if she'll shed any light on my quest to discover my own identity.

Obviously we eat Fettuccine Alfredo. I watch the waiter mix the pasta with the cheese and butter. He has an amazing wrist movement, a sort of flick and a turn at the same time which must come from years of practicing. The pasta is good: light, cheesy and comforting.

Valentina and I talk about Italian versus Anglo-Saxon characteristics. She has lived in England so knows both.

"I think the main difference is that the English don't like to talk about anything personal or emotional without drinking," she says. "We Italians are much more open and honest. It's hard work sometimes being with English people, they rarely open up."

"What about Italian passion?" I ask.

"Italian passion is a bit of a cliché," says Valentina. "But like all clichés, there is some truth to it. Like the Italian temper."

I don't know whether I'm more passionate than my English

friends. I'm certainly more short-tempered, which could be from my Italian side. Although my stepfather was impossibly short-tempered. Any little thing could send him off into a total frenzy, and what was so awful was that it was impossible to predict what it might be. My overriding memory of childhood is him shouting at me on street corners. Oddly enough, when I did truly stupid things, like shoplifting a plastic horse from Debenhams in Oxford aged ten because a friend put me up to it, or getting arrested for some drugs that weren't mine aged seventeen, he was always remarkably calm. Although my mother and he split up when I was nine we kept in touch until I was almost thirty. Then we fell out over his inability to stop shouting at me on street corners. I walked away from the scene, suddenly realising that this had been going on since I was three and I had just had enough of it. I had my own flat around the corner from the scene and I felt it was time to make a stand. So off I went, trembling with fear as I walked. But I kept going despite him ordering me to "get back here this instant". He never spoke to me again.

With my mother though, he was just furious most of the time. I remember one incident when they were arguing over a deep-sea diver who had come to stay. He was one of those gorgeous-looking Aussies with big muscles and floppy dark hair. His name was Dave. My mother of course fancied him and being a supremely honest woman did nothing to hide it. One night I came downstairs while they were arguing about the hunky diver. My stepfather had a machete in his hand.

"Do you mean to say," he was yelling, "that you would risk everything, our marriage, our family, for a fling?" He was foaming at the mouth by now and practically spat the last word out.

My mother looked at him, and the machete, and then, unaccountably, inexplicably, completely stupidly, said "Yes," in a loud firm voice.

I thought about calling the ambulance then and there, but was transfixed. My stepfather made a terrible growling sound and raised the machete above his head ready to bring it down on her. Mercifully we were living in one of those little old English cottages with beams in the ceiling. My stepfather had raised the machete with such force it got stuck in one of the beams. I started giggling. We weren't sure whether he meant to hurt himself. My mother grabbed my arm and we ran out into the fields behind the house, where we hid until it was safe to come back. It was safer to laugh away from the machete-wielding potential cuckold.

So when I lose my temper now, I wonder if it's as a result of being partly brought up by a short-tempered man, or if it's my Italian nature. Sometimes when I shout at my children I see him in me, which more often than not makes me stop. But then my Italian family is not famous for its patience either. I remember one of the first times I was with my aunt and uncle. We were driving from their house to the port of Amalfi.

"Where do you think we should park?" my uncle asked innocently.

Big mistake. Huge. My aunt went into an hysterical outburst about how she didn't give a shit where they parked, was that really all his tiny brain was capable of thinking about, how she wanted to share many beautiful things with him but the parking of the car was so out of her area of interest it wasn't even worth talking about and so on. The poor man. I bet he never asked her that again. Sometimes I feel like asking her where we should park just to see what would happen, but my courage always fails me.

"So do you think you're more English or Italian?" asks Valentina.

"More English," I respond. "But I am beginning to see some of the Italian in me. I am more obsessed with pasta than anyone else I know and also more emotional, especially when it comes to my children."

"Yes, and you'll totally spoil your son, like all Italian mothers, making him a total nightmare for any other woman. I have a friend who has a daughter but she tells me she has two children: her daughter and her husband."

The pasta is nice but forgettable, the whole operation slick and practised. As we leave Alfredo's and walk back into the Fascist square, I wonder if I have been a victim of propaganda.

The next morning my aunt confirms I have. We inch slowly past a restaurant called, amazingly, Alfredo's on our way to the Piazza Farnese. Outside a sign proclaims it is the home of Fettuccine Alfredo.

"That's impossible," I say stopping outside to gawp. "I thought the real Alfredo's was in the Piazza Augusto Imperatore."

"No, this is where you eat the real Fettuccine Alfredo," my aunt tells me. "It is the original one. The other one is just a tourist trap, no one except foreigners goes there."

I am too embarrassed to tell her where I ate lunch.

We walk into the Piazza Farnese. If Piazza di Spagna is my spiritual home, this is my uncle's. The French embassy is here and the cafés are full of French people. In the square are two fountains that look like they have been made out of giant bathtubs. My aunt tells me they are just that. They were found in the Baths of Caracalla and converted into fountains in the early seventeenth century.

We walk towards the Tiber and stand on the Sisto Bridge looking at the view. It is an autumnal day; the leaves that have fallen off the trees along the river have gathered on the paths that line it. It is tempting to run down and kick them. But I don't think my aunt would approve.

"Over there is Trastevere," she says. "The name comes from trans Tiberim, over the Tiber. They are a rebellious people, but you can eat well there." Food and clothes are the only mundane topics of conversation my aunt allows.

This is not the first time I have heard the name Trastevere. My father taught me a poem with its name in it that first summer.

"As it is July 29th, the birthday of the big stronzo Mussolini," he announced one morning, "we are going to dedicate the day to Fascist monuments and the Duce. It's a shame Nonna Settimia isn't here, she loves nothing more than a few Fascist monuments."

"Is she a Fascist?" I couldn't believe my lovely grandmother would approve of Mussolini.

"Of course, like all good catholics. They see no difference between the Pope and a dictator. And they have a point. Andiamo."

We left Via Margutta and walked towards Piazza di Spagna. My father's plan was to hire a horse-drawn carriage for the tour.

"What do you know of il Duce?" he asked me.

"I know he was a friend of Hitler's." In fact this was the only thing I knew about him. One of the benefits of an English education is that you get to learn who the goodies and the baddies are early on.

My father nodded. "For a while, and this was his downfall. He came from a typical Italian family, where the father spent most of his time and money on his mistress. From a very young age he showed signs of being a stronzo. His favourite trick was to stab his classmates with a penknife. But he had a gift of public speaking and the ability to catch the imagination of the proletariat. This is something Hitler understood very well too. Mussolini became so powerful partly because he was the only one that sounded like he knew what he was doing and the stupid people needed a leader."

We arrived in the square. There was one rather sad and scrawny-looking horse with his nose in a bag. His owner was chatting to a taxi driver close by.

"These kinds of people," said my father, moving closer to me and motioning to the owner of the horse, "are terrible. They are a waste of space. They are the typical Italian shitting stronzos who know nothing apart from how to abuse animals and pick their noses. In fact their only use is for a tour of Fascist Rome."

He motioned to the man, who quoted him some outrageous sum of money. My father laughed and asked him if that price included the horse. Eventually they agreed on an amount and we got into the carriage. As a method of transport it wasn't hugely comfortable; the combination of the cobbled streets, the thin metal wheels and no suspension grated after a while. But the view of Rome was splendid; it was a bit like being in a convertible car, only I could turn around and look behind me without feeling sick.

"There is a rhyme that will help you learn Italian and it is also about Mussolini," he said as we headed out of the Piazza Augusto Imperatore. "There is a part of Rome called

Trastevere which is famous for restaurants, artists and libertines. It was the only area of Rome that refused to become Fascist. Mussolini decided to try and woo the people of Trastevere with a brand new street light that lit up the central square. He had the light put up and a big banner that went across the square on which was written: Trastevere, shine with new light. The Madonna, King and Duce all wish you well. The people of Trastevere took the banner down and replaced it with one of their own. This is what they wrote:

> Questa luce non vogliamo
> Vogliamo star in pace
> Andate a far in culo
> Madonna, Duce e Re.

Loosely translated it means, we don't want this light, we want to be left alone, go and get fucked, Madonna, Duce and king."

"What did Mussolini do?"

"I don't know, probably stabbed them all with his penknife. Now try to learn it. Maybe without the Roman accent. You have to understand that most people in Italy, especially in the south, speak a kind of shitting Italian that you must not learn. We Benedettis speak the Italian spoken in Siena. The equivalent of your Queen's English."

By the time I had learnt the rebellious ditty, we had arrived at the Axum Obelisk, which Mussolini stole from Ethiopia.

"Mussolini had a very small penis," explained my father. "So a lot of Fascist monuments are phallic."

I wasn't sure whether to believe him or not. I mean how would he know?

"One day I will show you my film I made about Mussolini, it will be better than reading history books. But really bella, your ignorance is amazing. How did you get to this age knowing so little?"

"I did well at school," I tried to defend myself.

"Maybe at the kind of shitting school your mother sent you to. We have to think about it seriously or you will always be a poor stupida."

I must have looked upset as he grabbed my cheek and gently shook my head.

We continued the tour. "In Mussolini's time the roads of Rome were empty," said my father. "He had an agricultural policy that forced a lot of people out of town. Foreigners would come here and be amazed at how calm it was. 'Your Excellency,' they would say. 'How come in Rome the roads are so empty?' Mussolini would reply 'The roads are for me.'" My father laughed.

"But enough Fascism for one day," he said. "Now I will show you Roman Rome."

He took me to see the Colosseum and the Forum. I had only seen the Colosseum in films, most notably *Roman Holiday*. I looked in vain for the marble bench Audrey Hepburn falls asleep on.

"I organised all this for you," said my father, pointing at the Colosseum. "They had to work all night and as you can see it's not quite finished." We walked around it and I imagined lions eating slaves. Then we wandered around the Roman Forum. Or rather we fought our way around it with thousands of tourists. At the time, Roman ruins meant nothing to me. I was deeply superficial and mad about the film *Grease*. My father talked about the Romans while I thought about John Travolta.

Me in our home in Rome.

I now find myself back at the Forum but looking at it from a most unlikely place. I have said goodbye to my aunt and uncle, who have a meeting that afternoon. I decide to walk from Piazza Farnese towards the Colosseum. On the way I pass the Capitoline Museum. I remember from that first visit there seeing a huge hand and a foot in the courtyard. I have a picture my father took of me in front of the foot. It is a picture I have looked at often. I am trying to smile, but trying too hard. My expression is fake. I remember what I was thinking at the time. I was thinking how stupid I looked trying to smile next to an over-sized foot and wondering how I could become less stupid. I want to see these statues again.

I find them surprisingly easily. The statues are not as big as I imagined they would be. Maybe I was a lot smaller when I last saw them. I am certainly a lot more confident and happier in my own skin as the French put it. The white clean marble is just as I remember it. It has the same effect on me as the Fra Angelico in San Marco, making me feel peaceful. I walk into the museum. The most famous monument there is the Capitoline

She-Wolf from the fifth century BC with the founding twins of Rome, Romulus and Remus. The boys are a little kitsch—they were added later—but she has a weary dignity about her. She looks patiently into the distance as they feed from her.

I wander around for another hour or so before seeing an alleyway that has an intriguing look about it. I decide to follow it. I go up some steps and along a bit, up some more steps and then out onto a terrace. Suddenly I am in front of one of the best views in the world. At my feet is the entire Forum, bathed in sunlight. And best of all I am alone on this terrace to enjoy it. Below me tourists battle their way between the ancient remains and other tourists. Here, above it all, I am like a bird surveying them from the sky.

To my left is the pink neo-classical church of San Giuseppe dei Falegnami. It is a soft colour, almost pastel. Next to it stands the Baroque church of Saints Luca and Martina, white marble and extravagant statues, a perfect foil to the pink church. Next to that is the Senate House, or Curia as it is known, the seat of the government. This is a building the Japanese would describe as Zen. It is positively plain, basically four brick walls and a roof, but it has a grandeur about it, mainly due to its imposing size. To my right are the Roman remains of temples, roads and basilicas. Bits of grass sprout out of buildings like unruly bits of facial hair. Tourists walk up and down the Via Sacra, trying to take it all in. Beyond them I can see a fragment of the Colosseum rising above the forum. I see my father never finished building it. I feel like a time-traveller, with all of civilisation laid out before me.

The Palatine Hill makes up the backdrop. It is covered with trees: cypresses, olives, pines, sprouting palms. In the bright sunlight they all look the same greeny-black colour. The Roman ruins look mysterious half-hidden in the foliage.

The foreground is dominated by the remains of two temples: the Temple of Vespasian and Titus and the Temple of Saturn. All that is left of the first one are three columns, which stand alone like giant tripods. Close by is the Triumphal Arch of Septimius Severus, which is remarkably intact. There are four detached Corinthian columns in front of the façade. The front is decorated with small figures. The top looks like a giant tomb that has been airlifted down to its final resting place.

To the left of the arch seagulls fly over the roof of the Curia, as if to remind us how close we are to sea. The shadows of their wings create a strobe-light effect on the terracotta tiles of the roof. The columns down below cast their shadows on the grass. In the distance a bell rings from a Venetian-looking bell-tower behind the Colosseum. The fact that I can hear it reminds me that I am in possibly the only place in Rome where there are no cars. Even an aeroplane I see flying high above is silent.

It is partly the light that makes the view so exceptional. The sky is bright blue and the sunshine strong, but it is autumn, so the shadows are longer and the effects more dramatic. It is almost as if someone had thrown millions of minuscule diamonds from the sky and they are falling in slow motion over the Forum. Everything glistens, even the tourists.

I spend an hour looking at the view from the balcony of the Capitoline Museum. When I finally drag myself away and back down into the street below I feel like a Roman emperor who has been deposed. I am a mere mortal again, mixing with the proletariat and risking death by scooter with every step I take, instead of surveying my empire from the privacy of my balcony high up above the city.

6

Truffles with Everything

I am with my aunt when she gets the call. She is silent for a while, an unusual occurrence in itself. Then she panics. "But what can we do? Where can we cook it? This is terrible. Our flat is a shell." She listens to the other person for a while then carries on. "OK, bring it, I'll sort something out." She hangs up. She turns to my uncle. "That was Marco, he has a truffle which he wants to bring to Rome for us."

My uncle looks ecstatic, an occurrence that is even more unusual than my aunt's silence.

"But where do we cook it?" wails my aunt. "It's a disaster. I couldn't tell him not to bring it though."

Bertrand suggests they cook it at their friend Sveva's house where they're staying while their flat is redecorated.

"But she's so boring," says my aunt. "And she'll just want to get involved. And Marco is so ugly, I can barely bear to look at him." My aunt is not keen on ugly people. If a person is ugly, he's not worth knowing. Unless he's got a bloody great truffle of course.

My uncle points out that we have no other option on the cooking. The flat I'm staying in is too small. Marco is coming with the truffle and a young woman. There will be seven of us. And anyway, they've known Marco is ugly for fifteen years. Why should it suddenly bother them now?

"Is the truffle big enough?" he asks. "That's the really crucial question."

My aunt immediately phones the ugly truffle-dealer. Yes, he tells her, it's vast. She is delighted and starts planning the menu immediately. I am terribly confused. This much fuss over some fungus?

But as with anything concerning my Italian family, this is something unusual and exquisite. It is a white truffle from the Le Marche region of Italy, or to give it its proper and more reverent name, a tuber magnatum pico. These truffles can sell for anything up to £1500 a kilo depending on the quality and supply that year. They are found between twelve and fifteen inches below ground, usually in a circular formation around four feet from the base of an oak tree. The truffles are hunted by dogs or pigs. Only sows are used for white truffles as they contain pheromones that they find attractive. The downside with using pigs is that they tend to devour them once they've found them.

Up until 1945 all truffles in Italy were the property of the Vatican, to which they all had to be delivered. But I'm sure the canny farmers of Le Marche hid a few and pretended the pigs had eaten them.

Brillat-Savarin, the seventeenth-century gourmet, says: "Whosoever says truffle, utters a grand word, which awakens erotic and gastronomic ideas." He tells the story in his book *The Physiology of Taste* of a young lady who has supper with a trusted friend of her husband's, while her husband is detained on a business trip.

"The principal dish of our supper," says the lady, "was a

magnificent truffled fowl. The truffles above all were delicious." Once they have eaten, she recounts how the gentleman, who had been completely trustworthy until that moment, becomes "flattering, unreserved, affectionate, caressing," and makes advances towards her. She manages to keep him at bay, mainly by pretending she will give in and being "artful enough to make him believe that all hope was not forbidden to him". She concludes: "I blame the truffles for this. I am really persuaded that they were the cause of some predisposition, which might have become dangerous." She adds that she will, however, not give them up as that would be "too severe a punishment" but that she will choose her dining partners more carefully in future.

Aphrodisiac or not, this particular one has certainly got my aunt and uncle excited. There is a discussion as to how we will eat it. Pasta is decided on. Then we have to decide what kind of pasta. Then we have to think about whether there should be a sauce and so on. The truffle discussion takes up almost the whole day, and we haven't even got our hands on it yet.

The pick-up is at six o'clock that evening. My aunt, for as long as I have known her, has always been late for everything. You can set your watch by her lateness. If she says she'll be somewhere at one, you know she'll be there at two. But for the truffle rendezvous she is early. I see her from a distance as I approach the Bar Canova in Piazza del Popolo. She is standing outside looking around nervously, like someone waiting for a drug dealer.

I walk up and kiss her. She is truly fretting. I have never seen her so agitated. "He's so provincial," she tells me. "He can't even be on time. It's not like he's a woman making a lover wait, that's different." Her mobile phone rings, which makes her jump. It's him. I can tell from the urgency in her tone.

"He's late," she tells me as she hangs up. "He's been delayed by traffic or something. He won't be here for another half an hour at least. This means we'll hit the rush hour as we leave town, the whole thing is a disaster."

At that moment my uncle arrives with the car, ready to transport us and the truffle back to Sveva's house. He is equally disappointed by the delay. But we can't stand in Piazza del Popolo with a great big four-wheel drive all night. We arrange to meet the truffle man outside the Hotel Locarno around the corner.

It is a tense half hour. My aunt provides some light relief by taking me into a clothes shop she knows nearby. So here I am in the Via dell'Oca trying on clothes designed by Maria Vittoria, whom my aunt has apparently known for twenty-five years. I don't think there's a street in Rome without a shop my aunt knows intimately. They are all rather eccentric outfits, with crazy colours and even crazier prices, but as a way to spend half an hour waiting for a truffle it's not bad. Although there really isn't an outfit there I'd like to buy, even if I could afford them, which is unusual for me. I wonder who her clients are. Women with what the French would call "eccentric" taste, I guess. I quite like that about the Italians though, they're not as regimented as the French, they have more flamboyance, more flair really, and they're a whole lot more relaxed. Perhaps because they don't have the spectres of Dior, Saint Laurent and Chanel hanging over them. I remember one French woman telling me that for them to veer from the conservative is next to impossible. Italians with their modern, flamboyant designers like Dolce & Gabbana and Versace have no such qualms. My aunt was always telling me that first summer to be more "disinvolto" which means relaxed and like you don't care. Of course that was impossible. As a gawky teenager trying to reinvent myself, "disinvolto" was about the last thing I was.

Finally my uncle comes running into the shop. Marco is here, he's just seen him pull up in a taxi. There is a lot of frenetic scrambling as we rush to get into the car. Poor Marco is not even allowed to draw breath before he is bundled into the front seat. His date is told to get in the back with me and my aunt. My aunt looks horrified when she sees her.

"She's very fat," she whispers. "I hope she doesn't eat too much."

Bertrand speeds off in the direction of the sea.

"I'm so sorry we're late," says Marco. "I forgot the truffles."

"Stop the car," screeches my aunt. "Turn around."

"No, no," says Marco. "I have them, don't worry, but we had to go back to the hotel to get them."

There is silence for a while. Then my aunt and uncle both speak at the same time.

"Let me have a look, please."

Marco delves into his briefcase and brings out a glass jar. It has a silver lid with some kitchen paper underneath it. Bertrand tries not to crash into the Tiber as he gazes at the jar.

"Let me hold it," says my aunt.

Marco hands it over. She looks at the jar then opens the lid. Suddenly the whole car is filled with an aroma that is strong, peppery and musty.

"Quick close it," shouts Marco. "You'll lose the flavour."

My aunt takes one long last smell and then closes it. She reluctantly hands the jar back to Marco.

"I have one for you as well," he says, handing her another jar. "A present."

My aunt is visibly moved. She clutches her jar to her chest.

The picture from my grandmother's house.

"I'll have to hide it in the car," she says. "Or Sveva will steal it."

We arrive at Sveva's house by the sea after about forty minutes. The truffle for dinner is taken inside. In fact it is not one big truffle, but about twelve little ones. Marco assures us the flavour of the little ones is far superior. My aunt hides her truffles in the boot of the car, making it the most valuable four-wheel drive in Rome that evening.

Once we're inside the truffle discussion starts in earnest. Of course no one cares about the two magnificent turbot we will eat as a main course along with sliced roast potatoes with rosemary and sea-salt. All the arguments concern the truffles. What sort of pasta should be used? My aunt has bought tagliolini egg pasta made by Cipriani, the founders of Harry's Bar in Venice. "It is very delicate," she says. "You need something delicate with truffles." Then there is the question of how long the pasta should be cooked for. The box says four minutes, Sveva says it should be cooked for three minutes maximum. She is a formidable blonde woman with a booming theatrical voice and large breasts. She looks like she would know how long to cook a piece of pasta, but it's too dangerous to take sides.

Then they discuss the sauce. They agree it should be butter, but should the truffles soak in the butter sauce before to enhance the flavour? And if so for how long? How hot should the butter be? Should it be mixed with olive oil?

The truffles are brought into the kitchen and my aunt carefully opens the lid of the jar. Everyone rushes forward to get a smell, like a bunch of supermodels at a party lunging for a line of coke. Then they argue about how to clean them. Sveva and Marina (the voluptuous date) say they should not be touched with water. Marco says a little water is OK, but you should wipe them with a nail brush. My aunt is put in charge of the cleaning. Everyone watches in horror as she uses a knife to remove some of the more stubborn bits of mud. I swear bits of the actual truffle are coming off as well. It's like watching liquid gold being poured into the sink.

The table is laid and the pasta water is boiling. Sveva grates the parmesan in a Magimix. The house smells of truffles and rosemary from the potatoes. The anticipation is almost too much. I accept a glass of wine from my uncle with relief. Marina joins me. She is one of those women the Italians refer to as morbida, literally meaning soft. She is voluptuous, bordering on overweight. Her face is very pretty. Like most Italians she has lovely long dark hair. I wonder if Marco, who is not the most attractive of men as my aunt says, would have had such a date had he not had a couple of jars of truffles stashed away in his briefcase.

Finally we sit down. Minutes later my aunt appears with the pasta. It is a golden colour. The smells are butter, parmesan and truffles. It is an intoxicating combination. She starts to serve. I am at one end of the table and almost break into a cold sweat from thinking that there won't be enough for me. Finally a bowl is handed up to me. Along with a small plate filled with truffles.

"Mangia," I hear someone say. The word rings around the table like an echo as the others repeat it.

If you were an alien with extra-sensory hearing hovering above Italy at meal-times, you would hear the command "Mangia" being shouted from Bologna to Brindisi. You might ask yourself what it means. Is it some kind of prayer? Or maybe a call to arms? In fact it's a bit of both. Mangia or eat is the first Italian word I learnt at my grandmother's house on that first day in Italy more than twenty years ago.

O nce my grandmother had stopped weeping over my return, it was time for lunch. The table had been laid and the pasta was ready. Luisa, as my grandmother's maid who had opened the door was called, served us. I looked around the dining room. The floors were marble, the ceilings high, the furniture was antique and expensive. There was a vast chandelier over the table. This was not the sort of place I visited when we lived in England. I realised my Italian family was rich, something my mother hadn't told me. I suppose she didn't think it was important.

I was served a plate of spaghetti with tomato and basil sauce.

"Mangia, mangia," said my grandmother, beaming at me.

My mother translated and I obeyed.

The spaghetti was hard to handle. I watched the others who effortlessly wound it around their forks. Any bits that were left over were allowed to hang loose until they were chewed off. This slightly shocked me, but I soon realised it was the only way to eat it. The sauce was sweet and deep red. It was the first proper meal we'd had since leaving England. In fact my grandmother would probably have argued that it was the first proper meal we'd had since leaving Italy eleven years earlier. I finished mine quickly. Luisa was called for and gave me some more.

"Mangia, mangia," came the command from my adoring grandmother.

I did as I was told. By the end of the second bowl I could hardly breathe and was longing to fall asleep. Then the roast chicken arrived. When I made a sign that I couldn't possibly eat anything else, my grandmother looked as if she was going to burst into tears again. I accepted some chicken and a few vegetables. With a great effort I ate them. All the while my grandmother watched me intently.

There was a bit of talking after the chicken. I didn't understand anything as it was all in Italian, but they all seemed to be getting on well. I noticed a picture of me as a small baby on the chimney piece opposite me. It was in a silver frame. I looked very Italian, with big brown eyes and almost black hair. I saw that the carpet in the picture was the same as the one in the dining room now. It seemed impossible to me that I had been here before.

"Mangia!" Suddenly the command rang out again. It couldn't be possible. It was. In front of me was a huge piece of lemon cake. I started to feel myself going green. This was a look my mother recognised.

"Just eat as much as you can and we'll hide the rest," she said quietly, so they couldn't hear.

I smiled at my beaming grandmother and picked up my fork.

At one stage I managed to manoeuvre half of the cake into my napkin, which I hid in my lap. An old trick I had perfected after hundreds of inedible school dinners. In those days they still made you sit in the refectory until you'd cleared your plate.

After lunch my father suggested we all have a rest. He turned to my grandmother and asked her what she thought of her granddaughter after all these years apart. She hugged me again and said something. I asked my mother to translate.

"She said you're lovely. But you don't eat anything."

"There's a truffle each," says my aunt. "Use the slicer to shave it onto your pasta."

I pick up the truffle, it is the first time I have touched one. It is a fairly ugly little thing, a little bit like a turnip. But it smells strong. Packed into that little fungus is a lot of flavour. I shave it over my pasta, which already has the truffle-infused butter sauce in it and has been mixed with freshly grated parmesan. It is strong yet delicate, peppery and mustard-like but not overpowering. It somehow tastes of underground, of leaves and the earth, but it is clean at the same time. It reminds me of the smell of a dog's paw. It is like nothing I have ever eaten before.

There is silence around the table as we eat. Everyone is in raptures. My uncle proposes a toast to the truffle-suppliers. Their journey was definitely worth it.

The turbot and roast potatoes are a triumph too. My aunt is amazed to see me asking for a second helping.

"I see you eat fish now?" she says. "When Helena was younger, she wouldn't touch it. I think she must have been sexually oppressed, which is normal for the English. But look at her now!"

Everyone does just that. I smile and try to think of something to say along the lines of "Nothing sexually repressed about me now after three children," but decide to keep quiet.

"Maybe it's the effect of the truffles," says Sveva. "They always make me feel quite odd."

Marco agrees. "My greatest moments of seduction have always been linked to truffles. There is something truly irresistible about them. After a truffle dinner, fidelity becomes impossible."

Everyone around the table is asked to tell a story about infidelity. Sveva begins. She was married to a man who, until his death a couple of years ago, was one of Italy's leading theatre directors. They travelled to Paris together in the 1970s. He was directing a play there. After the play he decided he wanted to go to a lesbian bar. Sveva went along with this, although she has never had any lesbian leanings. They met a very pretty girl and they all ended up back at her flat, in bed.

"This girl of course was a lesbian," explains Sveva. "So she was far more interested in me. Umberto got very grumpy and tried to get her off me. I was beginning to enjoy myself. After all, he had been unfaithful to me for years. And in addition what she was doing wasn't unpleasant. Lasciala stare, I told him, leave her alone, she's doing fine."

This infuriated her husband who physically pushed the lesbian away from his wife. The lesbian then grabbed hold of Sveva's arm.

"Come and live with me," she pleaded. "Leave this monster. I love you, I have lots of money, I'll look after you."

Sveva's husband grabbed hold of the other arm. "So they were both tugging at me, pleading with me. In the end of course,

I left with my husband, but I can't help wondering how my life would have turned out if I hadn't."

Marco tells the story of a woman wearing a black dress and no knickers who seduced him at a conference in Pisa.

"It was terrible," he says. "She just had sights on me from the minute she saw me. At first I told her I was gay. Then I didn't want that rumour going round, so I said I wasn't gay but married. No problem she said, so am I. Then she jumped on me and violated me."

There is a great argument around the table about whether or not a man can physically be violated. Marco maintains he was.

"I was left in a terrible state," he says. "I couldn't get an erection for a year. Finally I said to my wife, let's go to the car, where we first made love. Suddenly it worked. I drank champagne and made love for the rest of the week."

Marina tells us that if you're truly in love, you won't be unfaithful. Everyone protests but forgives her idealism as she is so young. My aunt tells a story of a former girlfriend's of Bertrand's telling her she spent the night with him in Paris.

"I know Bertrand's not made of stone," she says. "But what do I care?"

Sveva agrees. "To have a successful marriage you have to learn to close your eyes," she says.

My father always used to say you couldn't eat the same pasta sauce every day and that fidelity was impossible. As my uncle drives me back into town I wonder if I have an Italian attitude towards fidelity or an Anglo-Saxon one. I conclude that it's probably more Italian. I certainly couldn't eat the same pasta sauce every day. Unless of course the pasta sauce were made with truffles.

7

Dinner with a

Princess

I am late for the princess. The train that is taking me from Rome to the town of Orte, sixty kilometres north of Rome, refuses to leave the platform. There are two main reasons for coming here. One is to meet the princess, a friend of Mariella's, the Rossini fan I met in Florence. The other is to see the place my life changed for ever. It was at Orte railway station that my future stepfather plucked up the courage to speak to my mother.

There is nowhere to sit, so I stand in the corridor with all my bags, being bashed from one side to another as people walk past to find their seats or the toilet. The train is shabby and old-fashioned; it could even be the same one my mother travelled on. I call the princess. No problem she says, I'll wait for you at the station. Considering she has just flown in from Marrakech and is on her way home to her castle for the first time in a week, I find this a very generous response.

I am curious to meet a real live princess. For as long as I can remember, I have wanted to be one. I wonder if there is anything that makes a princess identifiable. Some charming scar, rather like Harry Potter's. Or a special way of walking or talking. She doesn't know me, but being Italian and therefore very hospitable, she has invited me to break my journey from Rome to Venice with a night at her home.

"There is a dinner in my cellar," she says. "Come along, stay the night and then go to Venice the next day. You have to see my castle at Vignanello."

I am terribly excited by the prospect of dinner in a castle. I imagine footmen and butlers bowing as I glide into the dining room. The food will be served from silver platters and the company covered in diamonds. I wonder what on earth to wear. I didn't exactly pack for dinner with a princess in a castle.

I read in my guidebook that the castle was originally built as a monastery for Benedictine monks in the ninth century. It ended up in the hands of a Scotsman called Marescotti (Mario the Scot) when he married Beatrice's daughter Ortensia.

Ortensia was the first in a long line of powerful women to rule the castle. Ortensia ended up murdering Mario the Scotsman, clubbing him to death with a fire poker. She then eradicated his half of the family crest on the chimney piece in the great hall on the first floor of the castle. Her crest remains there to this day, but where the Scotsman's was it is just blank. He has been erased from history. Ortensia married twice again, killing both her subsequent husbands, as well as a daughter. Eventually she was thrown into prison, but only for a few years.

As I am reading this history, the train starts to move. I can't wait to see the castle. I wonder whether her evil ancestor is one of the reasons the princess, who is also known as Claudia Ruspoli, never married. In 1617 the name of Ruspoli first appears in connection with the castle when Vittoria, daughter of Orazio Ruspoli from Siena, marries Sforza Vicino Marescotti. The terms of the marriage stipulate that one of the sons take the name of Ruspoli in return for the Ruspoli fortune. Since then there has always been a Ruspoli at Vignanello. I suppose having the same house for four hundred years means you are unlikely to ever go through the pain of forwarding post or packing your belongings into a removal van.

It is only a half-hour train journey from Rome to Orte, but when I get off the train it feels like I have arrived in Russia. I left a warm and sunny Rome, despite the fact that it is mid-November. Suddenly I am plunged into sub-zero temperatures. The last time I was this cold, I was in St Petersburg in mid-December walking to the Hermitage.

The station is unremarkable. I look around for a minute or so before moving towards the exit. The architecture looks Fascist but could be later. There are two platforms and a subway. It probably hasn't changed much since my mother was here in the sixties. I call the princess. She tells me she is in the café and will meet me at the front of the station.

She is very attractive, around fifty, with lovely thick dark hair and light brown eyes. She is in black and has an incredibly warm smile (the only warm thing I am to encounter for the next twenty-four hours).

"Welcome," she smiles, hugging me. "I'm so glad to meet you." As we are driven towards the village of Vignanello by her friend Olympia, I try to see if there is anything particularly princess-like about her. She is wearing black trousers, a black wool jumper and black velvet coat. Whatever happened to the tiara and satin slippers? Her character is vivacious, fun, outgoing. She is intelligent and speaks perfect English with a sexy Italian accent. The result, she tells me, of being brought up by an English governess called Hilda Payne. "Pain in the neck I used to call her," she laughs. "She was typically

Victorian."

Princess Claudia has been mistress of the Castello since 1997. Prior to that she worked as an actress in Los Angeles and a documentary film maker.

"I hated the place and never wanted it," she says. "It was always somewhere I was sent as a punishment. For example if I didn't study hard enough, my parents would send me here to stay with my great-grandparents. But I was always brought up not to question gifts from my parents so when my father told me he had decided to give it to me I just said 'Well, I didn't ask for it, but thank you.'"

At the time Claudia was recovering from a broken heart so she took refuge in the castle with a friend of hers from Rome called Cesare. "I came to lick my wounds," she says. "But slowly I started to develop an interest in the place, trying to see what could be done and then I started to get involved: to open it to the public, to get funding, to organise concerts in the summer and so on. Finally I started to feel protected by the castle."

Even though I have only known the princess for ten minutes, she doesn't strike me as the sort of person who would sit and brood for long. She is a doer, a competent and energetic type. And extremely down to earth.

We arrive at the castle after a twenty-minute drive. It is almost dark by now but beyond my freezing breath I can see a vast stone block perched in the middle of the village. The walls are grey and at least two metres thick. The castle is square-shaped with four sturdy towers in each corner. I call them towers but they are not the elegant image one has of a castle tower; they are rather squat and ugly. But the effect is impressive. It's certainly a real castle, unlike some castles in France, which turn out to be nothing more than glorified stables.

We walk over a moat and a drawbridge to reach the vast wooden double door. Claudia fumbles around in her handbag for her keys while I stand there marvelling at the moat like an American tourist visiting anything over two hundred years old. Claudia can't find the keys so we knock. The door knocker doesn't look too imposing but the sound it gives is almost like a death-knell. Claudia bangs three times, slowly. The sound echoes inside and out. It reminds me of the commendatore in the opera *Don Giovanni* when he bangs on the door to be let in for supper.

The first time I saw *Don Giovanni* was with my father at La Scala in Milan that first summer in Italy. My father and I travelled up from Rimini on the train. He bought two Walkmans and we sat listening to it all the way there. He always told me you need to know an opera well to appreciate it.

"You must know it in your heart," he told me. "Every bar and note must be familiar to you, there must be no shocks, only joy at hearing something you know so well."

We sat in a first-class compartment with our tapes strewn around. I was told to read the English translation of the libretto. My father lectured me as we listened. Although the story interested me immediately, I was more worried about him yelling over the sound of the Walkman and the looks of disgust from the other passengers than learning about the opera.

"The thing to remember," he yelled, "is that Mozart had to kill his hero. There is no way a man who had sex with half of Europe and didn't repent could be allowed to survive. For a catholic Europe it was just not possible. But the truth is, like Dante and his Paola and Francesca, and Milton with his Devil,

Mozart loved Don Giovanni and despised the petite bourgeoisie that surrounded him."

I tried to tell him that we were disturbing the other passengers but he told me that was nonsense and Mozart was more important.

He was amazed when I admitted I had never heard of *Don Giovanni*.

"Your ignorance is incredible," he shouted over the sound of the opera. "It is like you came down to earth from another planet. How can you not know *Don Giovanni*? It's not possible. Without music we are nothing. And you must always remember that people who listen to classical music as background music are common criminals. If you listen to say Mozart or Brahms you have to concentrate on the music you're listening to and repeat the path he's taken. This is a path that didn't exist before."

We listened to Don Giovanni seducing Zerlina. I read the libretto in English while listening to the words in Italian. The music was seductive enough without any words, delicate and flowing in a rhythm that made you want to follow.

> Là ci darem la mano,
> Là mi dirai di sì,
> Vedi, non è lontano,
> Partiam, ben mio, da quì.

"Zerlina shows all the emotions we feel when faced with something we want to do but know we shouldn't," said my father. "She is tempted, but knows she should resist. "Vorrei e non vorrei," she sings. "Mi trema un poco il cor." I want to and I don't want to, my heart trembles. She is a butterfly, fluttering close to fire and then saving herself, but finally, he is too strong for her and "tack"—my father made a swooping gesture with his hand—she is taken by the flame. So the choice for the Italian woman is either good girl or whore. Now, for the finale."

He fast forwarded the tape to the final act. "The commendatore demands that Giovanni repent, but he won't, and Mozart won't either. The character of Don Giovanni is, obviously, loosely based on himself. Listen."

He turned the volume up and we listened to the final act, my father acting as conductor throughout. The deep bass of the commendatore booming, "Pentiti" and the reply "No", and again, this time more urgent, "Pentiti" and the confident "No" until finally he is swallowed up into hell, still shouting "No".

We listened to the most famous arias several times. My father's favourite was Leporello's catalogue of his master's conquests.

> In Italia sei cento e quaranta,
> In Alemagna due cento trent'una;
> Cento in Francia, in Turchia novant'una,
> Ma, ma in Ispagna, son gia mille e tre!

One of the things my father did when he chose to earn a living was to work as an opera critic. He had given up directing films several years before and decided, as he put it, "to throw money away on more useful things, like perfectly shaped bottoms in the South of France".

On account of his contacts, and the fact that we had a relative who worked at La Scala (who was later fired for having a homosexual affair with one of the male ballet stars), we were given the Royal Box. A man showed us up the stairs and we were then handed over to another black-tie-clad usher who stood guard at the door of the box. He showed us into an ante-room where chilled champagne was being opened by another Scala representative in black tie. Pictures of great conductors hung on the walls, which were clad in red velvet, matching the carpet.

At the front of the box were four chairs lined with the same material. I gulped down my champagne almost in one, partly from nerves and partly out of excitement. The bell rang once, signalling the performance would start in ten minutes. The box was right in the middle of the theatre, carving a hole in the upper and royal circles. I walked to the edge and looked down at the orchestra warming up, while the rest of La Scala looked up to see who was in the box. My father joined me. He was wearing a dinner jacket, white shirt and black bow-tie. He told me this was his uniform for La Scala. I wore a short black dress he had bought me in Rimini especially for the occasion and sandals with heels. It was the first time I had ever worn heels and although these were not high I felt quite insecure on my feet. I also kept fiddling with the dress which kept riding up, threatening to expose my Marks & Spencer's knickers. My father told me to stop fidgeting.

"Look aloof," he said. "Like you're a Russian princess or something. All these peasants will be consumed with curiosity." He gestured to the crowd below us and raised his glass. "To you, cara, and your first date with *Don Giovanni*. May there be many after this."

As soon as the overture began, the hairs on the back of my neck stood up. It was the most powerful sound I had ever heard. The music took over the theatre, flowing effortlessly all around it. It filled me with energy and anticipation. The curtain went up and I saw Leporello, Don Giovanni's servant, skulking among the trees, waiting for his master. His voice was so strong and clear. It was as loud, if not louder, than the music. It was a completely different sound to the one I had heard on the Walkman. He sang his famous aria about not wanting to be a servant any more. Then the hero appeared. He was dashing in a large hat and cape. I wondered briefly what I would do in Zerlina's position.

Below me people sat holding up their opera glasses. Some looked as if they were nodding off. My father sat to my left, silently conducting throughout the whole performance. I was glad we were in the privacy of the Royal Box, his arm movements would have driven the people sitting next to him mad.

During the interval we left the luxurious surroundings of the box and toured La Scala. As soon as I stepped out of the box, I felt I had lost my royal status. We headed for La Scala museum, which takes up one wing of the theatre building and is filled with original scores, portraits of singers and composers, batons that belonged to significant conductors and other items from the Scala's glorious past. There was a large portrait of Maria Callas.

"La Callas," said my father. "A genius with a truly genial bottom."

We walked back towards our box arm in arm. I noticed women look at us. My father was still a very attractive man, tall and distinguished with his thick hair slightly greying at the temples. He was dressed impeccably and carried himself well. He was also an attentive suitor, treating me like a precious object. He opened doors for me and looked after me very well. I think he treated all women the same; he needed them to fall in love with him, whether they were six or sixty. I only met a couple of his girlfriends, one a Lido stripper from Paris and another a rather glamorous lady from Rome, but I was constantly aware of them lurking in the background. He would sometimes vanish off for an afternoon and I wondered whether he was meeting some woman or other. Women liked him, especially younger women who I think loved his intellect as well as his money. I expect he treated them well when it suited him but was not the most faithful of lovers. I was his only daughter though, as far as he knew, and always felt like a princess when I was out with him.

The memory of feeling like a princess brings me back to the present and the fact that I am on a drawbridge, with a real princess, slowly freezing to death. I have come out in my hipster jeans, leopard-print corset and a cashmere cardigan. As a way of training your stomach muscles it's marvellous. Your stomach instinctively contracts with every gust of icy air. As a sensible outfit it scores about nought out of ten. I can hear my Italian grandmother's voice from the grave: "La bambina è tutta nuda." The child is totally naked. Eventually a short, ancient retainer answers the door of the castle. He is wearing faded blue trousers, a thick brown jumper, a coat and a faded blue waistcoat on top of the coat.

The man is called Santino, which means little saint. He invites us to come into the entrance hall. Incredibly it is even colder in here than it is outside. It is a grand room, with a herringbone patterned brick floor. Suits of armour of armour decorate the walls. Big cast-iron candle holders hold lights that are designed to look like candles. Maybe the real thing is a fire hazard, but it seems a shame. Candles might at least warm the place up a bit.

The princess insists on showing me the garden before it gets dark. I am delighted to escape from the cold room; at least there might be some heat from the street lights. The garden was planted in 1610. Claudia tells me it is one of the most beautiful and famous parterres in Italy. I nod knowingly and assume a parterre is something to do with the layout of the garden. It is rectangular in shape and divided by four paths. In the centre there is a large pond. It is subdivided into twelve sections, or parterres as I now call them. It is very elegant but, as Claudia explains, the lemon trees have all been put away for the winter. There is a secret garden on the lower terrace that I can imagine is charming when all its roses are out, but in the grey dusk in the middle of November it looks a bit sad. Claudia and I walk back to the house and she asks me why I speak such good Italian. I explain that my father is Italian but that my parents were divorced when I was very young.

"Are you in touch with him?" she asks.

"I saw quite a bit of him when I was younger," I explain. "But he's very difficult."

"Where's he from?"

"Rimini."

"Well there you are," she says. "They're all mad in Rimini. Look at Fellini."

When we get back inside the castle, Santino shows me to my room so I can get ready for dinner. He leads me up a wide stone staircase with extremely high steps. We walk through a dining room into an apartment of two rooms and a loo. "This is where the princes always slept," he tells me in his wonderfully deep and crackly voice. "It's south-facing, so the warmest room in the house."

Thanks to a gas heater that has been on for most of the day, the evil nip in the air I felt downstairs has been eliminated. But I would struggle to describe the room as anything approaching warm. Santino shows me around then, just before he leaves, he almost stands to attention, smiles, nods and says "Con permesso," with your permission. Amazing, I feel like a princess.

My bedroom is dominated by a large wooden bed covered with a fur blanket. The sheets are linen and crisp. I lie down on the bed and look up at the ceiling. There is a pastel-coloured fresco painted on it showing Modesty and Justice floating on clouds, surrounded by birds and blancmange-shaped forms with trees growing out of them. These I learn later are the family crest of the Cesi family. Maria Isabella Cesi married Francesco Maria Ruspoli in the early eighteenth century. He had the fresco in my room painted to please Pope Benedict XIII who came to stay for four days in 1725. According to Claudia, he was trying to acquire the title of prince, so he also built the church opposite the castle, which still bears his name on its façade. His efforts were rewarded: he became a prince shortly after the Pope's visit. Rather sweetly, or perhaps absent-mindedly, the Pope left his slippers, night-robe and hat for posterity and you can still see these objects in a glass case in the sitting room on the first floor. I must remember to bring a spare set next time I go and stay with someone; such an unusual gift.

I go downstairs to join the party. I have been told my outfit will be fine for dinner, which is slightly disappointing. I was looking forward to getting dressed up. Claudia is in the entrance hall with two other people. One is a lady of about sixty, who I am later told was the head of PR for Bettino Craxi when he was Prime Minister of Italy between 1983 and 1987. The other is a tall, good-looking man with longish straight hair, deep brown eyes and a sensitive mouth. He reminds me of St Sebastian from a painting by Mantegna. He is wearing jeans, a black jumper and leather jacket. "This is Raphael," says Claudia. Of course it is, I think to myself, what else could he possibly be called? Graham? I don't think so.

We go into the kitchen, where there is a roaring fire and a girl called Maria cooking chestnuts. The smell is intoxicating. The taste of them is even better. They are almost sweet. I have tried to cook chestnuts for years but without success. Either they burn, or they explode in the pan leaving traces all over the kitchen. People have told me to soak them and then slice them, or not to soak them and not to slice them but to poke holes in either side. This is all nonsense. What Maria does is this: she slices the rounded side from one end to the other. Then she puts them in a pan with holes in the bottom (don't try to make one at home; you can buy them all over the place). Then she cooks them in the embers of the fire. The result is a perfect chestnut, browny-black on the outside, moist and warm on the inside. To break them open she puts them in between two bits of kitchen paper and pushes them. The burnt skin cracks easily.

We are given wine in what I think are Ikea glasses; at least I have some at home that look like this. It is deep red wine, with a real rustic flavour, earthy and honest. In fact the whole scene is more farmyard than castle. In contrast to the grand entrance hall, the kitchen is small and simple. Along one side runs a stone range. It is decorated with tiles on the top, painted with small blue flowers and a deep yellow centre. Underneath the structure are semi-circular holes for logs. The fire takes up about one metre. In the corner there is an old marble sink with a large silver tap. The floor is terracotta bricks. There is a wooden table in the middle of the room, around which we are gathered, although I am staying close to Maria and the chestnuts. All along the far wall of the kitchen hang copper pans; they are so gleaming I wonder if they're ever used.

I ask Romantic Raphael if he lives in the village. He smiles, leans closer to me in a way that men who are truly interested in women do, and tells me he lives in Viterbo. Princess Claudia joins us and says that this year he was responsible for designing the statue for the Festa di Santa Rosa. This is one of those festivals you get in Italy, a little like the Palio in Siena. It is a festival that celebrates the Virgin Mary (what else does one celebrate in Italy?) but has some extremely pagan elements to it. Romantic Raphael has pictures of the statue on his mobile phone. It looks like a vast gold penis to me so I nod and smile in admiration. It is about thirty metres tall and is carried through the village by the men-folk. It is lit, while everything else in the town is in darkness, so the effect must be spectacular. Princess Claudia talks proudly of the event and Romantic Raphael's involvement. "He is the first local architect to be chosen to build the statue," she says. I wonder if her interest in his enormous erection is purely professional.

It is time to go to dinner. Princess Claudia leads us outside and we walk down towards the cellar. After the warmth of the kitchen fire and the chestnuts the outside air is even icier than earlier. On the way we meet Pippo, who is joining us for dinner. He also lives in Viterbo. I assume in a castle of some sort. To my amazement, there appears to be loud music coming from the cellar. These Vignanello aristos certainly know how to throw a dinner party.

As we approach the door, a young man comes out to smoke a cigarette. The cold hits the young smoker as he exits the party and he exclaims "Porca puttana," a rather untranslatable Italian phrase that literally means pig of a whore, just as we arrive with the princess. He is immediately very embarrassed and apologises. The princess doesn't seem to care. I wonder if all the guests are swearing smokers.

As soon as we get inside, I realise my mistake. This is not your run of the mill castle dinner gathering. It is a village feast to celebrate the new wine. There are no butlers or servants, instead around fifty villagers carousing and countless children playing. It is a jolly scene, rather like a Breughel painting, and who needs all those servants running around anyway? Fetching my own food will keep me warm.

Inside we are led to a table with benches either side. The tablecloth is paper and the glasses plastic, as is the cutlery. The noise inside is deafening. But it is not talking or shouting, which the Italians do well, nor is there an orchestra playing Italian music. The noise is the unlikely sound of Italian men standing around, arms wrapped firmly around each other, singing along to soppy Italian pop songs. Welcome to Karaoke Italian style. I don't know whether to laugh or cry. Partly it is such a sweet, almost pathetic sight, but mainly I wonder how I'm going to get "Hotel California" on and have a go myself.

Almost as soon as we sit down, the first course arrives. It is a mixture of things, Pippo explains to me, all very local. There is some salami, some scrambled eggs with garlic (interesting combination; I wonder if Jamie Oliver's onto that one), some chick peas, and an orange slice. The wine, which is the reason for the party, is a local one. It is called Castello Novello 2005 and has a very pretty label with flowers on it. Sadly the label is deceptive as the wine is filthy, but I follow Romantic Raphael's lead and mix it with water, which makes it taste better.

The next course looks like a pizza to me.

"Polenta with meat and tomato sauce," announces Pippo.

It's delicious, just what you need on a freezing evening, warming, rich and tasty. Basically it's a bit like eating semolina with a sauce, but not at all an unpleasant experience.

Romantic Raphael and I try to have a conversation over the din of the enthusiastic singers. It is terribly difficult to hear anything without leaning very close to him. I can't decide whether this is a good or a bad thing. He tells me a little about his work and I tell him about my children. The princess and he are both astounded to hear that my husband and I have five between us. She shakes my hand and congratulates me. In Italy the norm is to have one, at least among the more educated classes.

"Five children," says Romantic Raphael to the princess but loudly so I can hear too. "She looks like a child herself." The princess ignores the comment and starts clapping in time to the music. The rest of the guests follow suit.

Another course arrives. I knew this would happen so I held back on the semolina, a tough decision but I have a steel will. This time it is meat. Pippo tells me it's pork with a chestnut sauce. I don't really like pork but feel it would be impolite not to try it. It's delicious, charred in the right places to give it a bit more flavour, with a creamy sauce. The vegetables arrive.

"Peas," says Pippo helpfully. Maybe he thinks we don't have them in England.

Olympia, who drove us from the airport, is by now up and dancing. She is a pretty blonde woman who tells me she is forty with two children and works as a photographer. Despite her light colouring, I find her typically Italian. She is not wearing any make-up and looks great. She dances towards our table, pauses when she reaches us and puts her hand on my shoulder.

"Are you having a nice time?" she asks.

"Lovely, thank you."

"I adore these sorts of parties, I love to see people having fun and I love dancing," she says before she dances off again, encouraging us to join her in a conga. Romantic Raphael and the princess get up. "Come on," Olympia encourages me to join in. For some reason I can't move. Maybe I'm just too cold, but to be honest I think I'm a bit shy. I plead tiredness and smile.

The atmosphere is great, everyone is laughing and dancing and eating. One man keeps lifting his toddler above his head and swinging him around. The child's head does look a rather strange shape and I wonder how many times he has been dropped. I can hardly bear to look. His sister has a slight humpty-dumpty air about her as well.

Another course arrives, it is something white in a plastic container with tomato sauce.

"No, no, no," says Pippo. "Tripe." How he knew I hate tripe I have no idea, but I am glad he stops me piling in.

"Spinach," he announces as the serving lady arrives with something green on a plate.

Suddenly the music stops. Olympia and her dancers return to the table. It's someone's birthday so we all have to sing happy birthday to him. At last a tune I know. After the song the birthday boy goes on to the stage. I say boy; he is clearly about ninety. He takes the mike and sings a moody, evocative love song. His voice echoes around the cellar, but his eyes are fixed firmly on the floor as he sings the ballad. Everyone else is silent; they even stop eating. It is a touching scene.

Opposite me Romantic Raphael is drawing on the tablecloth. He uses a thick pencil to create the figure of Christ on the Cross. The princess looks on in admiration as he dips his forefinger in the red wine to add shadows and colour to his creation. I suppose it is as good a use as any for the wine. He expertly flicks his pencil and smudges wine, looking like a true professional. He is totally absorbed in his creation, but at the same time aware of the women around him. I am reminded of Sergeant Troy in *Far from the Madding Crowd*, who seduces Bathsheba by showing off his sword-skills. I wonder whether he is trying to seduce me or the princess, or maybe both of us.

After twenty minutes the masterpiece is finished. Everyone is impressed. Romantic Raphael dedicates it to Santino.

"Pudding," says Pippo as a plate of cakes arrives.

I say goodnight and make my way up through the icy corridors to my bedroom. I try to work out how to get undressed, take my contact lenses out and take off my make-up without freezing to death. In record time I am under the fur blanket. I wonder briefly if Raphael is still holding court with his painting skills. Then I remember something my father told me about the original artist Raphael when we were wandering around the Vatican looking at his paintings. "He is papist and conformist. Not terribly interesting." Romantic Raphael immediately loses some of his appeal. I look up at the fresco painted for Pope Clement VII. The colours are bright and clear, the theme simple and easy to understand. And there's not a trace of cheap red wine anywhere.

I think about the princess. I suppose if I had been brought up in Italy I would probably have had a similar education to her. Maybe not the same—my family are not royalty—but I would certainly have been spoiled and rich. Of course I have sometimes wondered if spoiled and rich wouldn't have been a less miserable way to go through childhood. But I'm not sure it would have made me happy.

As a young girl, when things were really bad, I would console myself by thinking that I was getting all my suffering over with now. I imagined that life as an adult would be pain free. It isn't, of course, but I wouldn't swap my life now with the princess's for all the castles in Italy. She is lovely, but there is an underlying sadness to her. One of the reasons for this is that her only baby has thick stone walls and damp problems. If the castle once protected her, it is now she that mothers it and keeps it from crumbling. To inherit a large building is both a blessing and a curse. You are tied to it. You could sell it and live in splendid isolation in an apartment in Rome, but then you would feel you had let down all your ancestors who struggled to keep the place going.

My early learning.

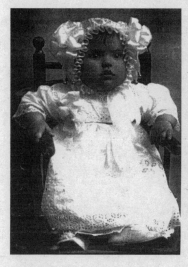

My father as a baby—not a great look.

Piera as a young girl.

Of course there is no telling how my life might have turned out had my parents stayed together. But I am glad I didn't grow up in the same mould as my aunt and father. And also relieved I will never have to live in a place that is as cold as this castle. I huddle under the fur blanket and fall asleep to the distant sounds of the party thudding away in the cellar.

8

An Erotic Tour
of Venice

I am at the home of the most famous man in Venice, surrounded by naked women. "I don't like Matisse, because Picasso didn't like him," he tells me. "But then I don't like Picasso either. Anyway, I don't much like to talk about art. I don't go in for all that intellectual bullshit; I just want to get the right shade of sunlight on a buttock." Geoffrey Humphries is a painter. His paintings of women smiling, sitting, posing, undressing and bathing in various states of undress gaze at me from the walls of his studio on the Giudecca.

Geoffrey's studio is a large room with four French windows looking out across the canal towards Venice. It has a stone floor and high ceilings; it is large, probably about sixty square metres. Inside there are Art Deco lamps, drapes, mounted elephant tusks, candelabras, a piano, a guitar and a skeleton wearing ostrich feather boas in various colours.

Furniture and things are crammed into the room, making it look a bit like an Aladdin's cave or even a junk shop. There is a double bed against one of the walls. It is draped with different bright-coloured cloths: red and gold, yellow and blue; over-sized cushions are thrown on top of it. Some of them have fallen off and lie on the floor beside it. Above the bed hangs a large drape made from red and gold velvet. A round old-fashioned wooden clock that ticks loudly is just to the right of it.

There are several chairs in the studio, most rickety and unre-markable but one upholstered in red velvet. There are lots of mirrors. Some are elaborate with gold frames, others simpler. There is one large free-standing one and the wall opposite the French windows is entirely mirrored. The rest are hanging on the walls. Geoffrey's studio is not a good place to have a bad hair day. There is an antique gramophone with a big brass horn sitting on a round table that looks like it used to be one of those old-fashioned sewing machine tables. Next to the gramophone, a game of patience is laid out. I see from the canvas on the easel that Geoffrey is working on a painting of a woman playing patience dressed in a short pink diaphanous dressing gown.

All around the studio there are paintings in various states of completion, mainly of semi-naked women. "I can never finish a painting," Geoffrey tells me. My favourite is of a girl sitting on one of the chairs dressed only in black stockings. She is demure, despite her rather minimal outfit. She has a full mouth and swept-back brown hair. Her breasts are rounded and not too big. There is a saying that if you're being erotic you use just the feather, if you're being perverted, you use the whole chicken. This is a feather-like painting.

But there is an air of debauchery mixed with art in the room, a carnival atmosphere. It is a room for partying, creating, seducing and drinking. The colours are vibrant and the setting is a mixture of the bohemian and the luxurious. The Marquis de Sade said of Venice: "Here the air we breathe is soft, effeminate, it is an invitation to pleasure." There is something of that in Geoffrey's studio. It has a seductive feel to it; I start to imagine Bacchanalian orgies, which is unusual for me. I wonder if it's all the naked bodies around, or maybe the smell of oil paint has got to me. There is oil paint everywhere: tubes of it lie opened on tables, splashes of it cover an easel and screwed up bits of paper that Geoffrey has used to clean his brushes lie on the floor.

As soon as I walk into Geoffrey's home I notice the smell of oil. It is a smell I recognise from my childhood. My stepfather painted with oils and the house always smelled of it. It seems fitting that I should be reminded of him as I walk into Geoffrey's: this is a house he also stayed in, just before he met my mother.

But as I am no longer in touch with my stepfather, my re-introduction to Geoffrey has come through mutual friends. I am curious to see this man who was a legendary figure to me throughout my childhood. If he ever visited us, everyone had to drop everything; it was like having the king to stay.

My stepfather would spend hours telling me about Geoffrey's womanising, drinking and parties with a sense of awe. I remember him as a figure with black curly hair, black hat and a cape, almost Byronic in style. I have one very clear memory of walking down Old Church Street in Chelsea with my stepfather and Geoffrey. We were on our way to the Chelsea Arts Club where he was staying. I must have been about thirteen at the time. A woman pulled up in an open-top car to talk to us. She was older than both Geoffrey and my stepfather, colourfully dressed and wearing a lot of make-up. They all chatted for a bit and then she drove off.

"Dreadful creature," said Geoffrey.

"But I thought you two had a thing together?" said my stepfather.

Geoffrey stopped walking and put his hand on my stepfather's shoulder. "You have to remember, dear friend, what one will do in Venice on three litres of wine is very different to what one will do in London on four pints of bitter."

He has changed. For a start he is now shorter than me, or maybe I am taller than him. His hair is now greying and he has grown widthways. But he is still immensely charming and retains his legend-like status. It seems I am not alone in adoring Geoffrey. In fact most of Venice seems to adore him. "Ah, our dear Geoffrey," a restaurateur says when I mention I am staying there. "I have known him since he was a boy. He is the most wonderful artist."

Holly, his American wife, tells me Geoffrey was the first person she heard about when she arrived in Venice.

"He is without doubt the most famous man in the city," she says. "The first thing I was told was to get myself invited to one of his parties. Which I did. I wasn't interested in him though, his reputation was too terrible."

Seventeen years later on they are married and have a daughter called Lucy. They also have a lot of wine. It comes in plastic bottles and gets drunk at an alarming rate.

The first night I arrive at their home, they have some guests coming for dinner. I get there at six o'clock.

"Oh my God, you're so early," says Holly, opening the door via a pulley-system and encouraging me to walk up the stairs. "There's no one here." She shows me to my room, which has a lovely view onto the Giudecca Canal and to Venice on the other side. "See you in a bit," she says and shuts the door. The house is eerily silent.

Venice in the fifteenth century had its own calendar. The New Year began in March and the day started in the evening. At Geoffrey's house, it still does. Come seven o'clock, the house is full of people drinking, chatting and laughing. I have no idea where they all came from, but they include a German lady who is married to a German film star, a Greek aristocrat and her daughter and a couple from New York. She reminds me of Diane Keaton: waspish and elegant. She tells me she used to live in Buffalo but that she left.

"To be the best dressed woman in Buffalo, all you had to do was put on a pair of high heels," she says. Conveniently her husband, the only other man at the party, is also called Geoffrey. He's also a painter, so I won't get confused.

I am placed next to Geoffrey the host for dinner. My husband always says that he is amazed by artists who paint anything other than naked women. If you can paint, what's the point in painting anything else, is his theory. It's not like you get up on a Monday morning and think "Oh bugger I've got some gorgeous bird showing up in half an hour and taking all her kit off, what a drag." You must greet every day with total enthusiasm. I ask Geoffrey if this is the case with him, as he paints predominantly naked women. And nice-looking ones too.

"Yes," he smiles. Geoffrey is a man of few words.

"Which artists have inspired you?"

"Degas, Whistler, John Singer Sargent," he says, serving me some Spaghetti Vongole. It has clams in it, which I have never eaten. But by now I have drunk around a litre of wine so forget that I don't like seafood and start extricating them from their shells. My aunt would be astounded.

"And do you have a technique that differs from other artists?"

"Not really. If it moves, I move with it."

I ask Geoffrey why he settled in Venice almost forty years ago.

"I have always wanted to live in the nineteenth century," he says. "And I had to leave England: I couldn't walk down the street without getting into a fight. So I came here to escape."

"But how come you stayed?"

"One morning I was lying in the studio. Your stepfather was here, sleeping in what is now Lucy's room. I hadn't sold any paintings and I was thinking about getting out, maybe moving on to America. It was dark in the studio and I thought 'Typical, a bloody grey day.' Then I realised it was actually a boat on the canal that was blocking out the sun. I could see the four letters of its name through each of the four French windows: H O P E. I took that as a sign and settled here."

After the pasta I turn to talk to my German neighbour a little. She is a strikingly attractive woman with a sharp black bob haircut and bright red lips. She reminds me of a character from the film *Cabaret*. In fact the whole evening reminds me a little of *Cabaret*. It is a long time since I was in such a bohemian environment. Probably the last time was when I was around six. My mother and stepfather had some friends round for dinner and they all smoked some pot. At one stage they stood up in a circle and passed me from person to person. I was very happy and kept telling everyone I could fly. I have a similar sensation this evening, though in reality I doubt I can walk, let alone fly.

"Who is looking after your children?" asks the American

lady who is sitting across the table from me.

I tell her my husband is, but that we also have a childminder.

"Is it easy to get help over there? Here we're so lucky, we have lots of Sri Lankans and Romanians," says Holly. "Tomorrow the house will be a disaster, but we always go to Harry's Bar for lunch on a Sunday and when we get back at six, the Sri Lankans have dealt with it all."

I turn back to Geoffrey to get away from the German woman's smoke (that's the problem with these bohemians, they chain-smoke). Amazingly he's fallen asleep. His arms are folded across his chest and his head is tilted downwards. But he's still wearing his hat. Now I'm no longer in *Cabaret* but in *Alice in Wonderland*. I need to move on before someone tries to stuff him into a teapot. I go and sit down next to Holly. I liked her before I even met her. She has read all my books and loves them. So naturally we have a lot in common.

"Geoffrey never gets a hangover," she tells me, pouring us both a glass of wine.

"I'm not surprised if he falls asleep half-way through dinner."

"Oh that," she laughs. "We've been to so many doctors about it. The thing about Geoffrey is that he works all day long, he's in his studio from nine having taken Lucy to school and then he's there until seven or eight. I've never met a painter who works so hard. Then of course he drinks fast and then, well, he used to seduce women, now he falls asleep. I suppose it's better this way. Anyway, the doctors say there's nothing we can do, he's just tired."

Holly, or "the woman who tamed Geoffrey" as she is also known, probably says more in ten minutes than Geoffrey says in a day. She is vivacious and intelligent (some posh US college, then Oxford to do a PhD: we're talking really brainy). She is short, petite, with greeny-brown eyes and blonde hair. Her lips are also, *Cabaret*-style, bright red.

"But don't you worry about all those gorgeous models undressing in front of him every day? I mean a man with his reputation and all."

Holly nods and fills up our glasses again.

"I'm always extremely nice to them," she says. "While keeping them at a distance. And at the same time dropping hints to Geoffrey that they may have some incurable venereal disease. I find that normally works."

"How did you manage to convince him to get married?" I ask. My stepfather always told me Geoffrey would never wed. It simply wasn't in his nature.

"It took me twelve years," she tells me. "Geoffrey never wanted to get married or have children. He really didn't want any responsibility. Now here he is with four goldfish, three galleries, two dogs, a wife and a daughter."

"Is he happy?" I ask.

Holly looks at the sleeping figure at the other end of the table. "I'd say he's pretty content. Geoffrey can get very depressed, especially about money. It's tough you know, we have all the galleries now and all this responsibility and payments to meet and he gets really wired about it. But I tell him lots of people we know fight because they don't like having sex together, or they hate each other or they disagree on just about everything. We only ever fight about money and that can be easily fixed, I just need to sell a painting or two. In fact tomorrow his agent is coming, she normally buys about five or six; he sells them to her far too cheaply but I suppose she buys in bulk. It's strange that he sells them so cheaply, he's notoriously tight you know. When we were dating, he used to ask me for dinner and say "I'll pay" and I was like, "Yeah, and your point is?" but then people started saying to me "Geoffrey took you out to dinner and PAID? He must be serious." Well, I didn't believe it for a long time. I just didn't trust him. Nor did my parents. They offered me a huge bribe to stay away. Then he took me on a tour of the Veneto. Everywhere we went, he was greeted like a hero. I started to realise there was something special about this man. Of course I was already in love with his painting, I mean, who wouldn't be? Then one day the prosecco flowed, a little too much, and well, one thing led to another and we didn't make it home for three days. That was it, and here we are. Cheers."

We raise our glasses to Geoffrey, who is still sleeping peacefully despite efforts from the other Geoffrey to wake him up by tickling him. I realise I would like to be asleep too. Katarina, the German chain-smoker, gets up to leave. This could be my chance. I start to say goodnight to Holly.

"You can't go now," she says. "Katarina has just gone to get Toto."

"Is that her film star husband?" Things are looking up. Maybe I'll stay on after all.

"No, it's her dog. He gets on terribly well with Perdita and Milo." Perdita and Milo are Holly and Geoffrey's dogs. They are lovely-looking, with wispy white fur and delicate features. They are called barge dogs or cane da burcio in Venetian dialect. They spend most of the evening on various guests' knees being petted and fed.

Katarina marches back in, cigarette in one hand, beast in the other. This is not a dog you would want on your lap. It is the size of a polar bear.

"What is it?" I ask, cowering behind my wine glass.

"He's a new breed called a Eurasian," says Katarina, nuzzling him affectionately. "Part Alsatian, part Chow and part Husky."

He's a nice-looking dog once you get over the fact that he could probably eat you for breakfast; very furry and with incredible dark eyes.

"He's very friendly," says Katarina, encouraging me to stroke him. They all say that, but I feel it would be rude not to trust her. I gingerly pat Toto's head. My hand almost vanishes in his thick soft fur. Toto doesn't think much of me and wanders off to smell Geoffrey, who is still sleeping. I feel a bit left out without a dog and wonder briefly how easy it would be to get our dog Wolfie FedExed over, but thankfully am still sober enough to realise that would be mad. He hates dinner parties.

I get up from the table and say goodnight to everyone. They all look amazed, as if to say "If you're tired, just have a kip here, now all the dogs are here the party's just beginning."

I make my way to bed and wonder briefly if I am still on the canal. There is something disconcerting about being close to water. For ages after you get off a boat, you find yourself swaying. It seems to me the inhabitants of the Giudecca spend most of their time swaying either from the water or from the alcohol.

I wake up at seven thirty and decide the only thing to do is go back to sleep. At ten I wake up again feeling slightly better. I am still swaying but as I'm about to get on a vaporetto to explore Venice I figure I'll just go with it. Venice is the final leg of my Grand Tour; I can't wait to see the city again. The vaporetto stop is just outside the house and I have been told the boats go every ten minutes. Of course I don't believe that anything could possibly run so smoothly in Italy and am feeling smugly English as I stand at the vaporetto stop and my clock hits half past ten. Then suddenly, out of nowhere, rather like Jaws, a vaporetto appears.

Truman Capote said that "Venice is like eating an entire box of chocolate liqueurs in one go". This morning I feel like I've eaten two boxes but I see what he means. As my eyes begin to focus in the bright sunlight and the city gets closer, I am astounded at how pretty it is. If I were American, I would call it awesome. Luckily I'm not. But the view of Venice from the Giudecca Canal has to be one of the most beautiful sights in the world. Paris from the Eiffel Tower seems sprawling in comparison; London from the London Eye has too many eyesores. This is as perfect a city as you can imagine. Even some of those Renaissance paintings purporting to be the perfect city don't come close. It is maybe because of the water that it seems so magical. The stylish buildings that line the canal are framed by the water and the blue sky. Their colours are muted. To the right I can see the top of the Campanile in Saint Mark's Square and the Doge's Palace, one of the only Gothic buildings I have ever seen that I really like.

I get off at Zattere, the first stop we come to, and wander down a small street. I have no idea where I'm heading to but Venice is famous for being a good place to walk in so I'm not worried. I suppose it's either that or swim. The streets are not busy, although I am surprised by how many tourists there are, even at this time of year. One thing that strikes me almost immediately is the lack of traffic. The absence of anything motorised, bar the elegant wooden water taxis or barges carrying goods, means the streets are totally peaceful. Another difference from other cities is that there are no ugly buildings. But the most memorable thing about Venice is the sound of the water. It is uncanny walking on a street and hearing water lapping as if you are on a boat. Maybe it's partly the water that makes Venice such a sexy place. It gives the air the humidity and sweetness Sade mentions.

I arrive in a square with a white-washed church in it as the bell strikes eleven. A charming-looking older man offers me a ride in his gondola. I ask him how much it will cost.

"It's □60 for the short tour of the small canals, □80 for the small canals and the Grand Canal and 100 for an hour incorporating more small canals, the grand Canal and a view of the Lido."

I tell him I'll go for the 60 one. He nods, springs up from his chair which he puts in the gondola. Then he helps me in and tells me to sit down on the opposite side of the boat to him. Just before he goes to take his position at the back of the boat, he asks if I wouldn't prefer the 80 tour. "It's much, much more beautiful," he smiles. Of course I agree.

As we glide off into the Grand Canal, I feel myself swaying again. Now I'm at home. I once read somewhere that sitting in a gondola is the closest thing there is to being in a coffin. Mine is an elaborate coffin. The black leather cushions are lined with fur; intricate carvings decorate the bow, a small Venetian flag sits in a brass holder in the middle of the bow. Either side of me small brass statues act as a support for a string of black pom-poms that I suppose are designed to stop me falling out of my coffin.

My guide tells me there are a total of 425 gondolas in Venice. There are only three men capable of making them and they run three separate workshops. Each gondola is handmade, eleven metres long and asymmetrical. They cost around ☐ 55,000 to buy and last on average fifteen years.

"They're a bit like a car," says my guide. "It depends who's driving."

He tells me the gondola was born in Venice to transport the nobles around. Each palazzo would have its front door on the water and the nobles' gondoliers would transport them to and from their homes.

"Oi," he shouts suddenly. I jump and look around. Am I touching something I shouldn't?

We go through a bridge and he shouts again. I realise it's a warning to whoever might be the other side of the bridge.

"Before they had motorised ambulance boats," he tells me, "the gondolas were the ambulances. You would have four gondoliers, two at the front and two at the back."

I wonder if becoming a gondolier is a little like becoming a black cab driver. Do you need to do the knowledge?

"Nowadays you have to pass exams and things, before it was always passed down from father to son. I started learning from my father when I was ten, just as he had done from his grandfather. I taught my son the trade too. He is thirty-six though, so he was obliged to take the exams."

Is there much of a future in gondolas I wonder? I mean, they do say Venice is sinking. Could be tough unless they develop a special submarine gondola; maybe James Bond's friend M could get onto it?

My gondolier nods. "It's sinking by ten centimetres every one hundred years," he tells me solemnly. So his family should be fine for another few generations.

We pass many other gondolas, mainly full of Japanese tourists, waving madly. I've never understood the compulsion people have to wave as soon as they see someone else on a boat. If you tried it on the vaporetto, you'd fall in.

"Are there any female gondoliers?" I ask. I wonder if they wear the same uniform of blue trousers and stripy jumpers. Maybe they have a sexy little skirt with a slit in it designed by Armani?

"No. One woman has tried the exam four times and failed. I don't think they have the strength. It's calm today, but sometimes the water is rough."

My gondolier lets me off close to Saint Mark's Square. I walk over a small bridge. A porter with a luggage trolley overtakes me. The sound of the luggage-filled trolley hitting the steps transports me back to my first visit to the city with my father when I was fourteen.

Back then I was not staying in a bohemian setting.

"I am taking you to your first luxury hotel," my father announced as we stepped up from a water taxi in front of the Danieli Hotel. "Try to look nonchalant. These people respect no one who is in awe of their establishments. You must act as if you live like this all the time. They don't know you have a shitting life and probably less money than they do. Let's go."

A porter followed us with our luggage as we walked into the entrance hall. It was as grand a place as I had ever been in. On my right was a polished wooden desk behind which various uniformed staff ran around. They seemed to speak every language known to man. My father dealt with the check-in and I walked up the entrance hall towards a stone red-carpeted staircase. It reminded me of the set of a production of *Romeo and Juliet* we'd seen with my school in England. The staircase was steep and tall, reaching in a zigzag pattern all the way to the ceiling. On the higher floors there were balconies and stone arches.

The entrance hall led off to a large room filled with tables and chairs. The floor was marble, as were the grand columns that lined the space. Great brightly coloured glass chandeliers hung from the ceiling. The chairs were plush and upholstered in green and gold. People sat around drinking tea; they were mainly Americans as far as I could tell. The sun outside shone through the stained-glass windows, creating patterns and colours. The sounds seemed louder than in a normal room, amplified, maybe because of all the glass and marble. A cup hitting a saucer sounded like a glass falling on a floor.

"Come along, we're going on an erotic tour of Venice," my father bellowed at me. His deep loud voice was of course amplified around the tea-room of the Danieli. Rarely had I been so embarrassed by him. A few tight-lipped tea-drinkers looked up in disgust.

"What's a neurotic tour?" I heard one woman ask her husband.

I followed my father outside into the sunshine. He was wearing a cream linen suit and Panama hat. I was wearing an olive green skirt and jacket my aunt gave me with a white T-shirt. We walked along the waterfront promenade outside the hotel towards Saint Mark's Square. I had never walked anywhere that was so busy. There were bodies everywhere. You literally had to push your way over the bridges.

Once we were in Saint Mark's, the crowd dispersed a little, but we had the pigeons to deal with. They were everywhere, like unguided missiles flying towards us. I was convinced one was going to crash into my head. Amazingly there were people feeding them.

"Bella, these sorts of people feeding the shitting pigeons," said my father taking my arm, "are the worst kinds of peasants. Because they can hardly afford to feed themselves, throwing food around makes them feel superior. Now, we must ignore them and the pigeons, who are the most stupid of God's creatures followed closely by sheeps, your mother, your aunt and you, and we must focus on the reason for our visit. Erotic Venice."

We walked to the Campanile and stood looking up at it.

"The largest penis in Christendom," announced my father, pointing towards the top of the building. "And a very royalist penis. It collapsed once on Bastille day, July 14th 1902. It was rebuilt brick by brick."

"Was anyone killed?" I asked taking a step away from the building and almost tripping over a pigeon.

"Just the Campanile cat," said my father. "It was a shame they rebuilt the tower, the square would be nicer without it. Now, onwards."

We walked to a large building on our left, which seemed to go on around the whole of the square.

"This building that lines the square is called the Procuratie. On this side is the Old Procuratie and on the other side is the new," said my father. "The interesting thing here for our erotic tour are the friezes carved underneath and around the arches. No one ever notices them, but they're magnificent. First we must find Cleopatra."

We walked along the vaulted walkway all the while looking up for Cleopatra. As we searched, my father pointed out one frieze of a man who looked like he was holding a large erection.

"Scholars deny it is his penis," he said, "but there can be no doubt. And a fine specimen it is too. Far superior to David's, don't you think?"

I wasn't amused by this erotic tour. In fact it was making me neurotic. I had never discussed penises with anyone; why would I want to start discussing them with my father?

"Really bella, you have to relax," said my father. "Fourteen and frigid is no way to go through life. Unless you want to be a nun of course. I'm sure your grandmother can introduce you to some nice sisters who will take you in."

"My sex life is none of your business," I replied.

"What sex life?" said my father laughing and grabbing my cheek. "When you have something wonderful to hide, then I'll be happy."

The whole idea of sex was quite scary. And the fact that he was so casual about it all made it even worse. I wondered briefly whether a life with nuns might be an easier option.

In fact my grandmother had already had a serious discussion with me along these lines. "There are two options open to a young girl in terms of career," she told me one day in Rimini sitting at her dining room table. "To be a nun or to be a teacher. I don't mind which one you choose, I'm sure you'll be very good at either."

"I was thinking more along the lines of model, film star or even pop star," I wanted to reply, but something in her eyes stopped me.

"Ah, here is Leda, with her swan, which she is using to amuse herself with. I once knew a Leda and was happy to be her swan," my father laughed, and we continued our search for Cleopatra. It was good to be out of the sun, underneath the arches of the building. At one point my father stopped and pointed towards the Saint Mark's Basilica.

"This is as close as you want to get to the ugliest basilica in the world," he said. "But the interesting thing for us is that she is made up almost entirely of breasts."

"They're not breasts, they're domes," I said.

"Really bella, you have no imagination," said my father and dragged me onwards. Eventually we found Cleopatra. She was lying down in a very sexy pose: a serpent lay across her body and nuzzled her nipple.

"Now we are going to continue our tour in a gondola, the preferred method of transport in Venice," said my father. "Say goodbye to Cleopatra. And try to have her a little more in mind as your role model instead of Mother Teresa."

We walked back towards the Danieli Hotel along the Riva degli Schiavoni, where there were gondolas tied up and waiting for passengers. I had seen gondolas and gondoliers on television but was surprised at how long the boat was. We stepped in and sat down on the cushion-covered seats. It seemed an immensely luxurious way to travel. It was very smooth and I couldn't understand how the gondolier managed to move us along with just the one oar. I had been on punts in Oxford, but this was totally different. The gondolier seemed to have an incredible ability to move the long boat and get it around even the tightest corners. I loved the delicate sound of the oar slicing into the water.

We floated up the small canals looking at the buildings and small bridges. I was intrigued by the steps of the buildings that were underwater.

"Venice is sinking," my father explained. "But not before the end of our visit." He instructed the gondolier to stop for a moment.

"We will start with the birthplace of what is possibly the greatest libertine known to man. Casanova. He was born in this house," said my father pointing to a building on our right. "Do you know who he is?"

The name meant something to me, but I decided not to bluff it. And actually I wanted to know. I shook my head.

"He was born Giacomo Girolamo Casanova on April 2nd 1725. He was a scholar, a writer and a rogue. He was most famous for having sex and also writing a huge memoir in French called *L'Histoire de ma vie*. The most astounding thing about him is how he found time to write so much as well as seducing most of Europe."

"Why did he spend so much time seducing people?" I asked.

"What an Anglo-Saxon question! Seduction needs no explanation. It is the most normal of pastimes. You see bella, you have much to learn about the Italian character."

We carried on along the myriad of small canals. Now and again another gondola would come towards us and I would be sure we were going to crash. It never happened. I loved the sound of the water lapping against the wood of the boat and the stone of the buildings. There was something intensely mysterious about the small canals; it felt like a surprise was around every corner. My father pointed out a white bas-relief of a woman on a wall. It seemed an odd place to put a mask; I wondered if it was some remnant from the carnival or something.

"This is the so-called honest woman," he told me. "There are three theories as to why she is called this and why the bridge here is called the Bridge of the Honest Woman. One is that she was the wife of a cutler who was dishonoured by a noble client of her husband's and killed herself with the knife this client had ordered. Two, a couple of friends were walking over the bridge

My mother in the mid-sixties—happy times.

discussing the virtue of women and one told the other that this was the only honest woman they would ever meet. Three, my personal favourite, it was the home of a beautiful and young prostitute who gave her clients discounted rates. So she became known as the honest woman."

My father was clearly enjoying the tour. I had begun to

understand that there was nothing my Italian family enjoyed quite as much as showing off their knowledge. "This is the Ponte delle Tette, or the Bridge of the Tits," my father said, pointing to a small bridge above us. "The authorities allowed whores to stand on the balconies above and show their tits and legs to potential clients in an effort to discourage homosexuality. Of course that would never happen in England, where all the men are gay," he added, grabbing hold of my cheek in his infuriating fashion.

We sailed on out onto the Grand Canal. After the little canals it seemed magnificent. It was heaving with gondolas, as if there were a regatta. Tourists stood along the side and on the bridges, admiring the view. We glided past palazzos painted different colours, some ochre, some red, others cream with bright green shutters. Some had been badly faded by the sun; others looked like they were still occupied by Venetian noblemen.

"Your Byron lived here," said my father pointing to a palazzo on our left. "He boasted that when he came to Venice he slept with two hundred different women on two hundred consecutive nights. Then of course he met the love of his life, the Countess Teresa Guiccioli, his last great love. She was only nineteen and married to an old goat at least forty years older than her. She was blonde and very pretty. From the minute he met her until his death, Byron didn't care for another woman."

"Have you ever felt like that?" I asked.

"Your mother was a great love for me, I was crazy about her. When I first saw her, I couldn't believe it. I had never seen anything so beautiful in my life. She was like a perfect creature, delicate and with the most incredible eyes I have ever seen. And she had had all her luggage stolen in Paris so showed up practically naked; intoxicating. After a few months of my trying to seduce her, she went back home. I was destroyed; partly of course because I was used to getting what I wanted. Eventually my sister went and got her. When she came back, we were both very happy."

"So why did it all go wrong?"

"After a few years we stopped getting on so well. She was much younger than me, rather like Byron's last mistress. She wanted to go out and meet people, I just wanted to study and not waste time. Then of course she met a stronzo on a train."

The gondola took us back to the Riva degli Schiavoni and the Danieli Hotel. My father took a wodge of cash out of his sock to pay for it. I had never seen him with a wallet.

"Why do you carry money in your socks?" I asked.

"It's very practical. People are unlikely to steal money from there without you being able to kick them." He lifted up his trousers to reveal two bulges, one on the inside of each calf.

"I have lire on the right and Swiss francs on the left," he told me.

"Why Swiss francs?"

"In case of an emergency." He took my hand and we walked into the lobby. The staff greeted him by name and nodded at me. We walked into a room just off the main reception area where there were people sitting about reading in large leather armchairs. My father walked up to a book case and started browsing.

"Ah, this will do," he said, beckoning me to join him. "This is a small book, so you'll be able to get through it. And the boy in it is the same age as you. It is very important always when travelling to read something set in the place you are visiting."

He handed me a copy of *Death in Venice* by Thomas Mann.

"It is more or less the story of an unfulfilled gay, but it has an important quote to learn when you're in Venice." He cleared his throat. By now the rest of the room was listening. This often happened with my father, I suppose it was a combination of his loud voice and the fact that he was usually talking about something relatively unusual.

"'This was Venice,'" he began, quoting from the book. "'The flattering and suspect beauty—this city, half fairy-tale and half tourist-trap, in whose insalubrious air the arts once rankly and voluptuously blossomed, where composers have been inspired to lulling tones of somniferous eroticism.' There, did you understand anything at all?"

"Yes, a bit, I'll read it," I said, willing him to get out of the room so all these people would stop staring at us.

"And you see it is not just me who sees the erotic in Venice, artists always have," he said as we walked up the stairs towards our rooms. "Now go and read the book or do whatever it is you do when alone. This evening we go to Saint Mark's for drinks."

9

A Figure in Black and Blue

The Rialto Bridge, like the Ponte Vecchio in Florence, is one of those things best viewed from a distance. Sadly I have not taken my own advice and am on top of it, looking out over the Grand Canal with around one hundred and fifty other tourists, all fighting for the best view. I can't go to Venice and not stand on the Rialto Bridge, was my reasoning. Big mistake. If anything ruins the romance of a visit to Venice it is the Rialto Bridge. Behind me vendors shout as they try to sell their goods, none of which is remotely useful or interesting. There is graffiti on the bridge itself, some in paint, some actually carved into the marble, mainly names and vows of everlasting love. Down below, the gondolas glide effortlessly through the water. The palazzos that line the canal are elegant and aloof, in stark contrast to the mess on the bridge. Their colours are muted reds, yellows and browns that look like they've been bleached by the sun and the water over the years.

Liz, the American friend of Holly and Geoffrey's I met at dinner who reminds me of Diane Keaton, suggested I visit the fish market, which is close to the Rialto. I don't like fish, but apparently the Venice fish market is a must-see and anything is better than the Rialto Bridge.

There has been a fish market on the same spot in Venice for more than six hundred years, but this particular one was built in 1917. It is housed in several grey stone buildings with green and red plastic drapes to keep out the sun or the rain, depending on the season. Actually the buildings look much older than they are. Maybe because you expect them to be as you're in Venice, but also partly, I think, because of the fish-like gargoyles at the top of the columns. They lend them an almost medieval feel.

There are around twenty-five stalls in total, each offering more fish and seafood than I have ever seen in one place before. The stall holders wear thick jumpers, white hats and white aprons. There is salmon, tuna, scampi, crabs, sole, sea bream and sea bass. The only one I am tempted by is the sole which is slippery, small and silvery. The swordfish are the most impressive. There is one cut in two; its bottom half has obviously already been sold, its sword points out towards the crowds, perhaps as a warning to those about to ask for credit. Its mouth is wide open and its eyes glazed. It looks as if it had a painful death.

The less dramatic and smaller fish are laid out in a fan on shards of ice. There is nothing random about the way the fish is displayed; it is done with a stylish Italian touch. There are also fillets on sale but they're not as much fun to stare at. The best things are the weird creatures from the deep. There are piles of cuttlefish, all squidgy and covered in ink, crabs looking most unappetising with their legs in the air, strange-looking see-through shrimp-like things and mad crustaceans that look impenetrable as well as faintly disgusting. There are also some lobsters, still living, vainly scratching at the ice trying to get away. There's no escape, I want to tell them. You'll leave here destined for a pot of boiling water. You may as well relax and listen to the bloke playing the accordion; this is as good as it gets.

One thing that strikes me as unusual for an Italian market is that rather than being filled with little old ladies dressed in black clutching their shopping baskets and Hail Mary chains, this market is full of tourists taking photographs. They outnumber the real punters by at least three to one. The stall holders must get so fed up with them. I mean when did you ever hear a tourist say: "Gee, that looks like a nice bit of swordfish, I must take that back with me on my twelve-hour transatlantic flight." I start to feel guilty snooping around with my notebook. Is there anything I could buy? Maybe Holly would like an octopus? No, you can't drink octopus. And as presents go, it's not really up there with champagne or flowers. I am almost tempted to buy one though just to keep as a weird-looking thing. I have never seen one close up, at least not in its entirety. I can't imagine how on earth you would start to cook it. I wonder who first came up with the idea of eating this beast? There is something sinister about dead fish. They just look so, well, dead. I think I have worried about them ever since I saw *The Godfather* and heard the phrase "he swims with the fishes".

I take one last look at the doomed lobsters and walk towards the canal. This is where the fish market suddenly gets sexy. There is a small corner stall here selling Italian cheese. There is parmesan, buffalo-milk mozzarella, pecorino, ricotta and gorgonzola. I spend a happy half hour tasting varieties of pecorino and discussing which parmesan to take home with me with the man behind the counter. The stall is curious: it is made of glass and tiny. There is a small opening at the front, either side of which are tall glass shelves stacked with cheese. In the summer it must get very hot and smelly. Around one side is a large closed counter with more cheeses on display. This is where the parmesan is. It is crumbly and creamy-looking; all of it looks better than any parmesan you get back in England, but which to go for? It has to be Parmigiano-Reggiano, parmesan from the region of northern Italy; they have been making it since the thirteenth century. But there are three varieties: new, old and extra-old.

"For Italians parmesan is a symbol of culture and civilisation," the cheese seller tells me. "And the stravecchio, extra old parmesan, is the apex of civilisation. You use it for very special occasions, like seducing someone."

The extra old parmesan is aged for between thirty-four and thirty-six months, as opposed to eighteen to twenty-four months for the old and just twelve months for the new. I taste all three. They get more peppery and tastier as they get older; the extra old one is almost too salty and strong. I buy a large chunk of the middle one. I wish I could take the whole round home with me but it weighs thirty-five kilos, more than my luggage allowance. I love Italian cheese. This could possibly be the most Italian thing about me. I must be the only person who, having lived in France, still prefers Italian cheese. I can't imagine life without parmesan.

Opposite the cheese man there is a fruit and vegetable stall that looks like a still life painting. The goods are beautifully polished and laid out. In the front row there are cherry tomatoes, artichokes, large, crisp pale-green fennel bulbs, deep purple aubergines and radicchio that look like elaborate flowers, sprouting out in all directions, red and white. The names of the vegetables and their prices are written in black ink marker pen. Behind the aubergines are more tomatoes, some plum-shaped, some round, some shaped like a Terry's chocolate orange, wedges making up the whole. The wedges are green in the middle. Next to the Terry's tomatoes are red and green peppers and delicate courgettes with yellow flowers. All the colours are startling, almost as if someone had come along with a paint brush and touched them all up. Perhaps Geoffrey was here earlier. On the third row there are salads, some whole, some leaves, as well as cabbages and cauliflowers. Beside the vegetables is the fruit. Again this is laid out with military precision: apples in front, then oranges, lemons and clementines, then kiwis, bananas and pears.

I buy an apple and carry on walking. There are signs for Saint Mark's, so I follow them. I wonder how many millions of other tourists walk the same way every year. It's no wonder the city is sinking. After a ten-minute walk I find myself outside the Museum of Erotic Art. This certainly wasn't here when I was last here with my father. It would certainly have been on our erotic tour if it had been. It seems rude not to go in, if only to discover exactly what erotic art is. I mean, how much of it is art and how much is erotic? I walk into a pristine reception area where a young girl sits selling tickets. She is obviously a student doing some work at the museum in her spare time, her notes and books are on the desk in front of her. She is slim, pretty and very smiley. In front of her are two TV screens, one a CCTV screen showing various rooms in the museum and another with a film about erotic art. I wonder if she ever gets confused between the two.

I pay 10 euros to get in (erotic art is not cheap) and am shown how to put my ticket under a laser that will let me in. The stairs in front of me are steep and painted with bright red lacquer. The name of the museum is written on each step in bold black letters. Maybe in case some easily shocked American tries to sue, rather like McDonald's now has to have the word HOT printed on all its cups after someone burnt their mouth on their coffee and made off with a fortune.

I walk up to the first floor. The walls are red. Cartoon-style drawings depicting women doing various things to each other hang on them. They are colourful, well drawn and amusing. One shows a female version of the 69, one a woman with her head tucked under the ample nineteenth-century skirts of another. All of the women seem extremely happy. In fact the only one who isn't happy is being approached from behind by the only man in the collection of illustrations. She looks positively horrified. I read that they are by a Danish woman called Gemma Wegener, who was born in 1885. She was married to a transvestite who used to model for her. In fact he was the first man ever to have a sex-change operation. Unfortunately it led to his death.

As I move into the next part of the room, I hear some other erotic art aficionados coming up the stairs. I long to turn round to see if they look perverted or really are here for the art, but I feel it's a bit cheeky. They make no sound for the first few seconds as they admire the work of Gemma Wegener. Then the man calls for his glasses in a southern American accent. He's in for a treat.

On the wall in front of me are ink drawings of couples in various positions. All of the drawings have one thing in common: the vast penis of the man. There is one position that looks particularly interesting but should not to be tried at home. The woman is upside down, bottom bare, propped up by a small wheel that she is holding onto, while the man holds her legs. He is about to take her. She is looking remarkably chirpy considering she is a) upside down and b) about to be penetrated by something the size of a large baguette.

I walk on up the stairs towards the next floor. As I leave the room, I hear the American exclaim: "That's one hell of a penis!" I am tempted to go back and tell him all European men are hung like mules but decide to move on to the next floor of erotic treats.

The second floor is all lacquered black, a bit like being in a gondola. There are some rather dated paintings and photographs on the walls of women in masks with pointed tongues and bare chests. They are all engaged in pleasuring each other or staring seductively from the canvas. The colours are garish and bold, the style very obvious. I move up a floor. Now we're into S&M. Maybe this museum gets pervier the higher up you get? There are whips and statues of vaginas and penises made of leather. Nothing very attractive. On the next floor are some interesting moving models. One of a bicycle seat and a bottom, another of a woman giving a man a blow job as he stirs his coffee. The top floor is all white. Again it is dominated by women. In one sketch a woman is sitting opposite another tweaking her nipples. It seems an odd thing to do. I mean, why would you bother?

I walk back down the stairs. That's enough erotic art for a day. I walk into Saint Mark's Square. It is full of people and pigeons, just as I remember from all those years ago. But the people seem grubbier, as do the buildings. The procuratie that line the square are almost black with dirt. There's no chance of finding Cleopatra under all that dirt. The cafés don't seem as grand. There is no band playing, possibly because it's winter. But Saint Mark's no longer feels like Napoleon's famous drawing room of Europe; it feels more like Grand Central Station.

Henry James once said: "Though there are some disagreeable things about Venice, there is nothing so disagreeable as the visitors." I decide to leave them to Saint Mark's Square and walk towards Holly's galleries. I have promised her a visit.

She has three galleries, all of them in Calle delle Botteghe, a small side street off one of the most charming squares in Venice, the Campo Santo Stefano. I decide this is the new drawing room of Europe and sit down in the Café Paolin for a coffee. An amazing cross-section of society walks by: some school children on an outing, chic Venetian women with Tod's shopping bags, perfectly turned out and slim, in stark contrast to the scruffy tourists, an intellectual-looking man in a raincoat reading the paper as he walks, policemen in perfectly ironed red and blue uniforms, tourists with maps, and a gaggle of Asian nuns. The waiter is charming and asks if he can help me when he sees my map. I tell him the name of the road I am looking for and he points it out. It's just next to the bar. I walk up the little road. An impeccably dressed elderly gentleman approaches a lady shop owner who is in the process of raising the shutters on her small delicatessen.

"Ciao bella, I need to kiss you," he tells her dramatically. She of course falls into his arms; who wouldn't?

I walk into the first of Holly's three galleries. There is no mistaking it. Apart from the name Gallery Holly Snapp on the door, there are some nudes by Geoffrey in the window. The floor is wooden and the walls painted white. It is a very different environment to their home.

"Hello, I'm James," says a good-looking young man who approaches me holding out his hand.

"No you're not, you're Prince William," I want to reply, but good manners prevent me. Have I stumbled on a *Roman Holiday* type scoop? *Roman Holiday* is the film in which Gregory Peck spends the day with Audrey Hepburn, who is pretending not to be a princess. If it is indeed William, then I have two options: one keep quiet and hope he rewards me with a title the moment he becomes king, two call the *Daily Mail* immediately.

"Shall I show you around?" says the reluctant prince. We walk along the street to the next gallery. As soon as he opens the door, loud salsa music comes blaring out.

"I crank it up in the mornings to get the punters going," he smiles.

"They won't like that at Sandhurst," I mumble, but the music is too loud for him to hear.

"These are some of Geoffrey's paintings of Venice." Prince William points towards some watercolours and pastels. They're lovely. Geoffrey is clearly very talented. But I don't think they're as good as his women.

The last gallery is the lightest and most airy. It is so Zen it has an almost Asian feel to it. Apart from the rag-time music, that is.

"So you go to each gallery first thing, putting on the music?" I ask.

"Yes," smiles the prince. "It's good, isn't it?"

"Great. Who are you staying with here in Venice?" I ask, trying to sound nonchalant. If he says he's staying with the consulate I'll know it's him.

"My godmother. I've been studying for three years but had enough, so decided to come out here and see how I got on. I love it. Holly's a great person to work for, such fun."

I thank him for showing me around; it is almost seven

o'clock and the day across the water is about to begin.

Geoffrey's studio is once more filled with people partying. This time, as well as the people that were there last night, we are joined by Rod, a *Herald Tribune* stringer, and his wife Christina, who is a translator, as well as a woman in her eighties who used to be the hairdresser to the Queen of Sweden.

Around this collection of guests Geoffrey and Holly's dogs, Perdita and her son Milo, run around.

"Perdita came cowering into the gallery one day, closely followed by some awful bag woman," Holly tells me as we share another litre of wine. "The next day I asked everyone around if they knew this woman and the dog. Several of them knew of her. I asked them to tell her to come to the gallery with the dog and that I wanted to buy it. Two days later she showed up, I gave her 100,000 lire and Perdita was ours."

As she is telling me the story, the doorbell rings. She doesn't move.

For a moment I wonder if I imagined it. "Shouldn't someone get that?" I ask.

"No," says Holly taking a swig of wine. "All our friends have keys, we're far too lazy to go and open the door."

Geoffrey joins us. Perdita immediately jumps up in his arms.

"I love your dogs," I say.

"They're the Kray twins of the canine world," he tells me. "They once killed an old lady on the Accademia Bridge."

"How?" I ask. The dogs are only about a foot high and two feet long. I can't imagine them killing a rat, let alone an old woman. And they look so sweet.

"I was painting from the bridge and they were with me. The old lady's dog saw them and ran after them, taking her with it. She fell over and died instantly."

"Oh my God. What did you do?"

"I carried on painting. What could I do? Another time they got me into a fight by peeing on a security guard's shoe. I came over all apologetic and so on, he wouldn't have any of it, so in the end I punched him and did my elbow in. I've got a metal plate in it now. More wine?"

I decide that if I stay any longer in Geoffrey's studio I will end up drunk again so say no thanks and ask him where I should head for dinner.

"Take the vaporetto across the water, walk straight down a narrow street and you'll see a little hotel called the Agli Alboretti. They have a good restaurant. If the Signora's there, give her this with my compliments," he says and hands me one of his latest catalogues.

"And if the Signora's not there?"

"Leave."

After a lovely dinner, despite the fact that the Signora wasn't there, I walk to Saint Mark's Square. It is better now that most of the tourists have gone and the pigeons are sleeping. I sit down in the Café Lavena, where my father took me for a drink all those years ago.

It was relatively empty then, despite the fact that it was a lovely summer's evening. There was a band playing some blues-type music. The band members were all dressed in black-tie; I remember thinking they were splendidly elegant and feeling like I was in a film.

"Did you read *Death in Venice*?" asked my father, removing his hat as we sat down at a table.

"I haven't finished it," I said.

"What do you think so far?"

"I found it quite hard going, a bit slow, nothing has really happened yet." It was a big change from Enid Blyton and C.S. Lewis. I found the long sentences as dull as the Venice canal water. I had struggled to keep awake.

"That is because your miserable uneducated brain has never read anything worth reading until now. But I agree the beginning can seem a bit like walking through a ploughed field. However it is a masterly portrayal of lust, and the dangers of becoming a slave to desire. I have to tell you, turning into a Von Aschenbach is my secret fear. And you must be careful too; we Benedettis are slaves to passion. It is one of our weak points and you must be on your guard against it."

A young man sat down at the table next to us. He was good-looking, with dark curly hair and rugged features. He took out a packet of Marlboro and lit one.

"Do you think he's Italian?" my father asked me.

"Certainly," I said. "Look how dark he is."

My father shook his head. "An Italian wouldn't be smoking Marlboro."

"Why not?"

"They're too expensive." My father took a sip of his coffee. "I'll have a bet with you. If he's Italian, I'll take you shopping tomorrow for the whole morning. You can buy anything you want."

"And if he's not?"

"Then you have to lose something more precious than the crown jewels to him: your virginity."

"Don't be so stupid," I said and got up to leave. He really was too much.

As I did so, my father turned to the man at the next table and asked him something in Italian.

"Sono americano," was his response.

"How interesting," said my father. "Won't you join us?"

"With pleasure," he said and moved over to our table. I sat down again. My father grinned.

"So, what brings you to Venice?"

"I'm on a tour of Europe," he told us. "Just trying to see as much as possible."

"And how do you like Venice?"

"I love it. I guess you Italians must be used to places like this but to me it's incredible."

"Are you a student?" asked my father.

"I'm an actor," the young man told us.

Just then a photographer approached us and asked if we'd like a picture taken.

"Yes, why not?" said my father. "I think my daughter would like a memento of this special evening."

As it turned out, I didn't lose my virginity to the young actor, but maybe I should have done. Years later I was watching a film called *While You Were Sleeping* with Sandra Bullock in it. The lead man looked incredibly familiar. For days his face haunted me; I just couldn't work out where I'd seen it before. Then I had an idea. I rooted through my old photo albums and found the picture in Venice. There he was smiling out at me. On the bottom right-hand corner of the photograph he'd written: "To my friends in Venice, Peter Gallagher."

As I leave the house the following morning to go to the Galleria, I hear a strange sound coming from Geoffrey's studio. It is the sound of someone reading something familiar but in a monotone German accent. I sneak into the studio. Geoffrey is by his easel while his model, an

attractive young German woman called Juliana, reads from
Pride and Prejudice.

"It's bringing tears to my eyes," he says as he spots me.

I'm not surprised, I'm tempted to respond. Jane Austen will
be turning in her grave.

"Why?" I ask. "It's not a terribly sad book."

"No, but it's all turning out well," he says. "And that always
makes me cry."

I leave them to it and get the boat over the water. It's raining
heavily and there's only one thing to do in Venice when it's
raining: head to a museum. The Galleria Accademia seems to
be the closest so I nip in there. It is like walking into a museum
in the old Soviet Union. The entrance hall is scruffy and old-
fashioned. I can't even see any tills, just two girls with bits of
paper they hand over in return for cash. The cloakroom
consists of a desk with one person behind it. In fact you
couldn't fit more than one person behind it. What must they do
when they get busy during the summer season?

I have been told by my art historian uncle to see *The Feast in
the House of Levi* by Veronese. "He painted it in 1573 for the
Convent of Saints Giovanni and Paolo. It was considered quite
scandalous because he included all sorts of things one
shouldn't include in a depiction of the Last Supper, like
drunken Germans and dogs," he tells me on the phone from
Rimini, where he and my aunt are staying while their flat in
Rome is being done up. "He was told to go away and rework it
after a trial, but all he did was rename it *Feast in the House of Levi*
and he got away with it."

The painting takes up the entire far wall of room ten in the
Galleria Accademia. It is a splendid work, with lots going on.
There is a long table behind three arches. Figures sit at the table

Peter Gallagher, my father and me in St Mark's Square.

or stand in front of it, eating, drinking and chatting. Everyone seems to be having a good time, even Christ. In fact with its dogs and drunken Germans, it's not dissimilar to a party at Geoffrey's.

It's almost time for my train to leave so I head back over the bridge to collect my luggage and say goodbye to my hosts. Geoffrey leaves *Pride and Prejudice* to come and embrace me.

"It was great seeing you again after so many years," he says. "Funny how neither of us are in touch with your stepfather. He's a difficult bugger."

I nod and smile, hugging him back and breathing in the smell of oil paint one last time.

"It's been great fun, thanks for everything."

Holly is going to the university where she teaches and so comes out with me.

"Let's grab a coffee," she says.

"I can't," I say. "My vaporetto will be here in five minutes."

"I'm catching one before yours, come on." She speeds out of the door with her handbag, dog and newspaper, her blonde hair tousled but her red lipstick perfect.

We are joined by the other painter Geoffrey and Rod the writer from the *Herald Tribune*. It's like a leaving committee. I'm touched. Or maybe they're just all here to make sure I go.

"I have to have a coffee," says Holly as Milo runs around her legs. "Come on, my boat is before yours. You won't miss yours, I promise. Let your Italian side out for a second, come on!"

I go with her but spend the whole time looking at my watch. So much for my Italian side. When we go back to the vaporetto stop, I look up at Geoffrey's studio. He is standing at the window, a figure dressed, as always, in black and blue with a white apron covered in oil paint. I wave at him, probably much in the same way my stepfather waved at him all those years ago before he caught the train on which he met my mother. Geoffrey waves at me before going back to his painting and *Pride and Prejudice*.

10

On Rimini Beach

I am in Valentina's flat in Milan when the panic attack hits me. I'm talking to my husband on the phone when I suddenly have an uncontrollable urge to see him and the children. I have spoken to them all several times a day during my trip to Italy but now I need to be with them. I start weeping. I have another week of my trip to go. I am in Milan for three days and then I go to Rimini, back to where it all started. The climax of my visit. But I can't face it. I just have to go home.

It is one of those things that just starts as an idea and then grabs hold of me with such force that I can't fight it. I need to be with them all. I need to hug my children and kiss my husband. I can no longer focus on work, anything else is irrelevant.

My husband calls our travel agent and she finds a flight which leaves two hours from now. It costs a fortune but by now I don't care.

"You'll be home in time for dinner," says my husband.

That's all I need to know.

But can I make it in time? The flight leaves in less than two hours and it's an hour-long journey to the airport. I call

Valentina to explain what's happened. She's not in her office. I call her flatmate Francesca. Thank goodness she is there.

"I'll order you a taxi," she tells me immediately. "Just leave the key with the porter and good luck."

I pack in a mad rush, hurling things into my bag and trying not to leave a mess. I run downstairs, the taxi is already waiting.

"To the Malpensa airport please," I tell the driver. "But my flight is at three o'clock."

The driver looks at her watch. "You might be better off on the train," she says. "But then you never know what time they go. It all depends on the traffic. Let's get going." She puts my stuff in the boot and we head off. She is a no-nonsense Milanese lady who hates Berlusconi.

"If he wins the next election, I'm moving to Switzerland," she tells me as she does a U-turn to avoid a traffic jam. "In fact most of the people I know will move. There will be no one left in Italy except for crooks and tourists."

I text my husband to tell him I'm in the taxi. He calls me to say a friend of ours has just told him the train is quicker. I look out of the window at the city which is speeding past. I don't believe anything can be quicker than this lady and the thought of lugging all my bags onto a train platform is not a nice one.

"Do you think we'll make it?" I ask her.

"Possibly," she says. "We should know once we get onto the motorway."

It takes another twenty minutes to get onto the motorway, possibly the longest twenty minutes of my life. The time is now quarter to two and I should be there at two at the latest; I still have to collect my ticket. I text my husband to tell him my progress. He texts back telling me he has bought some asparagus for dinner. Now I really need to get home.

"What do you think?" I ask my lady driver.

"We should be OK," she says reassuringly. "But you never know in Italy."

We get there at ten minutes past two, I pay her and give her a huge tip before running into the airport to collect my ticket home.

To get from Milan to Montpellier I have to take two extremely small planes. I am a nervous flyer at the best of times. These little propeller jobbies where you can feel every bump make my hands sweat just looking at them. I spend most of the journey thinking how ironic it would be if I left my children motherless due to my desperate urge to see them.

But I do land safely, to a text message from my husband: "Waiting for you: three beautiful children, two glasses of wine and one very happy husband". I start weeping again.

The last leg of the journey is perhaps the most harrowing. A friend of ours has just flown in from London and offers to give me a lift home. Just finding the car is stressful enough. Eventually he resorts to standing in the middle of the car park pushing the remote control key and looking out for which car lights up. Then we have to get out of the car park. He almost runs over a German couple innocently looking for a green Peugeot and then tries to exit through the entrance. The motorway is not easy to negotiate, as he is unused to driving on the wrong side of the road.

But at seven o'clock I've arrived, having left Milan at three. I have never been happier to be home. They are all in the kitchen, sitting at the table. Rupert is cooking dinner. I walk in and he puts his arms around me. Suddenly everything feels right again. I feel like a huge weight has been lifted off me and that I'm back where I belong. The smell of my son as I hug him is intoxicating. He has just got out of the bath so smells predominantly of apple shampoo and soap. But there is something else; something that is just Leonardo and that I would recognise immediately if blindfolded and put in the same room as him. I keep looking at them all; they seem miraculous to me; alive, happy, pretty and noisy. I can't stop looking at them, I'm like a wanderer in a desert who hasn't had a drink of water for days and finds a bottle of chilled Badoit.

I think about my Italian grandmother and how she held me after losing me for twelve years. At the time I was surprised by the force of her emotion. Now, as a mother myself, I can totally understand it and feel awful for all the years she must have missed me.

I spend the next few days being a dedicated Italian mamma. To my surprise it's a role I enjoy. The last few years I have been so focused on my career that my family has not always been my number one priority. My trip to Italy has made me rethink my attitude and realise how important they all are.

I throw myself into family life like never before. I even make homemade pasta with the children. This is the first time the pasta machine (a wedding present) has come out in the eight years we've had it. I supervise them all kneading the dough, covered in flour, and then winding the handle to make the fettuccine we're going to use to make Fettuccine Alfredo.

The children all love it.

"This is my best dinner ever," says Olivia, her face covered in creamy white sauce.

I read to the children from an Italian book every evening called *Questa è Roma*. I studied Italian at university so with that and my thorough Benedetti-style grounding as a teenager I cope quite well. The drawings are large and colourful and the text simple. I am surprised and happy that they seem to love the language. Bea is especially gifted and we are soon having a "how are you" and "what's your name" conversation in Italian. Leonardo just repeats whatever I say so it's easy to get him to tell me I'm beautiful. Olivia insists on watching the *Wizard of Oz* DVD in Italian and asking me to translate.

"There seems to be some mad Italian woman roaming around the house," Rupert says after a few days. "I rather like her."

I think one of the consequences of my crazy childhood is that I am a chameleon. Basically I learnt to adapt to whatever was going on around me and what I thought was required of me.

I wonder if my new-found Italian-ness is just another Chameleon-like phase, or will some of it stay with me. There is only one way to find out if I really have changed and that's to go back to where it all began; Rimini. I want to see how I feel when I get there. Now that I have a family of my own, how will I feel about re-visiting the place I first met mine? How different am I to that little girl who first got lost on the beach?

Although Milan was part of the original Grand Tour I made with my father I don't want to be away from home for too long so I decide to fly straight to Rimini.

I recognise the Via IV Novembre although much has changed since I was last here. It is now a pedestrian street with strange phallic lights lining either side. They are tall and grey, and lit all the way up. They remind me of a thicker version of the laser weapon Luke Skywalker uses in *Star Wars*. It is early December so there are Christmas lights stretched between the two blocks of buildings that line the street. The buildings themselves are made up of a ground floor, which are all shops, and then two or three more storeys of offices or apartments. The left side is taken up with a vast grey building that is almost Fascist in its architecture: stark lines with thick cement. The one on the right where my grandmother lived is not much better. It is also grey but a lighter shade. Outside my grandmother's house a section of the original Roman road has been dug up and illuminated for the benefit of passers-by. But the shops that make up the ground floor and the alcove where the entrance is are just the same as they were when I first came here.

On the left is a bar run by a man called Mario. He looks older and has dyed his hair a strange raven-black colour, a look I've seen a lot in Italy but never anywhere else. On the right is a jeweller's. Opposite is a linen and nightwear shop, which seemed old-fashioned to me twenty years ago. It sells dressing gowns that look like they belong in a jumble sale and the decor hasn't been changed since it opened, probably in the 1950s.

My aunt has collected us from the airport. I am no longer travelling alone, but with my son Leonardo. After my Milanese panic attack I decide to avoid travelling without at least one of my children. Leonardo is the same age I was when I was taken away from Italy. Apart from wanting him near me, I also want him to meet his family. My aunt has met the girls; she and Bertrand came to stay in France once on their way to their house in Burgundy. My aunt showed up with a suitcase full of clothes for me and then immediately started to spoil the children as well.

"I'll take you to the toy shop and you can chose whatever you like," she told them. On a scale of children's fantasies, that's pretty much up there.

My father, whom I haven't seen since he stormed out of my wedding eight years ago hasn't met any of them.

It takes my aunt precisely thirty seconds to fall in love with Leonardo and declare that she will leave him her flat in Rome when she dies.

"Amore mio," she says to him as we walk up the street towards the flat on a chilly Thursday evening. "Look at all the Christmas lights. All for you. They took all the stars from the sky and brought them here for Leonardo."

Leonardo likes this idea, jumps up and down a few times waving his blue and orange plastic aeroplane and looks at the decorations.

"And here," she points at a children's clothes shop close to my grandmother's house, "is the shop my friend Barbara owns. The first time she ever saw your mother as a baby, she stopped me in the street and asked if she was real, she was so beautiful."

Of all the places I have visited on this trip, Rimini is the most important to me. It is where I spent the most time, it is the home of the Benedetti clan and it is where I got to know them. It is also where I was reunited with my father aged fourteen.

Being in Rimini always made me feel secure. The Benedettis are a big family in the city and well known. My aunt and father grew up in an apartment in the main square, the Piazza Tre Martiri. You can still see it: it is the one with the bell tower. I never saw inside but imagine it must have been beautiful. My aunt told me it was so big it took her twenty minutes to walk from the kitchen to her bedroom. She inherited all the property in Rimini when my grandmother died. Most of it consists of shops, where they give her a discount.

"Don't go shopping without me," she warns before we've

even got into the house. "I insist on a discount."

We walk through the alcove, waving at Mario and his wife Bruna. We get to the door my mother and I first arrived at after that long drive through Europe. It is exactly the same. Brown painted metal. The bell we rang with Benedetti written on it remains unchanged. I half expect to hear my grandmother's voice over the intercom.

She died more than fifteen years ago, but because I haven't been to Rimini since her death, she is ever-present. She becomes even more so when we walk into the apartment. My aunt may have totally rebuilt it and changed most of the furniture, but it still smells of my grandmother, a sort of moth-ball mixed with cologne smell.

When I first met her, I didn't immediately see myself in my grandmother as I had my father. The main thing we had in common were brown eyes. She had very long, glossy, silver hair, which she tied back in a neat sausage-shaped roll. She had a habit of running her miniature hands along either side of her head to neaten any stray hairs every hour or so. My grandmother was living proof that your nose is the only thing that never stops growing. The rest of her seemed to hunch up and diminish, but her proud Roman nose would just get more and more formidable. It was almost hooked and, I remember, slightly blemished with blackheads, but it never looked obscene or out of place.

She was affectionate and kind, constantly touching me and repeating her mantra of "my little darling, my little beauty, my little star" while gazing at me lovingly.

My grandmother's name was Settimia and she had been a teacher before she married my grandfather, who was dead by the time I came back to Italy. My grandmother told me I had said my first words with him. One day while I was sitting on his knee, someone knocked at the door.

"Who is it?" he bellowed. "Chi è?"

"Chi è?" I repeated.

My father told me that Gigino was unfaithful to my grandmother the day after their wedding. "In fact in the eyes of the council they weren't even married," he told me. "They had a huge wedding and were married by a bishop, which for Settimia was the Ferrari of ceremonies. She didn't see any need to take the papers to be ratified by the Fascist council which at that time was basically against the church."

My father explained that Gigino married my grandmother because she was the only woman ever to say no to him. The other reason he married her was that he was secretly in love with his sister Valentina and that she approved a union with an ugly wife.

However Gigino was never going to be anything but unfaithful to such an unattractive woman. "She had a face like a goat, it was only when she was naked that she was beautiful," he said. "Then you could see she had breasts like Paolina Bonaparte, magnificent legs and a stunning lower back, but she was always covered head to toe in her dark school teacher's uniform which made her look dowdy. He deceived her day and night. She was under no illusions, she knew he would be unfaithful but she wanted a beautiful man and that's what she got. Occasionally she would challenge him and he would deny everything. 'You just believe whatever anyone tells you,' he would say. 'The only person you have to believe is me.' He was a sadistic man and would even bring his mistresses home for lunch to torment her with them. They were of course all extremely beautiful. Sometimes he would even admit to an affair here and there to give her something to weep about. But I think this insatiable appetite for women came in part from the fact that he couldn't have his sister."

My father's relationship with his father was not close. Gigino was extremely strict and never saw the children as anything but an inconvenience.

"As soon as he could he sent me away to school," said my father. "As far away as possible, to Savona, close to the French border. I would wake up in the mornings and see Corsica from my window. Gigino was too egotistical and vain to love anyone. I never once had a conversation with him." My father never referred to him as father. He would sometimes call him my grandfather but that's as close as he got. Settimia was always referred to by her Christian name. "She wasn't a mamma," my father told me. "She was always a teacher."

After the first lunch we had with my grandmother, my mother and I were shown into our room. It was a big room with a large double bed covered in a green and gold bedspread. There was a large window, which was shuttered. As soon as my grandmother left us alone, I drew up the shutter and opened it. The strong sun lit up the parquet floor and the room became hot almost immediately. I looked out onto the street below. There were people walking arm in arm, eating ice creams, scooters making their noisy way backwards and forwards, buses that ran on a tram-like system ferrying passengers down towards the sea. The imposing Tempio Malatestiano opposite looked unfinished.

I shut the shutter again and lay down on the bed next to my mother who was already asleep. I could hear my father's booming voice and my grandmother's shrill tones from the drawing room. I fell asleep thinking about how far away my den in the hay-barn seemed.

When I woke, I had no idea where I was. My mother was still sleeping and it took me a while to realise we had made it to Italy. My mother lay frowning in her sleep, a habit she had developed over the last few years. I got up and went into the kitchen, where my grandmother was preparing dinner. Her life was made up of work—she ran a shop where she sold materials produced in the family factories—religion and food. Her life followed a very simple pattern of eating, praying and working. Even though we didn't have a common language, I found from that first day I could understand her.

"Benedetto is out," she told me referring to my father. "Can you grate the parmesan?"

She handed me the biggest block of cheese I had ever seen and a grater. I started grating it. The cheese was cumbersome to hold and heavy, but it smelt lovely.

"No, no, no," she cried. "Not on that one." I had been grating it on the large holes. That was no good. It had to be finely grated.

I carried on until my arm was aching, lifted the grater, showed her the pile of cheese and asked her if it was enough.

"No," she replied. "Non basta."

This process was repeated three or four times, until I had grated a whole plate full of cheese.

"We are making pasta alla nonna," she told me beaming. "Grandmother's pasta."

She was very like my mother in that she never sat down or relaxed. She was constantly moving about the house organising things, her tiny slippers making a shuffling noise on the marble floors. Everything from the family silver to china and glasses to plastic carrier bags was kept in huge built-in cupboards that my grandmother kept locked at all times. She carried the keys to all these doors in the pocket of her apron, which she wore most of the day. Some of them reached all the way to the ceiling and I would often come into the drawing room to see my grandmother balancing on a stepladder locking away another treasure.

The most sacred cupboards were those in her bedroom. In one of these she kept a shoe-box stuffed full of cash, which would come out on the frequent visits of representatives from the church or when her children needed something. One day that first summer in Italy she gave me a crisp 100,000-lire note. I had never felt so rich.

My father came back and started picking at the parmesan until my grandmother took it away. He asked where my mother was. I told him she was asleep.

"Yes, she looks a little tired now, but when I knew her she was so beautiful," he said. "And what a bottom. One time we were in St Moritz and she was wearing, what do you call them?"

"Skipants?"

"Exactly. A group of maybe five men were staring at her bottom. In shock, mesmerised. When she skied off, they turned to me and said 'Is that all yours?'" He laughed loudly. "She was something special. I thought someone with a bottom like that could never be stupid, but sadly that was wrong."

Dinner passed quickly. There were only three courses. My mother and father laughed and chatted together. I had a brief fantasy that they might get back together. There was no animosity between them, they obviously got on well, maybe they had been wrong to split up?

When we went to bed, I asked my mother if she had ever

My father as a young boy.

considered it.

"No," she said firmly. "I don't want to live with a man ever again. Least of all Benedetto. But he's fascinating and I'm very happy you like him." She now lives alone in Devon with three cats. They are all female. She has not kept in touch with any of her other husbands. With my father, although things ended badly and they had years of estrangement, she never really felt anger or animosity towards him. Actually I can't imagine her being angry with anyone, even a man who thought a good way of spending an evening was beating her up, but I suppose there is no reason to be in touch with the others. She still has strong links with Italy through work and when she travels there she sometimes sees my father. I like the idea of them being together and have got over any childish desire for them to end up together. They're better off alone.

The next day my father took me out for lunch alone. I felt shy, like a girl on a first date. We walked to a restaurant close to my grandmother's house. We went in and my father showed me all the antipasti we could choose from. There were hams, char-grilled vegetables, pickles, tiny mozzarella balls, various seafoods and steamed broccoli. We sat down at a table. There was already a basket of bread on it.

I had always had a thing about bread. Much of my childhood was spent eating the inside of loaves after my mother had been to the supermarket. Sometimes I would roll the dough up into little balls before eating it. I would sit in the back of her mini-van with the shopping and munch my way through a loaf. She was very good about it and started to buy two loaves instead of one. But I had never tasted anything like the Italian bread and had almost finished the whole basket in five minutes. My father laughed and said I would be a cheap date if that was all I ate.

A round, middle-aged man with hardly any hair approached the table. My father introduced him to me as "il padrone", and said he was one of the most important men in the country as only he held the secrets of how to make perfect tortellini alla

My parents on one of my mother's recent trips to Italy.

bolognese. The man blushed and bowed and looked very pleased. They chatted for a bit and from what I understood we had ordered an amazing amount of food without looking at the menu once.

"So tell me about this madman your mother married," my father said.

"Which one?"

He laughed. "The second one, Barry, the one you ran away from."

I told him a bit about him and how awful it was. About how scared I was to come home from school, worried what I would find.

"I used to feel the same," he said. "Your grandfather Gigino used to beat me all the time. Mostly for no reason. I never knew what sort of mood he would be in."

"What did you do?"

"Nothing rational. But sometimes on the way back from school I would walk avoiding all the lines on the pavement, thinking that if I didn't walk on the lines he would be in a good mood."

I was amazed. I had adopted a similar strategy. "I used to do everything in threes," I said. "Squeeze my toes three times, or tear my loo-paper into three bits."

My father took my hand. "Doing things in threes is very catholic. This you must stop immediately. And remember, the best revenge is not self-pity or anger, but to write a book."

The antipasti arrived, a selection of all the things we had seen displayed as we came in. It was the first time I had ever tasted olive oil. It seemed quite strong and bitter, but I soon found that I liked it as much as butter. The antipasti were followed by the famous tortellini. They were small bits of pasta filled with a mixture of veal, parmesan, prosciutto and mortadella.

"Each one is hand-made by the man I introduced you to," said my father spearing a tortellini with his fork. "You will not taste a more delicate dish anywhere."

The only filled pasta I had tasted up to that point was Heinz Ravioli in Tomato Sauce, which comes out of a tin. All I can remember is that it looked like bits of pasta covered in ketchup. In fact it tasted like that as well. This was a different thing altogether. The tortellini were also covered with a tomato sauce, but it was delicate and sweet. They were filled with flavours; the different meats and the cheese combined to create something salty and succulent, something delicate and delicious, with a hint of lemon.

After lunch my father asked me whether I would like to go for a walk on the beach or go shopping for clothes. I opted for clothes. We wandered through the old town to the Piazza Tre Martiri, which was already busy with afternoon shoppers. He seemed to be recognised in every shop we went into and we were treated like royalty. I was the subject of much curiosity and exclamations. He explained that I didn't speak Italian yet whenever anyone tried to talk to me. He also said that if I ever came in on my own they were to give me whatever I wanted and he would settle the bill later on. I was amazed, and imagined days of shopping for anything I wanted to come.

We walked past an underwear shop. The windows were filled with models wearing lacy bras and knickers. They got more frivolous the further along we walked. The final window displayed a creation in pink and white lace, with satin ribbons.

"The more exaggerated they are, the more they appeal to women," said my father. "These things make them forget what a terrible life they have in reality. And they also make them forget all that is not angelic about them by giving them lacy wings."

It was in a small boutique just off the main square that he got down to the serious business of changing my image. I went into the cubicle and threw off my old shorts and T-shirt. Outfits would arrive by order of my father, who had the whole staff of the shop running around us. We came away with a whole wardrobe. I couldn't wait to wear it all, but especially an outfit made up of a skirt, vest and jacket. It was all white, silk and lace, the skirt was full and came down to below my knees. The vest was silk and the jacket lace, completely see-through and very delicate. I felt like a princess in it.

That evening I wore my new outfit. My grandmother said I looked like an angel and that she wanted to show me off in town. We went for a walk after dinner, which it seemed most of the rest of the city had decided to do as well. Rimini was full of people. We walked to the park where there are Roman ruins.

There were families there, children playing, parents strolling arm in arm. My grandmother told me she came to the park to do her breathing exercises and that they had kept her in shape throughout her life. She said she would demonstrate so I would be able to do them too. My parents sat down on a bench and I followed my grandmother to a grassy bit of land. She stood in the evening sun and raised her hands straight up in the air. She bent her knees slightly and breathed in and out slowly, lowering her arms and raising them again as she breathed slowly. She closed her eyes and stood still for a few seconds. Sometimes she varied the arm movement by holding them out in front of her chest. With the sun setting behind her she reminded me of a Buddhist monk practising some form of moving meditation.

My grandmother's bedroom has been turned into a kitchen. It is open plan, next to the dining room, which joins the sitting room. The only things that remain unchanged are the marble floor and the wooden cupboards all along the far wall. I open the kitchen window and look out on the street below. Whenever I stayed with my grandmother, I would have a room next to hers, now occupied by my aunt and uncle and their antique bed, which looks like I imagined the sleigh from *The Lion, the Witch and the Wardrobe* would be, only bigger. In those days I smoked. Of course my grandmother didn't know this, so I would lean out of the window smoking, watching the people walk by two storeys below me. My mother wasn't allowed to smoke either, but she never fooled my grandmother. I remember once when my aunt came to see her and asked my grandmother where Ella was.

"In the bathroom, smoking," she replied.

I hold Leonardo tight and we look down on the shoppers

below. Now it is all pedestrian, it seems very quiet. When I last looked out of this window, there were buses whizzing up and down the whole time. And of course cars and scooters; there is hardly anywhere in Italy without cars and scooters. Leonardo tries to wriggle free to get further out of the window so I take him back inside and shut it. To distract him we walk around the room. He opens one of the cupboards along the wall. In my

Nonna doing her exercises.

grandmother's day these cupboards would all have been locked

When she was on her deathbed, I remember a scene of intolerable cruelty. My aunt was by then in charge of things. My grandmother had moved out of her apartment and in with the nuns at her beloved church across the road, the Tempio Malatestiano. But somehow she had managed to bring with her all the lockable cupboards from her bedroom. I found my aunt going through her cupboards, throwing boxes of stuff away my grandmother had hoarded for years as she lay helpless in her bed, unable to move or protest. Her eyes were filled with fear. Maybe she realised Piera was getting the job done ahead of time. I can't imagine Piera didn't understand what effect her actions would have on her mother, we all knew how obsessed she was with her cupboards and little boxes.

I walk into what was the kitchen in my grandmother's house. It is now a bedroom, which I will share with Leonardo for the next four days. The floor is parquet and I recognise the double windows looking out over the inner courtyard. They used to be in my grandmother's dining room. I remember there were images of Padre Pio all over her walls, rather like I had posters of the Bay City Rollers. She would gaze at the Padre with tears in her eyes, making the sign of the cross and saying over and over again "È un santo." To me he looked like a fairly ordinary bloke, except for his rather odd clothes, but my grandmother would probably have said that about Les McKeown.

The dining room was where my grandmother would give me Italian lessons. We would study with the shutters shut to keep out the heat. Our lessons lasted for two hours a day. She was very precise about them and would put up with no interruptions. We sat down at the kitchen table with a dictionary. This was not English/Italian as would have been sensible, but Italian/Italian. My father had bought it for me that first day.

"There is no point in learning what the English word is," he explained. "If you can't understand one Italian word for something, you will understand another. This way your vocabulary will be richer. You must read dictionaries like novels."

My grandmother divided the lessons into two parts: grammar and vocabulary. She wrote out endless lists of verbs in her careful, elaborate handwriting. I pray, you pray, he/she/it prays. She would reel the verbs off in her high-pitched nasal voice and I would repeat them. She taught me to spell by laboriously pronouncing each syllable of words. "Abbbraccci" she would say, indicating that the word has two b's and two c's. For comprehension practice, she dictated passages from The Bible.

"This shouldn't take more than a few weeks," boomed my father. "Your mother learnt Italian in three weeks, there's no reason you can't."

I doubted his confidence but I liked being with my grandmother. She so obviously adored me. Even when she was telling me off for mispronunciation or for not sitting up straight, she smiled affectionately. She would constantly walk behind me when I sat down, grab my shoulders and yank them back with a strength you would have thought impossible from such a tiny woman. Even today, every time I think of her, I put my shoulders back and sit up straight.

After food the most important thing to my grandmother was religion. "Without God we are nothing," she would always tell me. The fact that I had never been to confession was of grave concern to her. She feared on a daily basis for my soul. In her view if I didn't go and confess my sins immediately, I was destined for hell.

"Vai a confessarti," she would repeat on a daily basis. "Go to confession, if you don't you'll end up in hell."

The concept of hell didn't really worry me, but I felt bad for my grandmother who was too sweet to deserve such a burden.

So one day when I found myself outside the Tempio Malatestiano, I decided to go in and tell all. I wasn't quite sure what I should start with. I really hadn't done much, but there had been some impure thoughts that could probably count as sinful. I had thought about kissing someone called Craig, probably enough to send you to hell without parole. If this wasn't enough, once I got going the priest would probably point me in the right direction.

It was a hot day and I was grateful for the cool of the interior, although I could see nothing until my eyes adjusted. The Tempio Malatestiano is vast. It is really a church that merits a bigger and more important city than Rimini. But its builder,

Sigismondo Malatesta, made a lot of money renting out his armies to the Pope and decided to build a church with some of the proceeds. He did a great job. Or rather the architect Alberti did. The proportions of the church are pleasing. It was built in the fifteenth century but totally destroyed during the Second World War, when the Allies bombed Rimini to bits. The Americans then paid for it to be rebuilt, stone by stone. The only real evidence of the fact that it has been rebuilt is the floor, which is a strange red stone and looks modern compared with the ancient chapels that line the walls and the Giotto-esque crucifix that hangs over the altar. The most famous work of art in the church is a fresco by Piero della Francesca. It is a portrait of the young Sigismondo genuflecting before Saint Sigismondo. There are two whippets on the right of the fresco, one white the other brown. In the distance through a round window you can see a city.

This wasn't my first visit to the church. My grandmother had already dragged me along to Mass three times. I had also been there once with my father, who explained to me that it was a church dedicated to a pagan God.

"Look at the cherubs with their ridiculously large bottoms," he said, pointing to a row of white marble statues that lined the wall of one of the chapels. "Sigismondo got around the church's veto of nudity by putting these vast bottoms on children. Very intelligent. This is a church which has nothing to do with the catholic religion, it is totally pagan. The images are not ones of the Pietà or the annunciation. They are of animals and bottoms."

He also told me how when Fellini was a teenager he had a shop opposite the church, where he sold cartoons. Fellini was always drawing, my father told me; it didn't matter whether you

My father on a rare visit to church.

were in a restaurant with him or wherever. He would draw on whatever was at hand, a tablecloth or a napkin or a scrap of paper. In later years a Swiss banker cottoned on to the fact that these sketches would become valuable so he struck a deal with Fellini to buy all his drawings and hired a man whose job it was to follow the director around and collect them. He then exhibited them and made a fortune from the sales.

"As Voltaire said," my father told me, "if you see a Swiss banker hurling himself head first out of a window, then you should follow as you can be sure there is something to be gained down below."

He described how Fellini was born from what he called the "smile of Rimini". He told me how the town grew from the most inhospitable place in Italy, where even the Roman emperors would exile people, to a magical place due to the beach and the night life that began at the turn of the century.

"This stretch of beach gave the city an unimaginable richness and from this richness the smile of Rimini was born," he told me. "Any pharmacist or butcher could come to the beach, once work was finished, and pretend to be an illustrious doctor or a rich industrialist. The women who came didn't care if it was true or not, they didn't come to the sea for the truth, they came for the adventure. In this way a theatre of lies was created. Fellini was like this. He told lies all the time, he was in his theatre. He never told the truth, to know his truth you had to go to the cinema. But he was born from the smile of Rimini once the beach had been discovered and it had become a pleasure-ground and not just somewhere to avoid."

My father explained how this was a time of debauchery. "There were two morals, one for inland and one for the beach," he said. "You didn't ask questions. And as there were two morals, there weren't any. Because you can't have two morals. This was the sentimental education of Fellini. He was born into the height of this in 1920. And in this church he used to come and give sermons to a non-existent congregation. He would close his shop, stand behind the altar and shout across the empty church."

I walked over to the holy water, dipped my fingers in it and crossed myself as I had seen my grandmother do. By now I was Julie Andrews in *The Sound of Music*, feeling very holy and sincere. A priest walked towards me and asked if he could help. He was wearing a long black robe with white trimming and a black hat. He spoke in Italian. My grandmother had prepared me and told me what to say.

"Vorrei confessarmi."

"Scusi?"

I repeated my aim. The priest then started talking to me. I smiled and waited for him to lead me to the little hut I had seen in the films. He didn't move. Eventually I understood that he was asking me if I had been confirmed in the catholic faith.

I had no idea what that was but it certainly hadn't happened to me.

"Well then you can't confess," he told me.

I left the church feeling disappointed. I had always thought churches were desperate for new sinners to convert. Clearly not in Rimini. When I told my grandmother of my efforts, she was very touched. She smiled and hugged me and said I was a good girl.

M y aunt and uncle are preparing dinner. We will be eating risotto with zucchini followed by sole fillets and broccoli. Leonardo has a chair piled high with silk cushions prepared for him. Behind his chair on the floor is a painting by my aunt's first husband, the Spanish artist. I suggest we move it. I have images of Leonardo falling backwards into it or spraying it with pasta. I heard one sold recently for over £100,000.

"It doesn't matter," says my aunt. "It'll be fine. Let him do what he wants."

Leonardo eats well; my aunt and uncle are charming.

My aunt kisses the palm of Leonardo's hand and closes his

fingers into a fist.

"Save this kiss for later," she says. I have never seen such a display of affection from her.

After dinner my aunt brings out a photograph of me.

"This was taken when your mother went back to England and you stayed with me," she says handing it to me. I must have been around two, I am lying on a towel or a blanket, it's difficult to say which, it is coloured with light and dark blue stripes. The picture is big, blown-up to A4 size. It is a head-shot of me. By now the black hair I was born with has turned blonde. My head is turned sideways, laughing at something out of shot. I am the spitting image of Leonardo. I show it to him. He of course thinks it's him and wants to keep it.

My aunt rarely surfaces before eleven o'clock, so the next morning I decide Leonardo and I will go down to the sea. I wake early and lie listening to the unfamiliar sounds around me. At first I think it is raining and that I can hear the sound of the rain on a metal roof, but I realise it is the tapping of the central heating system slowly waking up. Then I listen to the neighbours dragging their child out of the door and towards school. My aunt has told me they are from Naples. Even if I didn't know this, I could have guessed. A noisier neighbour you couldn't hope for. The other sound I hear is a comforting one. It is the sound of people pulling up their wooden shutter-curtains. These wooden shutters are something I have only seen in Italy. They totally block out the light. In fact if it weren't for the noisy neighbours I would have no idea of the time. As they are dragged up they make a sound rather like the cars on the cobbled streets of Rome.

The return of the Neapolitan neighbours wakes Leonardo. I get him up and dressed and we head to the bus. Leonardo's

My aunt's picture of me.

favourite thing in the world is a bus and he spends the journey shouting the word, refusing to sit down in his seat.

We get off at the Grand Hotel and walk towards the sea. We cross the main road that leads to the nearby town of Riccione and is full of cheap shops open only in the summer. I remember spending hours walking up and down the street at night as a teenager. It was full of pubs and clubs. Shouts of "ciao bella" were everywhere as the young Italian men tried desperately to impress the tourists, who were, in those days, probably more likely to sleep with them than the local Italian girls. I would hate it now, but then it seemed like paradise.

We walk into the Fellini Gardens in front of the Grand Hotel. The main attraction in the garden is a vast fountain with four horses. Leonardo is fascinated by the horses and tries to get in. Around us pigeons land waiting for something to eat. Leonardo runs towards them shouting "Get away" until they take flight. These were his first words. He was about one at the time and as usual I was trying to smother him in kisses—an instinct that may come from my Italian side. I notice that it is impossible to walk down the street with Leonardo without some stranger trying to touch him. In England people tend to avoid you if you have children; here it is the other way round.

I manage to drag Leonardo from the fountain towards the sea. I am longing to see the beach at Rimini again. Leonardo walks even more slowly than my aunt and uncle. I am tempted to pick him up, but he's having such a good time looking at everything and chasing the pigeons following us.

Eventually we get there. The beach is not covered with sun-bathing bodies and the smell of sun cream as it was when I was here twenty years ago, but with fog. It is a fog that starts on the ground and goes up to my chest. I can only see the grey sea in the distance above it. It looks cold and uninviting. The sky is the same deep grey colour.

Rimini beach is divided into sections, each of them run by a different person, from whom you rent your deckchair, water-skis or pedalo. We are in the domain of Luciano, who has the number eight on his sign. In the summer he would be running around carrying deckchairs to punters and chasing squatters off his turf. Today he, or one of his workers, is fixing a window frame on his white hut. I am surprised to see anyone here at all. There is no one else on the beach; it feels ghostly, like we're the only people alive and have somehow landed in this summer playground by accident.

"Good morning," says the man as we walk past. "Are you on a walk?"

I stop to chat with him briefly. When I start to walk on again, I realise Leonardo is no longer with me. I kneel down in

My father in his fedora hat.

the fog to try and find him. I can't see a thing. I panic and start shouting. How will I ever find him in this blanket of white? He could walk into the sea and never come back. The man drops his tools and helps me look. We decide to take one half of the beach each: he will take the top, I the bottom. I run towards the coastline. Still no sign of him. But he couldn't have got much further.

"Signora," I hear the man cry. His voice is almost muffled by the thick fog. "He's here." I run towards the sound. The man is standing by a small plastic house with a green door on it. Leonardo is inside, pretending to cook dinner for his sisters. I feel like crying with relief. I thank the man, who goes back to his window frame.

I look towards the Grand Hotel. I can just see the outline of the elaborate roof through the thick fog. I strain my eyes to see more. Something seems to be moving towards me. Something black. But it doesn't look like a bird. It has no wings. It is heading straight for me. I think about picking Leonardo up and running away. I've had enough excitement for one day. It's probably some psycho killer who only comes out when it's foggy and specialises in murdering women with young children. As it comes closer I recognise it. It's a 1920s hat, which seems to have a life of its own. The rest of the figure is shrouded in thick fog. It is only when he is less than a metre away from me that I am sure it's him.

"I recognised you by your hat," I say.

He laughs and holds me close to him. "Ciao bella. My sister told me I would find you here," he says. Leonardo starts to protest, already the jealous Italian.

"This is the last of the Benedettis," I tell him, motioning towards Leonardo.

My father leans down on his haunches and grabs Leonardo's cheek.

"Ciao bello," he says.

11

Tea at the Grand Hotel

Why did you storm out of my wedding?" We are in the Grand Hotel. I have never been inside before, but am curious to see it after all the Fellini films. The entrance is disappointing: a small modern door at the top of an unremarkable staircase. Nothing grand at all. But the entrance hall is better. It is huge with a high ceiling, large granite pillars and a vast marble counter. There are chandeliers evenly spaced throughout the ceiling. The one closest to the entrance is the largest. It hangs above a rotund sofa that Leonardo runs around. The carpet lets the whole place down. It is brown with large beige swirls.

My father and I sit on a cream sofa in the right-hand corner of the entrance hall.

"Weddings are so conventional," he says. "Don't be so bourgeois."

"Whenever you want to justify your bad behaviour, you say that to criticise it is bourgeois," I say. "It was not nice of you to storm out. It's not as if no one noticed, I mean fathers are meant to be at their daughters' weddings, that's just how it is. You were meant to walk me up the aisle. And you were meant to recite from Dante's fifth canto."

"Who recited Dante?"

It was typical of him to care more about Dante than who walked his daughter up the aisle.

"Piera. But she took some persuading. She said she didn't know if her hat would go with Dante."

My father laughed. "She should have been more worried about getting the canto wrong."

All the way to the hotel I have had my arm in his. He is still a good-looking man. I know from my mother he is now eighty-one. He looks about sixty. We take off our coats and sit down; he takes off his hat. Behind us is the famous terrace Fellini filmed in *Amarcord*.

"That's where the hotel guests used to dance," says my father when he sees me looking at it, perhaps in an effort to change the subject. "Fellini and his friends would stand at the gate and gaze at them. To them it looked like something from the Orient, glamorous and exotic. Once he was a success, Fellini always stayed here when he came to Rimini. He didn't pay; they let him stay in a suite now called the Fellini Suite. I suppose you could say he is the spiritual symbol of a non-spiritual city."

The terrace is more elegant than the interior. It has white metal chairs and tables. Palm trees grow beside it. Fellini was right: the grandeur of the Grand Hotel is in its exterior.

Leonardo comes running up. He has managed to get hold of one of the deep red apples they keep in silver bowls on the marble reception. He doesn't like apple skin so is standing in front of me like a small bird waiting for me to remove it from his mouth. Without even thinking I do so. He runs off again and comes back a few minutes later with another piece of apple skin in his mouth. This time my father intervenes. He takes out a bundle of napkins from his pocket. I remember on my first visit to Italy being astounded at seeing him stealing mountains of napkins from every bar we went into. His houses were littered with them. He obviously retains this habit.

"Take it out yourself," he tells Leonardo in Italian. "Why do you need your mother to do it for you? Dirty little boy."

Leonardo protests and looks at me. I don't move. After another minute of protest he takes the piece of apple skin and puts it in the napkin my father is holding out. He runs off again. I am amazed how easy it was to get him to do something he didn't want to. I'm not sure I've ever tried it.

"You know if you only lavish a quarter of the affection you do on this boy he will still be all right," says my father. "And if you continue to spoil him like you do, he will grow up a delinquent."

"Well, there was no risk of that with me."

My father doesn't answer, but I see he has a point with Leonardo. In fact this is something that has been bothering me. I know I indulge him, but can't help it.

"I don't understand," I say. "How do you always seem to know what's going on in my head? It's not as if we ever lived together or spent any time together."

My father takes my hand. "Bella, we are more intimate than you can imagine. The things I tell you infiltrate deep into your stomach and then take on a life of their own. Eventually they become your thoughts. They are things you already know, but don't know that you know."

He lets go of my hand and sits up straight. "As Dante said," he begins. I might have guessed Dante would be involved.

"'I see that you believe in what I say, because I say it, but you don't know why.' So you see, you believe it because I say it because it touches something inside you that you recognise. And I can do this because we are the same. For example, I expect you wake up in the night and then can't go back to sleep."

This is true. And since having the babies it has become worse. I often go for weeks without a decent night's sleep.

"So what do you do?"

I tell him I sometimes take a sleeping pill, but most of the time I just lie there, panicking about getting back to sleep.

"Stupida scema," he yells. Now I recognise the father I know and love. "Pills are for imbeciles, for people without the capacity to write. How dare you mess with your brain, your most important tool? It's criminal. When you can't sleep, get up and write. It doesn't matter what you write, just write."

Leonardo comes back with some more apple skin. This time he puts it straight on top of my father's napkin pile.

"Bravo, bravo," says my father pinching his cheek. "I also expect you are very tired once you've eaten," he says to me.

This is true too. Especially after pasta. All I want to do is sleep.

"You have to remember that we Benedettis have a very complicated digestive system," says my father. I am intrigued and as always surprised by the Italians' capacity to discuss digestive systems as if they were talking about car engines. "We need to eat very little. I for example can't think if I eat a lot and then I can't write. Terrible. We are also prone to diabetes, but it is not a diabetes that doctors recognise. It works away slowly and imperceptibly; your grandfather died of it. So you need to avoid sugar."

When I was pregnant with Leonardo, the doctors thought I might have diabetes. They did all sorts of blood tests but found nothing.

"That's going to be tough," I tell him. "I eat dark chocolate every day. I can't live without it."

My father looks unimpressed. "The phrase can't live without is a terminally stupid one, used mainly by whores frequenting the beach and women working in supermarkets. You can live without it. In fact you can live without most things, except food, water and writing. All you say to yourself is 'For me chocolate doesn't exist' and there we are. Finito."

Leonardo comes over to us again. He has finished running around the entrance hall playing with his aeroplane and eating apples. Now he's bored. We go on a tour of the hotel. First the Fellini Suite. I have to say if I were Fellini, there are a hundred places I would rather stay. It is drab and badly decorated. The suite consists of a bedroom, a bathroom and a dining room. The dining room is the most interesting part of the suite. It has a frivolous air about it, with strangely exaggerated lamé-gold chairs covered with red velvet material. There is a chandelier in the middle of the ceiling. I imagine Fellini at the table, feverishly sketching.

Next we go to the restaurant. Breakfast is laid out on a gigantic oval table with an arrangement of palm leaves and yellow and red flowers in the middle. At either end of the table there is a vase of white lilies. The cloth is thick white linen and hangs all the way to the floor. Above the table there are three chandeliers. On the table is a feast of food. There are several types of bread, everything from baguette to pumpernickel. There is fresh fruit cut up into bite-size portions, large cylindrical containers with various kinds of cereal. Yoghurts, jams, honey, tea and coffee are laid out. All along the wall there are silver containers that look like bread bins with cooked food inside them, such as tomatoes, blood pudding and porridge.

There are eggs cooked in every manner; scrambled, boiled, fried and poached. There is enough food to feed around one hundred people.

The dining room is about the same size as the entrance hall. It is light and decorated in an Art Deco style. There are chandeliers throughout and large windows that look out on to the famous terrace; the tables are covered in white linen cloths and the chairs wooden with high backs. A waiter walks around surveying the scene, polishing glasses and adjusting chairs. There are just two people eating breakfast.

When we leave the Grand Hotel, the fog is lifting and it is starting to rain. The kind of tropical rain that comes down in sheets and soaks everything. The fountain with the horses now looks even more impressive. Water cascades over the horses but it's impossible to see which is the water from the fountain and which is the rain. It's all just an orgy of water, splashing everywhere. I ask my father what happened to the fog. He tells me it often vanishes just as quickly as it descends.

"Once I was on the beach with a girl and there was a fog even thicker than there was today, all the way up to my chest. Suddenly she vanished. I looked around but couldn't see her anywhere. Then I felt something around my midriff. She was undoing my trousers. Formidable. Luckily that day the fog didn't disappear."

We run to the bus, despite my father's insistence that a taxi might be more practical. But I can't deprive Leonardo of his favourite thing. Once on the bus my father lectures me about Dante and Leopardi. I see the driver watching us. When I was a child he used to embarrass me with his loud voice and intellectual lectures, but now I don't mind it. When we stand up to get off the bus opposite my aunt's house the driver turns to my father.

"It's been a pleasure listening to you, maestro," he says.

"Thank you," says my father. I feel unaccountably proud of him.

"I found what you had to say very interesting," he continues. "I'd be very interested to talk some more with you as I'm a bit of a reader myself."

"Really?" my father said, raising his hat. "Complimenti."

"What is your opinion of Ken Follett?" asks the bus driver.

My father's face gives nothing away. "It's as if for me he doesn't exist," he says and walks off the bus.

He says goodbye to us outside the Tempio Malatestiano.

"It's been a pleasure meeting you Leonardo," he says taking his hand. "Please try to ignore your mother's need to kiss you at any given moment and you might grow up relatively normal." Next he takes my hand. "Remember that when you're not writing you are still very much in danger of relapsing into mediocrity and sentimentality. Two beasts that you have to fight at all times. It's normal, these are the same beasts I have had to fight."

Just then my mobile phone rings. It's Olivia who is calling to tell me that Bea has just scratched her.

"Send her a kiss from Benedetto," says my father.

I do as he asks. "It's already arrived," she says.

Later that day I borrow my uncle's car and head off into the hills outside Rimini. There is somewhere I want to visit. My family used to have a country house in a village called Carpegna, about an hour's drive from Rimini. It is the kind of village that hasn't changed much since the war, tucked away in the mountains, with its own prince and modest castle. This is where my father kept his horses. I remember it being very grand; the entrance had vast iron gates which led into a pebbled courtyard. On the left were the stables, kept in pristine order by a German girl called Helga. The house rose above them, white and elegant. The grounds were large; there was a lawn and a pond where two swans nested. Up above the house was the mount of Carpegna where we would go riding every day. The house was in a modernist style, which owed quite a lot to Le Corbusier. The most extraordinary feature was a vast window in my father's bedroom which looked like a mirror from the outside.

I call my father to ask how I will find it again.

"Just ask for the Casa Benedetti," he tells me. "But why are you going?"

"I just want to see it."

"So purely for sentimental reasons," he laughs. "Brava."

When I arrive in the village, I go into the butcher's to ask for the house. I have a vague memory of where it is but don't trust my sense of direction; it has never been a strong point. The butcher tells me to turn right off the high street and follow the road north.

I do as he says. The road takes me up a steep hill into a hamlet behind the main village. I remember the track to my father's house being gravel, but all the roads are tarmac now. I come to a crossroads and have no idea which way to go.

"Which way do you think?" I ask Leonardo.

"Car," he replies helpfully.

Then I see something through the foliage which looks like it could just be it, although it appears to be a smaller house than the one I remember. I drive up towards it and find myself outside the gates, or what is left of them. They are falling apart and rusty.

The house does seem less imposing, I suppose I was a lot

smaller when I saw it last. An elderly man wearing more jumpers than I would in a ski resort is turning the earth in his garden with a rotivator at a nearby house. He stops the machine as we park and walks to the fence to greet us.

"I've come to see the Casa Benedetti," I tell him.

"There are no Benedettis here any more," he says shaking his head. "He sold everything."

He is referring to my father, who inherited the house from my grandfather.

"Who bought it?"

"Some people from Cesena, but they don't come here."

The house is abandoned, the garden full of rubbish, the stables falling apart. Helga would be horrified.

"I used to come here as a little girl," I tell him. "I'm going to take a look around."

He nods and watches us walk through the gates.

Leonardo and I enter the courtyard. I look up at the house. The over-sized window is still there, but the reflection seems blurred. We cross the courtyard to where the pond was. It is totally dry; the swans have long gone. The paddock behind the house where the horses used to graze is now home to a modern-looking barn, probably belonging to the local farmer.

"House alive?" asks Leonardo.

I bend down to pick him up. "No, it's not alive any more," I tell him. I wonder why the people from Cesena bought it only to let it crumble. I feel a huge sense of loss, a sense of a world that is no more.

I remember my father telling me how my grandmother would drive my grandfather insane at weekends when they were preparing to come here. They would all be in the car ready to go.

"Every time, without fail, just as they were about to leave, Settimia would say she had forgotten something and go running back into the house," my father told me. "Gigino would fly into a rage and start shouting at my sister and me. I think it was a small revenge she took for his constant infidelity."

I imagine they must have been an elegant addition to the village, arriving in their car with an entourage of servants on hand to prepare the pasta and their fine clothes.

When we get back to the car the neighbour is waiting to talk some more.

"Do you remember Settimia?" I ask him.

His face lights up. "She was wonderful, the house was always immaculate and she would have lovely lunches. They came here a lot in those days," he says. "But he lost it all."

"Maybe it all came too easily to him?"

"Maybe," says the old man and goes back to his rotivating.

Leonardo meanwhile is drinking water from a small fountain I remember the neighbours used to wash their clothes in. I take one last look at the Casa Benedetti. If I had the money, would I buy it and restore it to its former glory? Would I replenish the pond, bring the swans back and restore the stables? I decide I probably wouldn't. The Casa Benedetti has lost its magic.

That evening my aunt, uncle, Leonardo and I are invited to dinner. As it is half-way between Rimini and Carpegna I meet them there. We won't be eating at the friend's home, but at a restaurant called Gino. This is not a normal restaurant. It is a family-run place that serves only fish. It is run by Gino's widow and looks more like a home than a restaurant. It is in the hills above Rimini. I'm already dreading it as we drive up the mountain towards the house. Ever since I came back to Italy that first summer, this fish thing has haunted me. I used to get sweaty palms as a teenager going to a restaurant with my aunt and uncle, worried they were going to make me try some awful creature from the deep and then look on disapprovingly as I turned green.

A present from my father at Carpegna.

You walk into Gino's via the kitchen. On your left is a large open fire where the fish gets cooked. In front of you is a sturdy wooden table full of dead fish, ingredients and knives. There are unnerving blood stains on the table. Beyond that is the kitchen where all the cleaning gets done. The women who work there are all sturdy, obviously brought up on fish. They are short, broad and healthy-looking. They wear pinafores and their hair up. They look perfectly friendly but to me they seem like torturers, preparing my evening of seafood hell. Already I feel my aunt is watching my every move. I have to pretend to like everything on offer or she'll tell everyone I'm sexually repressed. In fact I do like fish, but only white fish that doesn't taste of fish. According to my aunt you have to devour all sorts if you're to be considered anywhere near normal.

We sit down at a long wooden table covered with a paper tablecloth. I try to sit as far away from my aunt as possible and start feverishly collecting napkins I can either throw up into or hide my fish in. We start with sardines. Next to anchovies they're as close to hell as I can imagine. As bad as it gets. The whole rest of the table, consisting of my aunt, uncle, their friends, and their two daughters, one a rather charming twenty-three-year-old poetess and the other a schoolgirl, are in raptures.

"You'll see," says my aunt, oblivious to my panic. "This is one of the best things you will ever eat."

At Gino's there is no menu. You're served whatever the fishermen catch. I'm already wishing their trip had been less successful. There will be around ten courses, the poetess tells me helpfully. But at least the wine has appeared. The white is slightly sparkling and fairly rough. I try the red, which is marginally more drinkable. There are displays of boat knots on the walls. It is not an exquisite place, but I already love the easy atmosphere and the formidable women who stomp around cooking, cleaning and serving.

Cries of ecstasy come from everyone else. I briefly contemplate my age-old trick of shoving my food into my napkin, but with all that tomato sauce it could get messy. Especially as I'm wearing cream. Then I see him. My secret weapon. Yes. Victory is mine. I pop Leonardo on my lap and feed him my sardines, while pretending to eat them myself. He gobbles them up eagerly. What joy. I knew there was a use for children.

The next course is canocchie, little shrimp-like creatures. I am at least tempted to try these, for two reasons. One, Leonardo and I saw them in the market earlier that day. They were alive, squiggling about oblivious to the fact that for them it was all over and their short lives were about to end in a pot of boiling water. The second reason is that when Fellini was a young man one of his nicknames was Canocchia because he was so thin. The other one was Gandhi, for the same reason. I am rather intrigued to know what his namesake tastes like.

The canocchie are seasoned with lime and mint. They're delicious. Leonardo does less well with this course. I am amazed to find myself eating seafood; perhaps I have finally got over whatever deep sexual aversion I had.

The next course is just the sort of fish I hate, what I call really fishy fish, in other words it doesn't taste of nothing like cod or sole but it tastes of the sea. It is also small, red and full of bones. Yuk. This one's for Leonardo. And so it goes on, more sardines arrive, this time grilled with breadcrumbs, so tightly fitted onto the grilling rack that they have merged together, then we have squid, then prawns. It just goes on and on until the seafood risotto, which is followed by sole (miniature sole from the Adriatic, delicate and delicious) and sea-bass. Half-way through my secret weapon is taken away for a walk with Lorenzo, the father of the two girls. Lorenzo is a lovely man. He lived in France for a year so is able to communicate easily with Leonardo. They vanish for about ten minutes. When they come back, my aunt asks them what he's seen.

"He's seen dead fish," says Lorenzo.

Finally the pudding arrives. It's a cake called a ciambella, made with flour, eggs, sugar and butter. The crust is crunchy and tasty, the inside light and fluffy. We drink a sparkling wine to go with it, which tastes like cider. I ask the owner for the cake recipe. She can't tell me, she says; only Gino's wife knows it and she's gone home.

Lorenzo pays for us all and refuses to let go of Leonardo.

"We'll see each other soon," he tells him in French. "D'accord?"

"D'accord," Leonardo responds.

Leonardo and I have an appointment the next morning with my father at the Café Antiqua in the Piazza Tre Martiri. He has picked this café, he says, because they make good tea served with milk. Drinking tea is my father's only English habit. We sit in large wicker chairs, close to the outside heaters, watching the Christmas shoppers go by. On our knees are blankets provided by the café. It's a little like being on a cruise liner. Except that our sea is inhabited with people and bicycles instead of fish.

"In the rest of Italy, tea is the negation of civilisation," he tells me. "But here it is good."

Leonardo is not pleased to see him. In fact I feel like a woman with two lovers, trying to keep them both happy at the same time. Every time my father talks to me, Leonardo starts whingeing. My trying to pacify Leonardo annoys my father and so it goes on.

My father says the problem is that Leonardo doesn't understand who he is.

"I am your mother's father," he tells Leonardo. "Me, daddy, to your mummy." Leonardo looks confused and calls him daddy.

"No, he's your grandfather," I tell him.

My father grabs my arm. "Never say that," he says. "Teach him to call me uncle or something."

"But why?"

"Because being a grandfather obliges you to be older than someone."

"But anyone can see you're older than him. It's pretty damn obvious."

"That's your opinion," says my father, sipping his tea. "But it is incredible. Me, you Leonardo." He grabs Leonardo's cheek. "Inside him, there is something of me."

I am going to ask him a question and I don't know if I want to know the answer.

I once found a newspaper cutting in my mother's bedroom that was all about some Italian film director flying to England twenty-two times to see his daughter. It was only after I read it three times and saw my mother's name in it that I realised it was about me. I also had a vague memory of someone coming to find me at playschool and my mother rushing over and dragging me away. I thought at the time it was some dangerous man I should be scared of.

"Why did you give up trying to see me when I was a child?"

"Your mother made things very difficult," he says, taking off his hat. "She sent me that letter telling me you no longer looked like me and severed all links. Also when you moved, I had no idea how to find you. You had a different identity, given to you by a stronzo who thought his role as father was to make you do what you didn't want to."

"What did you think when she came back with me? Weren't you furious with her? How come you got on so well?"

"I'll tell you what I thought when she came back with you," he says. "I thought: it's extraordinary but I can see my legs walking towards me. I know I am attached to them, but there they are. That's what I thought."

The waitress brings a cheese and ham toasted sandwich.

"Don't you look like your grandfather?" she coos at Leonardo.

My father grabs a fistful of napkins and starts to eat.

"More," says Leonardo pointing at it. My father tears off a piece of his sandwich and hands it to him. Could this be a truce?

"What did she say when she left you to go to England with my stepfather?"

My father laughed. "She left a note saying 'Gone fishing'."

"And you think that's funny?" I say. For some reason it annoys me he can laugh about it.

"Listen bella," he says leaning closer to me. "The important thing to remember is not that I didn't stay at your wedding, which by the way was because your mother annoyed me, but that you were born from a grande amore and a great desire. You were really wanted. One day I took your mother to the sea at Ostia outside Rome in my convertible car. On the way to the beach we were caught in a gaggle of schoolchildren coming back from a walk. The car was surrounded by them. We were stuck as if in a traffic jam but instead of cars we could hear little voices jabbering away. We looked at each other and we both knew we wanted to have a baby. So you must remember you were not born by chance. And do not dwell on the past and the mistakes made or not made. Think what a miracle it is that we're here; you, me and your greedy son."

"More," says Leonardo, finishing off my father's sandwich. After another ten minutes or so my father says he has some work to do at home. He lives down by the sea. I say I will walk him to the bus. This is our last night in Rimini and he is coming to dinner at my aunt's house. We leave our surrogate cruise ship. My legs feel suddenly exposed to the cold without the blanket. We walk towards the bus stop; Leonardo stops at every shop and sits down on the step.

"It's like you," says my father, grabbing hold of my arm. "Formidable!"

My father's bus stop is down past the Tempio Malatestiano but Leonardo is pulling me in the opposite direction, keen to try another step further up the street.

"See you tonight," says my father and walks away. I watch him go, an elegant and stately figure with a black hat on, carrying his cache of napkins.

12

Unconditional Love

We are all dressed for dinner. Leonardo is wearing a tie for the first time ever, I am wearing some purple velvet trousers and a purple jumper my aunt has given me; she is wearing something black from Emporio Armani. There is a joke in Italy that you can always tell if a woman is from Milan as she is dressed all in black. Last time I was there, I even saw an advertisement for a washing powder that you use just for black clothes. It was on a vast billboard by the cathedral, the city's prime advertising spot. Imagine wearing so much black you can fill your washing machine with it? I suppose Piera does, although she's not from Milan. And I can't imagine her washing her own clothes.

My father arrives as always wearing a hat, cashmere coat and gloves. Underneath he wears black trousers and a black and white jumper. He carries himself well, always standing up straight. I wonder if my grandmother used to pull his shoulders back as she did mine. He has bought a selection of cakes for pudding, and marrons glacés. His voice fills the whole apartment rather like an opera singer's, even drowning out the television on which Leonardo is watching Italian cartoons. My aunt says it's impossible to invite him to dinner with other friends because he so dominates the conversation. This is in part due to the loud voice, but possibly also his personality.

Bertrand offers us all a glass of wine. Being French he prides himself on his knowledge and good taste in wine.

"This is a nice Italian wine from near Pesaro," he tells us. "With the pasta I will serve a white Croatian wine made by a friend of mine."

"Is this the same friend of yours who committed suicide because he wanted to make a decent wine and couldn't?" asks my father.

Bertrand laughs nervously. "It's not a great wine, but it's perfectly pleasant."

Bertrand gave it to me on my first night here; I'm with my father on this. It is terrible. There I was after a seven-hour journey with a hyperactive child who didn't relax for a second, totally desperate for a drink and what do I get? Something I wouldn't use to remove my nail varnish.

"Oh no, this is no good," says Bertrand. He is talking about the Pesaro wine he has served us.

"What's wrong with it?" I ask.

"It's slightly corked," says Bertrand. "Can't you tell?"

"It still tastes better than the Croatian's," says my father. "Stop fussing."

We eat a starter of smoked salmon, small goat's cheeses, avocado and rocket. Leonardo refuses everything bar the salmon, which he eats in industrial quantities. Even my father is impressed.

"When he eats, he eats, doesn't he?" he says.

We are all holding back because we know what is next. Truffles. During the truffle season my aunt cooks with them almost every day. The pasta is boiling and the sauce is made. There is an instantly recognisable smell of moist earth mixed with anticipation.

"I always remember the first time I met Ava Gardner, we ate pasta with truffles," says my father. "It was in a restaurant in Rome."

"You met Ava Gardner?" I ask. "What did you think?"

"I thought I'd like to fuck her," says my father.

"And did you?"

"No, she was married to a very good friend of mine, and I didn't think I could get away with it. Besides she was intolerably stupid, like all these actresses. I have fucked hundreds of them, one more stupid than the other."

"That seems to be your opinion of most women," I say.

"Not true, not most women. Most people. But there was one woman I was truly mad about, apart from your mother, she was my first love and was called Leda."

"Why was she so special?"

"I was twenty-something, a more cretinous person you'd have difficulty imagining. Even more stupid than you. I was the world champion of stupido stronzos. Leda taught me a lot, but most importantly she taught me how to make love. This is something a young man never forgets. She was a sexual saint, the patron saint of love-making; she saw it as her mission to give pleasure to men. Leda was a colossal woman, not in size, but in character and passion. Sadly people misunderstood her and saw her as a whore not a saint. We carried on our relationship even after she married. She didn't get on with her husband and asked me to take her away. I did but her brother came after us and begged her to go back to her husband. She loved her brother so much she went back. But even after that we would meet often.

Eventually her husband found out and we had to stop."

"How did he find out?"

"She came back one day with leaves all over her coat: we had made love under a tree in Rome."

"What happened to her?"

"She died aged forty-five from a brain tumour, while making love to a man half her age. I read about it in the paper. Can you imagine?"

My aunt arrives with a large serving plate of pasta and truffles. It smells enticing. The pasta is pale yellow and gleaming with a buttery sauce. The truffles are shaved over the top.

My father immediately forgets about Leda.

"I am fainting from pleasure," he says. "You, Piera, are the bearer of joy, happiness and the meaning of life, the truffle."

"What shall we drink now?" says Bertrand.

"As Benedetto doesn't like the Croatian wine, we'll have to find something else," says my aunt.

"It's not a question of liking it or not liking it," says my father, helping himself to the pasta. "It's a terrible wine. I understand he's a friend of yours and if you hold a knife to my throat and say I have to say it's good, then I will. But it's not."

"No, I'll get something else," says Bertrand. "Maybe something from our friend in Sangiovese."

My father turns his attention to Leonardo.

"I'm Benedetto," he says.

"Bedenetto," says Leonardo.

"Bravo," says my father. "Over there is Piera. She drinks lots of wine, have you noticed?"

Piera ignores him and starts to talk about how clever Leonardo is. We spent the afternoon in the cinema watching a film about penguins.

"He understood everything," says my aunt. Not true. He understood less than nothing and spent the whole of the first half climbing on the chairs and menacing me and the unfortunate people behind us, who refused to be drawn into conversation. It was only when I bought him a bucket of popcorn that was practically the same size as him that he sat still. Probably weighed down by the popcorn.

B‍ut my aunt has always had a strange relationship with the truth. I remember one Christmas dinner in Rimini several years ago with my grandmother, my aunt, my mother and my father. After that first summer my mother and grandmother, who had been very close, rekindled their friendship. They used to write to each other every other week, long letters describing what they'd been up to and news from the family. My grandmother would invariably urge my mother to take me to church and suggest that she too could do with a bit of religion. She didn't mind if it was protestant, her coming from Northern Europe, even that was better than nothing. She would send little messages to me calling me her "little far-away flower", telling me she thought of me always and missed me. My mother and I often visited her in Rimini and this particular Christmas the rest of the family was there as well.

We all sat around in our Christmas best (mine obviously chosen by my aunt) and ate vast amounts of food prepared by my grandmother's maid Luisa. I remember the lunch so well partly because it was the smartest event I had ever been to. The glasses were so delicate they looked like they would break if you touched them. All the cutlery was silver, the crockery china and monogrammed. The tablecloth was made of thick white linen and the napkins were big enough to make me a toga. The bright winter sun made the chandelier glitter. We started with various anti-pasti; porcini mushrooms in oil, prosciutto and salami. Then we were served cappelletti in brodo; small ravioli-type pasta filled with capon, beef, cheese and spices in a clear capon broth; these had been handmade by Luisa and were traditional at Christmas. I was ready to go for a sleep but we hadn't even finished the starters. Next came passatelli; a kind of pasta made from bread and cheese, also served in the capon broth. This was followed by spit-roast beef and potatoes cooked in rosemary. It was served with a deep red wine. Pudding was an amazing creation consisting of meringue, biscuits, cream and chocolate in the shape of a boat. We finished with fruit and roast chestnuts.

Between the main course and the pudding my father raised his glass.

"I think we should toast our dear mother and grandmother Settimia and hope this will not be, as she says every Christmas, her last. For my part, I wish her a happy year full of messages from the Pope and other excitement." Everyone joined in the toast. My father continued. "Maybe Settimia would like to tell us what she wishes for each of us for the next year?"

Everyone agreed this was an excellent idea. My grandmother beamed from her chair. Although she was sitting on three cushions, she was still about a foot lower than the rest of us. She was the picture of innocence and Christmas cheer. She smiled and looked at her son.

"I wish for Benedetto that he will take religion to his heart," she said. "Without religion we are nothing."

"Bah, stop it," said my father. "Always the same old chant."

My grandmother undeterred looked at my mother. "I hope for Ella that she will find peace, wherever she goes."

Next it was my turn. "I wish for my little beautiful one, my little star, my little darling,"—like all good catholics my grandmother did everything in threes—"that she will study and become as clever as she is beautiful."

"Ha, some hope," said my father. My grandmother silenced him with a stare. Now it was Piera's turn.

My grandmother took a deep breath. She looked straight at her daughter.

"I wish for Piera that she will have more concurrence between what she says and what she does," she announced.

The words hung around the table for a second or so while everyone took them in. Then my mother covered her face with her napkin. My father was less subtle. He started laughing out loud.

"Brava, well said. I'll drink to that," he said raising his glass.

Piera was not amused. Shortly afterwards she excused herself from the lunch to join Bertrand in their hotel. My grandmother knew of his existence of course, but as they weren't married Piera never brought him into her house.

I wonder if there will be any similar drama this evening. After the pasta there is sea-bass with roasted vegetables. My father declines, saying he wants to savour the taste of the truffles. Leonardo starts to make a fuss so is allowed to get down to watch television.

"You shouldn't let him watch television straight after eating," says my aunt. "He'll get a fat stomach." I nod in agreement but am tempted to tell her that in babies fat stomachs are actually acceptable. I decide it's not worth it. For my aunt, fat is akin to the devil and must be avoided. In fact it's worse than the devil.

"When you were a baby," says my father, "you would scream like a Wagnerian soprano until I picked you up and put you just here, on my chest." He points to a spot just below his neckline. It is the same place Leonardo slept when he was tiny. He would lie there with his little face on his hands, his legs curled up beneath him and sleep for hours. Olivia and Bea did the same before him.

It's time for pudding. My father calls Leonardo, who is totally wrapped up in Tom & Jerry.

"He's so used to doing what he wants he doesn't listen to anyone," he says.

"Nonsense," says my aunt. "He's very obedient." She really has been drinking too much if she believes that.

The pudding is a selection of small cakes, some lemon, some zabaglione, meringue, fruit and pistacchio. They are pastry and cream; I feel like eating them all but limit myself to the meringue and the zabaglione. Then we eat one marron glacé each.

"You know it wasn't until I saw my legs walking towards me that day on the beach that you passed from a theoretical daughter to a practical one," says my father. "It was a miracle. But what is even more important is the feeling between us now. Whenever you have any doubt, ask yourself what I would do. And remember that the cure for everything is writing. You just need to be careful to avoid your sentimental side, which of course you get from your mother. And maybe a bit from your grandmother."

My father leaves soon after dinner; he is not one for late nights. He tells me his best writing time is the early hours of the morning when everyone else is asleep. "Remember bella," he says taking my hand as he leaves. "Now that you have found writing you have found your god. It is very important that we find our god, otherwise we find a man who drives his car through our hedge."

I get Leonardo ready for bed. He has been playing a game of puppets with Piera and some priceless antique Chinese dragon. I have never seen her so besotted with anyone. In fact this trip has shown a softer, warmer side to her I have never seen before.

"Since meeting Leonardo, I'm no longer free, his presence is everywhere," she tells me while smothering him with goodnight kisses. "I'm so sad you're going tomorrow."

I lie in the double bed next to my son unable to sleep. My aunt is always criticising me for appearing tired, especially after food, so this evening before dinner I snuck down to Mario's and drank several espressos. They have had the effect of a gram of cocaine. I am in bed, listening to my aunt and uncle wash up and Leonardo snore, my brain totally wired with all sorts of thoughts.

Suddenly there is a loud crash as either my uncle or aunt drops something. The noise makes me jump. Luckily Leonardo sleeps on. Ever since our years with Psycho I can't hear a door slam or a sudden noise without jumping. I am straight away transported back to my bedroom at the last farmhouse we lived in with Psycho in Berkshire.

I would often be woken up by a bang in the night, which would be a signal for me to rush out of bed to help my mother. If I was lucky, my mother had escaped after the first bang. This was a strategy she adopted after being caught a few times. Psycho would drink and then get violent. My mother would run away and hide in the woods. He would tell me to come and call her. I would call her, but try to make my voice sound different and will her to stay where she was. Strangely enough he never hit me when she wasn't there.

During the last two years with him, until the last beating that made her decide we had to leave, she escaped more often than she was caught. But sudden noises still terrify me.

I try to go to sleep by thinking about nice things, like getting home. But I have an awful going back to school feeling I often get before journeys, even if I'm looking forward to them. My father once said that if I was troubled and needed some help I should "ask Bach". By this he meant listen to Bach and let the problem resolve itself. Every night at home I go to sleep listening to the Goldberg Variations. Sadly here I don't have that option.

The main thing that's worrying me is that tomorrow we leave to go home to France and I don't know when I will see my father again. Our relationship has always been stormy and intermittent. Almost every time I visited him after that first summer, he would get furious about something I said or did, usually quoting Dante incorrectly or confusing Mozart with Rossini. The result would be the same: he would call me a stupida stronza, march me to the nearest station and put me on a train back to England. Once in Florence I remember the man at the ticket counter asking if he wanted me to travel first or second class.

"Second class," my father told him. "She'll have more in common with her fellow travellers." The result was that I only saw him about once every seven years. Who knows if he will be around in another seven?

Looking back on our history I wonder why I'm so drawn to him. He's hardly been a good father in the traditional sense. Here is a man who practically gave up on me me as a child, then when he found me did nothing but shout at me and make me learn Dante, stormed out of my wedding (leaving my mother to walk me up the aisle) and is only now beginning to be nice to me. In fact the last time I saw him, apart from briefly the day before my wedding, he was dreadful. It was about ten years ago, before Rupert and I were married. Rupert was renting a beautiful old farmhouse in Sussex and I was living in London. It was a large farmhouse with an oast house in the grounds. It was owned by a rather eccentric couple called Lord and Lady Delamere who lived on their vast estate in Kenya for nine months of the year and came back to England for three months during the summer. Living in their home was a bit like walking into a scene from a film made in England during the 1950s; willow-pattern china, inglenook fireplace, large shabby armchairs with blankets thrown over them. On the wall they had paintings of hunting scenes and Sussex landscapes.

This was my first Christmas with Rupert and his children who were then aged four and two. I was really looking forward to it. The children and I decorated the tree together, we wrapped up presents, went shopping for all the food. I loved being in the Delamere's house, I felt totally at home there and was excited about my father coming to stay. I wanted him to see the England I loved. Where better than an aristocrat's farmhouse set deep in the Sussex countryside with views over green rolling hills?

The first night of his stay I cooked Pasta Siciliana (penne with a fairly heavy tomato, parmesan and aubergine sauce) for him, Rupert and my stepchildren Hugo and Julia.

"In Italy you could be sent to prison for serving this," was my father's comment as he pushed his plate aside.

The following morning when I got up he was already in the kitchen, dressed in his coat and hat.

"Look at this bird," he said pointing to a robin on the bird-table outside the window. "He is very intelligent. He comes and eats and then flies away to watch from a vantage point to make sure there is no danger before coming back to eat again. He is not greedy enough to risk his life."

We all went for a walk after breakfast. I was keen to show him the beautiful countryside behind the house. But rather than look at it he spent the whole time lecturing us about anything and everything (mainly involving Dante). My stepson Hugo still imitates him to this day: "Example!" he says. "Example!" That's how my father would start yet another sentence. Sometimes when his English failed him I would have to translate. A less enjoyable walk is hard to imagine.

On Christmas day we all got dressed up to go for lunch with Rupert's parents. I was wearing a beige cashmere suit I had had made at great expense by a designer friend of mine in London. It consisted of a tight-fitting knee-length skirt, brown and silk cap-sleeved top and a long jacket, tight around the waist and then very slightly wider until it stopped just above the hem of the skirt. The buttons were made of brown silk to match the brown in the shirt.

As we took our seats for a glass of champagne my father turned to be and said in Italian: "What assassin made that suit? It looks terrible on you, makes your bottom look too low." I was devastated. I hated the idea of looking terrible of course, but also the fact that he'd been so cruel to me. My perfect family Christmas had not worked out as I'd planned. He wasn't impressed with me or our life or our lovely farmhouse. He was his caustic, arrogant self at his worst.

When we got back to our farmhouse the antique oil-fired heating system had broken. There was no one around we could get to fix it so we had no hot water or heating. It was an idyllic white Christmas—absolutely freezing. My father spent the next three days in bed, in his hat and coat, covered in blankets. Thankfully on the third day my mother arrived. She made the whole Christmas experience a good one by being lovely about the house, the children, us and generally helping all the time. The most helpful thing she did in fact was to take my father away. They went off to Devon where she lives.

"You can't have him hanging around in bed here," she said. "I have an aga, he can sit next to that until it's time for him to go back to Italy."

I asked her if she minded being lumbered with him. He was hardly charming company. "No, I'm used to him," she told me. "The only thing I'm dreading is the drive down there. He won't stop talking all the way and it could take six hours."

I can't say I missed him once he'd gone. In fact I wondered at the time whether I'd ever bother to see him again. But something has changed now. Maybe it's since he lost all his money he's become more reasonable and kinder. I say lost his money, he actually spent it or rather frittered it away, amazing though it now seems as he had so much. I asked him recently why he didn't just give it to me.

"You were even more stupid than me," he told me. "Imagine what a stupida stronza you would have been with all that money. You would never have become a writer." His argument is that he couldn't do anything sensible when he had money because all he did was race around the world staying in luxury hotels seducing women and sending postcards from the luxury hotels to my mother "mainly to annoy her". His theory is that I would have done more or less the same if I'd had unlimited funds. Maybe he has a point.

Leonardo turns and kicks me in his sleep. I stroke his head. At that moment I realise my son and father have something in common: my unconditional love.

Leonardo wakes early the next morning and starts telling me about his aeroplane. I am still semi-high on caffeine so we get up and head to Mario's for another hit. We are alone apart from the owner of the jewellery shop across the alcove, also called Mario. In fact I have never met so many Marios as I have in Rimini. We went for lunch in the Chinese restaurant there one day and even the Chinese waiter was called Mario.

My father phones me while we are there and says he will join us for breakfast.

"I just want to say goodbye to you again," he says.

This surprises me. It's the first time he has ever shown any signs of not wanting me to leave. I am as happy as a schoolgirl in love by the time he walks in the door.

Leonardo doesn't eat but plays with the sugar packets. Mario's wife Bruna comes and chats to him. It's our last day and he finally responds to "ciao" with "ciao". My father is delighted. "Bravo," he says, pinching his cheek.

"Doesn't he look like his grandfather?" says Bruna. My father is less delighted by that.

After breakfast we walk into the Piazza Tre Martiri. A small white train we have seen every day is parked there. Leonardo starts running towards it. It looks like a tourist attraction but is actually a council-run train that transports people into the centre of town for their Christmas shopping. I ask the driver if we can hop on. He is typically regional, extremely well fed and sporting an impressive moustache. Must be called Mario. He tells us to get in. My father declines and says he will wait for us at the café with the blankets. Leonardo and I set off. It's early and we are Mario's only passengers. There are loudspeakers and we are being forced to listen to "*Love lifts us up where we belong*"—a cruel choice after a sleepless night.

I remember an advertisement I saw a few years ago that said something like "No one in Italy grows up wanting to be a train driver". The implication being they all want to drive Ferraris or Maseratis. And even if they don't actually get to drive Ferraris, they act like they do. Our train driver is no exception. We take off at high speed, careering around the small cobbled streets and then up past the Augustus Arch towards the old market and the out of town parking. We whiz through housing estates leaving a wake of barking dogs and wailing women. I'm amazed when he stops at a traffic light. An elderly couple take advantage of this rare stationary moment to get on.

"Where will it take us?" says the lady as they get into the compartment in front of us.

"To the centre," I tell her. "Very quickly."

We're off again. We are now on our way back into town. We race past most of the cars on the road. The only one that manages to overtake us is an Alfa Romeo Spider. As soon as we hit the cobbled streets of the town centre again, the journey turns into a tour of the elderly couple's life.

"This is where we had a shop for over fifty years," says the woman, pointing to a building that is now a mobile phone shop. A rather nasty-looking man dressed in black with a red belt is outside it smoking. He waves at the old couple.

"And this is where our daughter was married," says the man, pointing at a church.

"This is where she taught for several years," says his wife showing me a school. "In fact all our children went to school there too."

"That's where we lived for over fifty years," says the man, pointing out an apartment block.

The train takes us down a cobbled street. Now it's my turn to show them a sight.

"That's where my grandmother had a shop," I say as we pass it at breakneck speed. It is now an optician's. "And down there is my aunt's house," I say pointing towards the Via IV Novembre.

The couple turn round and smile at me.

"Ah, so you're a Benedetti?"

I have never been called that before. When I was four, my mother remarried and my stepfather adopted me. Since that day I have taken his name, which is Frith Powell. Although my Italian relations complained about it, to me a name didn't seem so important, I was just who I was. My father talked about me changing my surname back to Benedetti. My aunt was adamant I should.

"You're the last of the Benedettis," they would argue. "You have to have your proper name." We even went to see a lawyer about it. But by then I had my life in England, I had my identity there. I didn't want to be a Benedetti. It was bad enough at school having a double-barrelled name; imagine the grief I would get with a silly Italian one?

I remember my stepfather once asking me who I loved most, my mother or him. Because he was a sensitive and difficult character, I lied and said him of course. My father would never ask that question, partly because he doesn't need to. It doesn't matter to him who I love more or less, if I live in Italy, France or England, if I feel more English some days and more Italian on others. Actually after this trip I have come to realise that I do feel more English than anything else. I love the English way of life, the courtesy, the green fields, Marks & Spencer. Even the humidity agrees with me. Having lived there almost all my life I don't feel as comfortable anywhere else. And although I live in France, I have done my best to create an English environment for me and my family.

Another reason I know I am more English is that I can never imagine supporting Italy against England in the World Cup. And although my father is a football fan, he doesn't mind. He knows all about me and what I am and he accepts me. I think now that I am following the career he set out for me all those years ago and admits I'm not quite as stupid as he first thought he loves me, maybe even unconditionally.

But this trip has made me realise that my mother didn't take away my roots. She may have transplanted them, but they're still there. At the Palazzo Medici in Florence the girl selling guides asked me why I wanted to buy one in English. I realised then that I could be Italian. I can speak the language, I look Italian and in some small ways I am Italian. When I first went to Piazza di Spagna in Rome as a teenager, I felt at home and I continue to feel at home in Italy. I felt the same way when I got on the sleeper at Nice and was suddenly surrounded by Italian voices. Although I haven't lived with my father since I was a toddler, I feel intimately close to him. There is something about him that feels right.

He said to me recently that when I first arrived in Italy that summer I was only operating with half my body and brain. The Italian half had been completely forgotten, it was dead and buried. There is no doubt that when I come to Italy it comes alive. Suddenly I feel Italian and have an insatiable urge to speak Italian, wave my arms around and eat pasta. I sometimes think we should all move to Italy for a while, a plan that invariably gets forgotten as soon as I get home to our lovely house and the relative calm of France. But when I heard a little girl of Bea's age talk to her mother in Italian recently I had a pang of sadness that my children won't ever be Italian. But at least they will have the choice. They know about their Italian roots and can make the most of them if they want to.

Leonardo's middle names are Thomas Benedetti. This might not seem that significant, he'll never be known as Leonardo Benedetti, he'll be Leonardo Wright, but it makes me feel like my whole Italian identity hasn't been erased and that the Benedetti name will live on. For some reason this is important to me. Perhaps because I have come to understand what it means to have roots and how important your identity is. Mine was temporarily taken away from me, but my children can do whatever they like with theirs. I will encourage them, by bringing them to Italy and teaching them about the culture. In fact they can all already swear in Italian and eat pasta without resorting to the English habit of using a spoon. And obviously they'll be expected to learn the whole of Dante's Divine Comedy off by heart by the time they're ten.

My mobile phone rings. "I assume you've gone to Milan," says my father. "But I'll be waiting for you when you get back." I can see him sitting at the café as our train approaches its final stop in the Piazza Tre Martiri. He holds the mobile phone in one hand and with the other he is stuffing napkins into his pocket.

"Yes," I tell the nice old couple. "I am a Benedetti."

We get off the train and walk back to the café. My father stands up when he sees us approaching.

"I ordered you a cup of tea," he says. "You're so lucky to have a father like me," he adds, pinching my cheek.

We all sit down.

"In fact I'm lucky to have a daughter like you," he adds. "To be honest I never expected it."

A reluctant grandfather and grandson.

"Why?" I ask him.

"Because I thought your mother would totally ruin you. In fact she did everything she could, but she failed. You're just like me."

He's wrong; I'm not just like him. Though there are many things that bind us together despite our many years apart. But he is right that I am lucky to have a father like him. He may not be the most conventional of parents, but he's taught me much more than a traditional father would have. Maybe not about how to drive a car and other practicalities, but about myself and how I should live. He has encouraged (almost bullied) me into writing. Nowadays he is always there if I need him. Some might say it's a bit late, but I don't agree. More than anyone else he responds to my innermost fears and worries, almost without being asked.

And for all his faults and eccentricity, he's never short of a napkin, which is essential for someone like me who always forgets to bring a handkerchief with her.

Afterword

My life is very different from when this book first came out. There is a new man in my life; he wears linen suits, has a head of thick grey hair, always carries a hat and still quotes Dante on an hourly basis. Those of you who have been paying attention will recognise this character as my father.

As I write he has just left my home after his third stay with me since I wrote *Ciao Bella*. My father and I are in constant touch since I wrote *Ciao Bella*. I have seen more of him in the three years since the book came out than I have during the last twenty years. He calls me every week.

"*Ciao Bella* is the biggest declaration of love I have ever had," he says.

Sadly his sister, my aunt, doesn't feel the same way. In part I blame myself for giving her the book. But she kept asking me for it and I didn't think she'd ever bother to read it.

I knew there was trouble when she called me.

"I am a bit upset about the thing you wrote about my first husband," she told me. "I never said he made love like a beast. I hope he won't sue me."

I assured her making love like a beast is seen as the highest of compliments in English and prayed that would be the end of it.

Two days later I got a call from my father.

"Your aunt has finished your book," he said.

"Did she like it?"

"She's furious. No, she's more than furious, she's apoplectic with rage. In fact I daren't go within a three-mile radius of her."

"What bit doesn't she like?" I asked.

"She hates all of it, especially the bit where you say she can't open her mouth without telling a lie. She is calling you all sorts of names and says you're ungrateful."

I very much regret hurting my aunt's feelings. I am extremely fond of her and thought that came through in the affectionate and humorous account I have written of her. Apparently my uncle is even more furious than she is, mainly due to the butler reference. I am very sorry to have upset him as he has always been very kind to me. Maybe I was too honest.

Graham Greene once said that a novelist's only responsibility is to his novel. A writer friend of mine says that as long as you don't get anyone in trouble with the police or his wife, everything else is fair game. I am very happy with Ciao Bella. The book wouldn't have been as good without my aunt roaming around buying designer clothes and lying. Which is what she does; most of the time and always has done. This is not a criticism, it's just the truth. Or at least it's my version of the truth, but as a senior judge in England summed up recently: There are three versions of the truth; yours, mine and the truth. Maybe I have been unfair on her and if I have, I apologise. I wrote what I remembered. I am happy to say that her anger with me has not meant that she doesn't see the children. They are going to stay with her this summer. They also talk to my father on the phone quite often. They speak in French or pigeon Italian. "Buongiorno parmiggiano," says Bea.

I do think that if anyone could have been upset by the book it is my mother. Her life, and many parts of it I am sure she would rather forget, is written about in great detail. When we discussed my aunt's reaction and I asked my mother what she thought of it she said "we all have to live with our mistakes".

Maybe writing an honest account of my family was a mistake and now I have to live with that.

It seems my father is now willing to take the same risk. After the publication of *Ciao Bella*, his first novel was published, to great critical acclaim. It is called *La Signorina Notte* and won one of Italy's most prestigious awards, the Frontino Prize. He is now working on another novel that he says will be about his sister, among others. I am thrilled, not only is at amazing effort for a man in his mid-eighties, but it might take the heat off me.